T0116092

*f*P

ALSO BY RAFAEL AGUAYO

*Dr. Deming: The American Who Taught the
Japanese About Quality*

RAFAEL AGUAYO

THE METAKNOWLEDGE ADVANTAGE

THE KEY TO SUCCESS IN THE NEW ECONOMY

Free Press

NEW YORK   LONDON   TORONTO   SYDNEY   SINGAPORE

FREE PRESS
A Division of Simon & Schuster, Inc.
1230 Avenue of the Americas
New York, NY 10020

Copyright © 2004 by Rafael Aguayo
All rights reserved, including the right of reproduction
in whole or in part in any form.

FREE PRESS and colophon are trademarks
of Simon & Schuster, Inc.

For information regarding special discounts for bulk purchases,
please contact Simon & Schuster Special Sales at
1-800-456-6798 or business@simonandschuster.com

Manufactured in the United States of America

10 9 8 7 6 5 4 3 2 1

Library of Congress Cataloging-in-Publication Data.

Aguayo, Rafael.
　　The metaknowledge advantage : the key to succcess
in the new economy / Rafael Aguayo.
　　　　p.　cm.
　　Includes index.
　　　1. Intellectual capital. 2. Knowledge management.
　3. Knowledge workers. 4. Communication in management.
　　I. Title.
　　HD53.A38 2004
　　658.4'038—dc22
　　　　　　　　　　　　　　　　　　　　2003049311

ISBN 978-1-4165-6828-5

Dedicated to and in memory of my parents
Juan Roberto Aguayo (1907–1993)
Aida R. Aguayo (1920–1994)

CONTENTS

FOREWORD

Writing a book is much like having a baby. After a few years one forgets the difficulty and pain involved and embarks on creating another. Both are time-consuming and frustrating, but they can be the most gratifying and fulfilling experiences in one's life. Each book, like each child, is different. To expect each to be the same, with the same joys, is to invite disappointment. This book has been like the difficult child who was always getting into trouble, leaving the parent unsure if he or she would amount to anything. Whether he or she does or not is determined after the child or book is launched and has to make its way in the world alone.

This book started out with the intent of answering a question: What was going on at the height of the economic boom of the late 1990s? Was it a bubble, or was there a fundamental change in progress? And if it was a bubble, was anything really changing? The market answered the first question—it was a bubble—but did not answer whether a fundamental change was occurring. To answer that I had to explore my understanding of business and human society.

Much of the early literature of business dealt with individual, personal motivation and relations with others—in other words, people issues. But a separate although not unrelated line concerned with process can be traced to Frank Gilbreth (1868–1924), who had a natural sympathy for workers and believed that most problems lay with the management and not with the worker. He studied every job thoroughly and was able to improve productivity many times over by redesigning the way the work was performed. Frederick Taylor (1856–1915), who is probably better known today, also believed he could find the best way to perform a job but his writings showed much less sympathy for the worker. His underlying presuppositions were of a linear world, without probability, where workers were basically unwilling to work. But his work was influential and to a large degree formed the basis of industrial engineering.

Walter Shewhart (1891–1967), while working at the Bell Laboratories of AT&T, discovered that improving quality not only improved productivity, but that statistical thinking was required to avoid errors and waste. He developed Statistical Quality Control. Process improvement was then given a modern scientific basis that could deal with nonlinearity, or what we now call Chaos through statistical thinking.

My belief is that any very successful person of the past dealt, to some degree, within two areas: people and process (or systems). But their successors often focused on one or the other and rarely met with the same level of success. Normally, working on these two levels is enough to ensure reasonable success, but when a company meets turbulence either because of changes in the environment or stagnation from within, a third level needs to be addressed and that is beliefs.

To answer my question concerning whether society was going through a fundamental change I needed to examine the basis of successful management. My answer was MetaKnowledge—a system of knowledge based on modern thought in diverse areas such as statistics, psychology, mathematics, and ecology—which is a basis for understanding excellent management. Because it deals with beliefs MetaKnowledge also serves as a theory of transformation in an organization.

Readers familiar with the work of W. Edwards Deming, Walter Shewhart's best-known disciple, may recognize similarities between Deming's profound knowledge and MetaKnowledge. To Deming, profound knowledge was a system of knowledge with four branches: appreciation for a system, knowledge of variation, theory of knowledge, and psychology. From these his management teachings could be derived. I am indebted to him, especially for the idea that several branches of knowledge need to interact together as a whole system.

But I found myself disagreeing with him on several fronts. He often stated that one counterexample could disprove a theory. As I state in the text of this work, I believe that is true only for those laws that are assumed to be universal, such as physical laws. It may also require an exact model of reality as opposed to a probabilistic model. In any event it is my feeling that there are many cases where a single counterexample does not disprove a theory.

Deming also stated that until a system is in statistical control you don't have a system. I have to disagree. It seems to me that this is an overly restrictive definition of a system and I don't believe Shewhart, whom Deming referred to as The Master, would have gone along with it. For the concept of a system to be useful a more generalized definition, such as the ability to self-regulate or return to a former state, is more appropriate. We do have chaotic systems and I think those are important phenomena that need to be included in twenty-first-century thinking. I have chosen to use Shewhart's terminology of assignable causes over Deming's special causes. Even though the two terms are operationally equivalent, the tone and coloration of each is different. A special cause is special to the system. It is not really a part of it. An assignable cause implies that it is a part of the current system but can be identified at its source and probably eliminated. I think that makes control theory more applicable and useful as an explanation of corporate success and gives it great applicability elsewhere.

While profound knowledge was a system from which Deming's fourteen points of management could be derived, I felt MetaKnowledge could be something larger and more comprehensive and needed to include Chaos theory or nonlinear dynamical systems theory, and much more human understanding, as well as insights from ecology, logic, mathematics, and other fields.

It should come as no surprise that a system of thinking with roots in management should have wide applications globally. In its most basic form business is the human effort to improve one's lot and shape one's immediate environment for survival and procreation. And while many of the principles of MetaKnowledge are quite new in their formulation, that does not mean that some form of these principles have not been at work for eons. Business, then, in this sense has application everywhere. We are all in business in some sense. The writer who puts down commerce, the minister who preaches to her congregation, the politician seeking reelection all need to earn a living. They all need to feed themselves and their family, and they all seek to improve their lot and perhaps the lot of others.

In this book I bring together knowledge of several logical types, including people, beliefs, and systems, to form a greater holistic understanding of commerce. The book touches on some difficult material. But if anything, and the last twenty years have strongly confirmed this knowledge, brains and smarts are not just something to be tolerated.

They are a strategic advantage. Probably no one has demonstrated this better than Bill Gates, the founder of Microsoft, who with little capital, some ideas, and some smarts was able to surround himself with the brightest people and trump not just other entrepreneurs of the personal computer industry but the giants of the computer and electronics industry. His dream of a computer on every desk has become a reality.

Beliefs, and in beliefs I include what most would call knowledge, make a big difference. In 1998 Daimler-Benz AG, the company that made Mercedes-Benz, merged with Chrysler in what was initially called a merger of equals. But since the merger, all Chrysler senior management left, American directors have been replaced by German directors, and the Daimler-Benz management emerged as the only senior management. What was originally billed as a merger of equals really became a takeover. And Daimler management took a global car company headquartered in Auburn Hills, Michigan, earning more than $4 billion a year and turned it into a money loser. None of the strengths of Chrysler survived the takeover.

On the other hand, in 1999 the Japanese automobile manufacturer Nissan was hemorrhaging money and had lost market share in Japan for decades. Their new car introductions were somber and slow. They owed billions of dollars in debt and talk of bankruptcy was in the air. Renault entered into an alliance with Nissan, injecting $5 billion in capital and putting Carlos Ghosn, one of their leading executives, in charge of the turnaround. His initial title was not even chief executive but chief operating officer. Just a handful of executives went in with Ghosn. In two years Nissan went from being on the verge of bankruptcy to having the most profitable year in its history. Further, more than twenty new models were introduced or scheduled to be introduced in a three year period. And this was done with almost all the same people. Several plants were closed but most of the changes were implemented by the same middle management that was there before. The same people, operating in the same locations, in the same industry, with the same plants and the same brands. Yet it was not the same people at all. Something had changed.

It appears to me that Daimler management had a very limited understanding of MetaKnowledge and violated key principles. They were interested in the plants, the brands, the corporate structure of Chrysler, all the nonliving aspects, and didn't appreciate the knowledge and unique skills of the organization. Ghosn, on the other hand, seemed to grasp the essence of MetaKnowledge and operated consistent with the principles. Ghosn seemed to have an innate appreciation for Nissan as a living entity with unique strengths that he could tap.

Writing is a process. The writer, like a parent, tries to shape his creation, but if the book is powerful enough it changes the author as well. This book took me to places I did not originally intend to go and led to conclusions I did not foresee. It took on a life of its own and forced me to redo, rewrite, and rethink. I went through a transformation and at the end I was not the same person who started it. This is as it should be. For me this book, while difficult and challenging, was worth the effort. If you the reader are also changed in some way, then this book will really be a success.

Rafael Aguayo
March 7, 2003

THE
METAKNOWLEDGE
ADVANTAGE

CHAPTER 1

THE WINDS OF CHANGE

America and the world are in transition. The basis of economic power and wealth is rapidly shifting. Whereas in the past economic power was determined by access to key physical resources such as petroleum, steel, or manufacturing, economic power is increasingly being determined by access to key knowledge resources. Evidence of the shift is seen in the profitability and valuation of different industries. US Steel, the pride first of Andrew Carnegie and then of JP Morgan, was once the largest corporation in the world. It represented real power. Today, while still involved in steel production, it is a minor company with paltry profits. Petroleum, while still a potent economic factor, is decreasing in importance.

In the nineteenth century, 70% of the population of North America was involved in farming. By the 1950s that number was down to 5%. Today it is down to 2%. There is reason to believe that that percentage will shrink further. Similarly in the early part of the twentieth century, 50% of the population was involved in manufacturing. Today that number is down to 14%. This percentage will also continue to decrease.

Several of the companies with the highest market valuation in the world did not exist twenty-five years ago—and neither did their industries. Among these are Microsoft, the leading provider of software for the personal computer, and Intel, the leading provider of the personal computer microprocessor. The company with the highest valuation (at this writing) is GE.

Amidst such obvious and dramatic changes it is easy to fall into the trap of assuming that management principles and the values we use to guide our lives must also constantly change. Thus in the recent past we have heard talk of a New Economics in which everything is in flux and profits are unnecessary. Before that the vacuous fad of Re-Engineering promised constant upheaval, but that just puttered before fading from serious discussion. For a management philosophy to be both effective and enduring it must be based on principles that transcend daily occurrences and swings in markets. Indeed it should help explain cycles and prepare managers to deal with swings in markets, cycles, and long-term trends.

Such a management system must be based on knowledge tested and confirmed over decades. That basic knowledge would change slowly only after significant evidence required it. The system would encompass knowledge from diverse fields, some of which are normally considered to be unrelated. Metaknowledge in the generic sense of the word represents the presuppositions and knowledge that each of us has and that, in large measure, frame our thinking and help determine our actions. But MetaKnowledge, with a capital M and K, is the specific system of knowledge put forth in this book that brings together some of the most advanced thinking in several fields into a system of knowledge. MetaKnowledge is a system of knowledge that serves as the foundation for management in the twenty-first century. It is a kind of metaphysics for management, or a metamanagement.

When Aristotle coined the term "metaphysics" it was meant to deal with topics beyond physics. In philosophy, metaphysics became primarily an examination of our presuppositions of reality, especially physical reality. The emphasis was often on a theory of knowledge. But the analogy with metaphysics is limiting for several reasons. Physics has often been called the queen of sciences. Models from physics and chemistry have been applied to most areas of our understanding, including psychology, biology, and economics, with some success. However it is becoming increasingly clear that biological phenomena operate in subtle and complex ways that often seem to defy basic fundamental physical principles without actually violating them. Life seems to operate at a different level, with principles and rules that we are just beginning to appreciate. Our MetaKnowledge must also include lessons from biology, ecology, and other life sciences. MetaKnowledge is a more accurate and descriptive term for the basis of our understanding than both metaphysics and metamanagement.

No single field of knowledge is sufficient to guide us in our actions, yet most of us are trained in just one, often narrow, area of expertise. But our knowledge base has become increasingly complex and diverse. Luckily it is possible to put together a system of knowledge that draws from many fields but does not require us to become expert in any of them. Yet each area of knowledge modifies the others and thereby creates greater wisdom than any single field on its own. That is one of the promises of MetaKnowledge.

MetaKnowledge also gives us an intellectual and moral compass independent of the personality or biases of the reigning management hero of the day. It is based on theory or knowledge and not on "gut."

The Knowledge that Binds

A story here may be helpful. In an interview in the January 11, 1999, issue of *Fortune* magazine, Jack Welch of General Electric enthusiastically proclaimed the success and value of his quality program. By instituting a Six Sigma initiative that focused on process improvement, profitability increased by 67% in a little more than three years. Six Sigma is the name of a quality initiative with the main goal of creating a defect rate of less than 4 defects per million for every part, compared to a more typical 35,000 defects per million. This remarkable interview brings out two very startling facts:

1. General Electric was considered one of the best-run companies in the world prior to instituting a quality program, their profitability and stock price had grown dramatically during Welch's tenure, and it became the most valuable company on the planet based on market capitalization. It was voted the most admired company in the world by other managers. Yet upon instituting their Six Sigma quality program they were able to make drastic improvements quickly. The more established belief is that once a company reaches a certain level of success it becomes increasingly difficult to wring out improvements. In the interview Welch praised his quality program and the remarkable effect it was having on his company. Besides the 67% improvement in profitability, working capital turns increased from four times a year to nine times a year. Other financial indicators were also affected positively.

2. Welch adopted the quality program fifteen years after other major organizations like Ford, Intel Corporation, Motorola, and Harley-Davidson, all of which had experienced dramatic improvements. It was Motorola's success with Six Sigma that eventually became the beacon leading to Welch's turnaround. It took Welch so long because he had a prior notion that quality would come from "acting well and fast."

How the Change Came About

Jack Welch decided to make the change only after speaking to his friend Larry Bossidy, whom he describes as being the only person in the country who hated quality more than he. Bossidy, who had been appointed CEO at Allied Signal, Inc., needed to improve results, and fast. Allied Signal, Inc., was in trouble and needed to try something different, so Bossidy went to Motorola looking for solutions. He then applied Six Sigma at Allied Signal. According to the *Fortune* article, Bossidy told Welch, "Jack, this ain't b.s.—this is real stuff, this is really great stuff." Welch then polled 10,000 employees who came back and said they desperately needed a quality initiative. Now Welch has only praise for the quality initiative. According to him, "The results are fantastic. We're going to get $1.2 billion of gain this year."[1]

Ten to fifteen years may not seem like a long time, but remember, we are talking about our managerial elite. Even though Jack Welch is generally recognized as one of the great managers and CEOs of the latter half of the twentieth century, it took him fifteen years to adopt a methodology that would bring fantastic results to his company. What about mediocre companies and those that are struggling? How long does it take them to adopt a better way? In some cases they won't, and in many cases they won't be around in the future. If it took the best manager of the day fifteen years to adopt a methodology that he now swears by we can each be forgiven if we are a little slow to embrace some required changes.

The first thing to note about Jack Welch's break with his old notion of quality is that he heard a strong message from someone he trusted and respected, someone who was the only "guy in the whole country who hated quality more than me." He heard it from a former non-believer, a friend who spoke his language. This opened Welch up to lis-

[1] *Fortune*, January 11, 1999.

tening to his own managers, who also strongly felt the need for improved quality at GE.

General Electric was not in any kind of crisis. As a result of strategic decisions Jack Welch had made fifteen years earlier, it was either number one or number two in all its markets. The company was thriving, as were its shareholders. Its management was among the most admired in the world. Why should it change?

Most companies that do shift radically are either in crisis or in the midst of a competitive challenge or both. The fact that GE made a big change when there was no imminent crisis demonstrates one of the real strengths that led to Jack Welch's reputation at the pinnacle of American management. But this book will not be a love fest for Welch or any other manager. We want to move away from accepting management ideas because of a strong personality and toward management ideas based on theory and long-term results. Let me give two examples where Welch's actions are directly contradicted by MetaKnowledge. One, his insistence on eliminating the "bottom 10%" of managers year after year, even when the company was doing well. He used loose statistical analogies for justification, but statistical theory, or what we call knowledge of variation, definitively and unmistakably contradicts his position. Two, he also produced precise increases in earnings that matched his forecasts for most of his tenure. Knowledge of systems and variations tells us that this is only possible in a fantasy world. In the real world there are and must necessarily be month-to-month and year-to-year variation. No one has a 100% prediction rate. If you want financial reporting to actually measure something then it must show these variations. Otherwise the financial reports are just psychological statements meant to assuage financial analysts and stock investors. They become nothing more than a form of the Emperor's new clothes. We will have a lot more to say about these two examples in later pages.

The story of GE's conversion to quality highlights two important points for managers to appreciate.

1. Ideas that work eventually get adopted, even when there is massive resistance. The direction is never straight. There is always some backtracking. The names get changed, in this case from Quality to Six Sigma. But the effective idea, almost always, wins out and gets adopted. There is a kind of evolution of the most fit idea and approach. This very

much mimics biological evolution. At any given time many ideas are being tried. Some last several generations and permutations. Others, like Re-Engineering, die quick deaths. But over time we see the survivors form a kind of species of ideas.

2. Major change, even among the smartest, most sophisticated people, comes not from hi-tech solutions but through human interaction. Welch made a 180-degree shift in his thinking, but only because a trusted friend told him it would work. Human nature is one of those areas that changes very slowly, if at all. Those futurists who predict rapid and instantaneous change often overlook the fact that people's habits would also have to change overnight, and that does not happen except in the most radical situations.

MetaKnowledge

General Electric's adoption of quality as a major corporate initiative was accompanied by a fundamental shift in its knowledge base and belief system—a paradigm shift. It involved not just an addition of facts or knowledge to the existing system, but rooting out a whole belief system and replacing it with something else. Welch went from believing quality was B.S. to becoming the leader of a quality jihad.

Understanding what occurred requires that we understand something about human knowledge. What is knowledge? How is knowledge related to skills and intelligence? This line of inquiry can be called metaknowledge or knowledge of knowledge. But metaknowledge can be a whole lot more, and MetaKnowledge *is* a whole lot more.

Today many corporations such as IBM and British Petroleum are recognizing the strategic importance of knowledge by naming the equivalent of a chief knowledge officer. If knowledge is of strategic importance, shouldn't it be one of the main concerns of the CEO? Just what is the role of knowledge in corporate success and economic well-being?

The Usefulness of MetaKnowledge

A robust management theory should be applicable to almost any business and industry. If someone versed in the theory were to fall asleep today and wake up one hundred years from now, he would still be able to apply it in a well-run organization of the future. MetaKnowledge as a system of knowledge is such a theory.

MetaKnowledge cuts across many disciplines, such as theory of knowledge, statistics, linguistics, psychology, systems theory, mathematics, and others. One doesn't need extensive training in any area, just enough to keep from getting into trouble. Knowledge from each area gives a new dimension to the other disciplines, and together they form a system.

In a real sense, what we know is rooted in our minds through beliefs that reach deep into our unconscious. We all know or believe things of which we are unaware and rarely question because they are so fundamental to our understanding of reality. Yet other people can have very different unconscious beliefs from ours. Two examples would be that the world was flat or the center of the solar system. Some people believe the average employee is lazy and has to be forced to come to the office or factory and then forced to work. Other people believe that given the proper environment, most people will flourish and develop an intrinsic motivation to excel. People with different beliefs often end up not talking to each other but talking through each other and becoming adversarial.

Never has the need to understand other cultures' views been greater. I don't just refer to people of different nationalities or those who speak a different language. Cultures are changing everywhere. While McDonald's is considered a symbol of the influence of American culture in other parts of the world, Chinese restaurants in my neighborhood are at least twenty times more numerous. When my daughter took me out for Father's Day we had a typical American meal—sushi. Today the leading Christian continent is arguably Africa, where there is an enormous demand for new churches and parishes are growing. In Europe and North America churches are regularly closing and parishes are being combined. Many North Americans and Europeans practice some kind of Eastern discipline such as Yoga, T'ai-Chi, Ch'i-Gong, or some form of Eastern meditation. Sometimes these changes lead to domestic clashes of culture such as the political clash between the organic food movement and those industries that sell pesticides and fertilizers to conventional farmers. Another is the economic clash between conventional medicine and so-called alternative forms of medicine. In each case there are differences of belief so deep that they can seem irreconcilable.

While major shifts in culture are occurring in society and business, substantive knowledge is also changing rapidly. The half-life of the knowledge of a computer programmer is six months. If he or she is away from the discipline for six months half his or her knowledge becomes obsolete. MetaKnowledge can help us adapt to change because it is one step removed from the frontline and changes more slowly. It is more fundamental and so provides a reliable reference. It is a technology that is not likely to change significantly. But when changes in MetaKnowledge do occur they have revolutionary implications.

I believe much of MetaKnowledge as developed here is timeless. It would have given a manager an advantage centuries ago and it will be useful a hundred years from now. Nevertheless we will discuss it in the current context of three major trends that are impacting us personally and commercially. First is our increasing ability to improve our knowledge of the world, and therefore our ability to produce in all areas of economic importance including farming, manufacturing, the service sector, and knowledge products. As a result we are mastering physical needs in the developed world. This is allowing us to redirect more of our resources to nonphysical needs such as psychological well-being, mental health, and personal achievement. It is creating a new post-industrial economy.

Our mastery of physical production is at the foundation of the second trend, an explosion of communication and processing tools that include phones, faxes, e-mail, computers, cell phones, and audio and video digital technology that are converging in the Internet. As a result communication is increasing throughout the world and we are all being connected. This in turn feeds into the third major trend of globalization.

In a sense MetaKnowledge can be considered a proxy to wisdom. Wisdom requires a big picture view, both physical and temporal, and therefore implies the ability to do things for which there is no current evidence. Wisdom allows one to go with the tide when it's appropriate and to go against the tide when it is not. With MetaKnowledge we hope to create a management wisdom that will help guide companies, individuals, and societies over the coming decades. We hope to create a framework for a management system that is truly international. MetaKnowledge offers us a window to the future.

CHAPTER 2

KNOWLEDGE AND REVOLUTION

Let's go back to an earlier time in world history when Europe was in the midst of chaotic change and the world was being stood on its head, at least figuratively. The period was similar to our own. A new era of globalization was afoot. From the European perspective, new contacts with Asia and Africa had already been initiated. Now a whole new world was discovered, a by-product of an attempt to find a new route to India and China. The proposal that the world was actually round was gaining credibility: Perhaps the earth was not the center of the solar system. The printing press had made the Bible accessible to masses of people instead of just the elite. Heretics who dared to challenge the orthodoxy were being burned or tortured or both.

Expeditions ventured to new continents. A successful expedition resulted in fame and fortune. Hernando Cortez, a Spanish explorer, traveled to Mexico in the early sixteenth century. There he met Montezuma, an Aztec king who offered him a cup of strange dark liquid. Montezuma might have said, "This is a most precious gift. We call it the nectar of the gods. I personally like it so much I have fifty goblets a day. Here, enjoy it."

To which Cortez might have said after tasting it, "Phooey. This is bitter. How can you drink the stuff?" To the Spanish man it was a bitter tasting drink that didn't look very pretty, either. So the Aztec added sugar to make it more palatable. It was appreciated a lot more.

Today we take for granted the existence and availability of chocolate, but the process of creating a cup of chocolate is complex and involved. Several varieties of trees exist, and all are quite delicate. Seedlings must be grown in nurseries before being transplanted to the fields. Even then the trees are fragile and require protection from the wind and sun, often by planting other trees such as banana, plantain, and coconut around them as a protective shield. Only certain climates and soil conditions are suitable. With careful pruning and cultivation the trees yield fruit in four to five years.

Once full grown, the pods can be harvested. *Tumbadores* (pickers) are sent into the fields to pick the pods. The *tumbadores* are given long mitten-shaped knives that can reach up and cut the highest pods without injuring the soft bark of the tree. It requires a high skill level to determine the appropriate time to pick a pod. After picking, the pods are hacked open with a machete and allowed to ferment. From there a long and complex process developed over millennia begins. The end result is modern-day cocoa and chocolate.

These few, highly condensed paragraphs give a hint of the complexity of cocoa cultivation and production.

Re-Creating Existing Knowledge

Suppose you tried to re-create the knowledge of modern cocoa production. Imagine being in a jungle or forest. There are thousands of plants, maybe tens of thousands. Each plant has various parts, each potentially useful. You have seeds, stems, roots, barks, sap, and so on. Which plant—which part of the plant is useful? How would you know? How would you learn to process it so it could be used?

If our knowledge of plants today were zero it would be a major undertaking to find a use for all or any of the plants that we currently take for granted. In fact modern scientists are trying to do just that for the plants of the rain forest. If we could discover viable economic uses for them we could provide strong financial incentives to prevent the destruction of the rain forests of the world. But even with the benefit of our knowledge and technology it is a long and risky project to develop commercial uses for plants with little human history behind them.

Our best anthropological guess is that cocoa first came under cultivation 3,000 years ago. Cocoa is one of many crops now enjoyed globally that originated in the Americas. Up to 60% of the foods currently in use around the world were developed by Native Americans prior to the arrival of Europeans. So much for the myth of primitive people inhabiting the New World.

The cocoa pods were taken back to Europe but didn't make a stir right away. In fact it would require several major innovations before chocolate and cocoa took on their modern form and gained universal appeal. The Spanish learned how to process cocoa from the Aztecs. Despite Europe being a so-called advanced civilization no other European nation was able to independently develop the cocoa process. For a hundred years the Spanish held a monopoly on processing and production. The rest of Europe learned the process only when some Spanish monks revealed their secrets to the rest of the continent. At that point it was a hi-tech industry.

It would take several hundred years of research, improvements, and innovations before cocoa took on its modern form. With each improvement cocoa became more popular. With each innovation, the market grew. *The innovations from our perspective did two things: They expanded the market of people who wanted the product, and they brought down the costs of producing and delivering the product to consumers.*

As more knowledge goes into a product or industry it goes from being hi-tech to low-tech. With each new piece of knowledge the mystery of cocoa diminished. In fact the term hi-tech implies that there is a lot of knowledge still to be acquired in the field. Low-tech, therefore, must mean a technology that is highly developed and where commercial success relies mainly on pure business functions such as marketing, production, finance, and management.

What happened in the cocoa industry is generally the same process that has occurred and is occurring in other areas of agriculture, manufacturing, technology, and science today. *The difference is the speed at which we now can learn.* What once may have taken a hundred years to develop might now be done in five, or less.

A Possible Difference

But is the rate of learning the only thing that has changed? Uranium in its natural state gives off heat and radiation as individual atoms decay. As a nucleus decays it gives off energy and a few particles. If those particles happen to hit the nucleus of another uranium atom they may split that nucleus. Most of the time when a nucleus decays the released particles just escape into the environment without colliding with another atom.

As you increase the amount of uranium, however, the likelihood of more collisions and therefore more energy and even more particles given off increases. When the mass is large enough, a threshold is reached and the reactions become self-sustaining. Now you have the makings of atomic energy, or an atomic bomb. This level is called critical mass.

At critical mass a change of state has been reached. The uranium, in a sense, is behaving differently. A linear incremental increase in the amount of uranium leads to totally different behavior at the threshold. There are other changes of state in nature, such as when water becomes ice or steam. Water and ice behave very differently even though they are made up of exactly the same substance. With all the changes that are going on in the world today, are we just getting an acceleration of change or are we reaching a change of state? Are the results so different that new laws apply? That is one question we will try to answer.

An Existing Plantation

It is clear that a great deal of knowledge is involved in growing and processing cocoa and chocolate, and there are different people in different positions with different degrees of knowledge on a cocoa plantation. At the bottom of both the knowledge and economic scale are the day laborers, in this case pickers or *tumbadores*. They need to be able to correctly judge when to pick the pods, something that is far from obvious, but their knowledge and skill can be learned quickly and inexpensively. Their compensation is on the order of several dollars a day. They get paid for time. No time working, no pay. They also do more physical labor than anyone else on the estate.

At the top of the knowledge and economic scale are two people. The agronomist has intimate knowledge of the plant; he knows how to grow and cultivate it for maximum production and quality. The entrepreneur or manager has knowledge of the commercial end of farming.

And that brings up an important distinction. There are two kinds of Economic Knowledge:

1. Knowledge of the subject matter that is specific to the field. In this case it's agriculture. We will call this substantive knowledge.
2. Knowledge of how to monetize or commercialize substantive knowledge. We will call this entrepreneurial knowledge.

The entrepreneur/manager and the agronomist are the highest paid people on the estate. They are paid on the order of $1,000 a week and up. They possess a great deal of knowledge, some of it quite subtle, and have spent years learning their craft. Training someone for these positions is lengthy and expensive.

In between these highly trained positions and the *tumbadores* are a group of intermediate people involved in several functions. These people are to a large extent under the direction of the entrepreneur or agronomist, and may include supervisors of the *tumbadores*, bookkeepers, secretaries, sales people, tasters, cooks, and various assistants. Each earns roughly from fifty to several hundred dollars a week. Training takes from several months to several years. Replacing someone is moderately expensive and time-consuming.

And this brings up another distinction. We have described *categories* of economic knowledge: substantive knowledge and entrepreneurial knowledge. The people that make up these categories work together to make knowledge work for humanity. There are also three *types* of knowledge.

1. To do anything and achieve any kind of result requires knowledge. This is knowledge that has already been developed. It may take skill and creativity to apply it but the process has been demonstrated to work. It may not be the best way currently available, but it does the job. We will call this existing, or technical, knowledge.

Our definition of technical knowledge is different than the conventional definition. In other contexts, technical knowledge implies engineering or related to technology. We use it to mean existing knowledge in any field. There are various ways of acquiring technical knowledge. One can be trained by someone else. One can observe others or learn at school. Let's call the acquisition of technical knowledge training.

Most of what we learn is technical (existing) knowledge. We learn to add numbers, read, write, sell, patch a cut, and diagnose symptoms. All these are existing processes developed by others. For the most part once we learn something we continue doing it as taught until we're taught a better way. A technician knows how to do something in a given way. He does not necessarily have the knowledge or skill to create new ways of doing the same thing or something new. His way may be the best way available—or it may not. It does produce some result, however.

2 and 3. The other types are totally new knowledge. That is to say knowledge that is not learned from someone else but discovered on one's own.

Innovations and whole new processes are being developed and discovered in almost all areas. The ability to create new knowledge is different from the ability to do an existing task well or learn something well from someone else. A lot of what we call education is really technical training. It is teaching what is already known. One needs to learn current ways or at least about current ways before they can be improved upon.

One has to master the existing in order to be able to add to it. I am not sure anyone can be taught to create new knowledge. Some seem to have a predisposition to it and some not. The same can be said of technical knowledge. Some people are better at executing than others. Some adopt new methods quicker and better than others.

There are two different ways of creating new knowledge. One is within the current paradigm of the profession. The other is by creating a new paradigm. A little story will illustrate the point. In one of my college courses' laboratory experiments we were measuring the electric charge of the electron. Everyone had partnered up since we had only so much equipment to go around. My partner and I very carefully conducted the experiment. We recorded our results and then wrote up our conclusions independently. When we got back our papers he had an A and I had a C. I looked at him and said, "How can that be? We had the same data, the form of the report is standard." I looked over his paper and the format was the same. There was no original thinking involved in his over mine. But in order to make his data fit the expected answer he had thrown out two data points.

In my eyes I had been truthful and honest, the cornerstone, I thought, of scientific thinking. But because my data had not completely conformed and I had looked at the data and reality as it was, my work was downgraded.

There are many ways of looking at this story. Today, having studied with one of the giants in the field of statistics, I know the statistical methodology used by that professor (and all other physics professors of the time) was incorrect. I also know some of his other assumptions were fallacies. But the main point I want to make here is that in every field people are rewarded for agreeing with the Orthodoxy. Universities and most established institutions of knowledge are notorious in this regard. They screen out anyone who too readily challenges the existing paradigm. As a result universities and other similarly organized bodies are good at doing research within limits. They generally do not create the major breakthroughs that lead to whole new fields and whole new vistas.

In the field of physics there are three recognized Giants: Galileo, Newton, and Einstein. Galileo so offended the orthodox establishment that he was excommunicated. Newton was considered an average student with little promise. When the War of the Roses broke out, he had some time to think and essentially developed physics, what we now call Classical Physics, on his own. Einstein couldn't get a teaching job so he took a job as a patent clerk where he had time to think on his own. He of course revolutionized physics.

In the field of nineteenth-century biology, Charles Darwin and Alfred Russel Wallace independently developed the theory of evolution through natural selection, creating an upheaval that revolutionized thinking. They took a great deal of heat from orthodox thinkers. Each was independent of any major institution. Gregor Mendel, a monk, did experiments with pea plants and developed a theory of genetics at about the same time. When Mendel passed away the succeeding abbot of his monastery was so outraged by his experiments that he burned his papers. When Mendel's basic work was discovered in the early twentieth century it transformed biology and evolutionary theory.

Thomas Edison and Henry Ford were both extremely creative and inventive but neither of them completed school through the sixth grade.

To sum up we have delineated two *categories* of knowledge:

1. Substantive knowledge is knowledge of the subject matter.
2. Entrepreneurial knowledge is knowledge of how to commercialize substantive knowledge.

We have also delineated three *types* of knowledge:

1. Technical knowledge is existing knowledge necessary to produce a given result.

2. New knowledge within the existing paradigm is required to create new processes or new results.

3. New paradigms are the earth-shattering breakthroughs that create new fields of knowledge or new industries.

Learning

With this framework we have to examine the way we use the verb "to learn." After all, if I learn from a mentor how he does something, that is certainly an achievement. It raises me to his level. But this kind of learning, as valuable and necessary as it is, is distinctively different from the process of creating new knowledge. In fact the processes are almost opposite. Learning from a mentor normally requires fewer questions and a certain level of acceptance of what is said as gospel. It requires respect. New knowledge creation requires much more questioning and a kind of disrespect for the existing way of doing things.

Creating new paradigms can also be called learning, but revolution is probably more appropriate. "Revolution" implies a desire to totally uproot the existing order. People who create new paradigms are often seen as outcasts or oddballs. Jim Clark, the founder of Silicon Graphics, Netscape, Healtheon, Inc., and myCFO, developed very different commercial paradigms in the companies he started. The book *The New New Thing* made clear that the CEOs of the firms he founded considered him to be not just eccentric, but erratic.

What should be clear is that as our ability to learn has increased and the speed of change has increased, the value of being able to learn has increased. The ability to create new knowledge has increased even more. I am addressing this from an economic point of view. The ability to create new knowledge has always been valued in scientific circles and among the cultured. But the implication is that the relative economic values of these abilities has increased and will continue to do so.

We can categorize four different types of people with four different kinds of talents. (1) People who, once they learn a task, do it extremely well for an extended period of time. (2) People who can learn quickly and very well from others. These people like to learn. (3) People who can develop new knowledge within the existing framework of thought or within the existing paradigm. (4) People who create new paradigms. Let's call these Doers, Learners, Discoverers, and Creators.

In the recent past the doer was highly valued. The stable worker who did her job consistently was highly rewarded. She will continue to be valued, but only up to a point. The learner, the discoverer, and the creator are becoming relatively more important economically than they were in the past. And the doer who can't learn new tasks, new skills, and new methods will encounter difficulty.

Doing It All

Let's return to our cocoa estate for the moment and note that it is possible for one person to possess both substantive and entrepreneurial knowledge. This occurs on small farms all over the globe. It is also possible for one person to do all the work and make the decisions. The neighbor who grows some tomato plants and then sells them on a stand on her property is one example. It is also possible for this person to be making some innovations in her growing methods.

Separating the functions is necessary for two reasons. First is for clarity in our analysis. This will allow us to trace how organizations shift when we move from an economy that is involved in physical goods to one where knowledge is the strategic commodity. The second is that there is real leverage in separating out functions. People have different strengths and the individual who excels in multiple areas is the rare exception. There are often inefficiencies or problems when one person tries to perform too many functions.

Competitive Edge

The ability to create or adopt improved methods is what gives an enterprise a significant competitive edge. Improvements and breakthroughs provide an advantage over competitors. It's useful to examine how this occurs.

At any given point in time a plantation owner has incentives to expand his production by bringing more land under cultivation, hiring more workers, or attracting more capital. He can generally increase his revenues and profits by increasing production. He can also increase profitability by adopting any innovation that improves his productivity, lowers his costs, or increases the appeal of the product. Those innovations could be developed on his estate or they could be developed elsewhere and then adopted by the estate.

Profit motive is a strong incentive to improve. But it is often not enough. Anyone who has worked in industry or in a bureaucracy knows that the profit motive is often the last thing to be felt, measured, or responded to. Other things such as power, the need to have position or respect, respect for past methods, and the need to look out for number one often play a much larger role.

An estate that successfully adopts better methods ends up being stronger. Those that fail to change experience a smaller market or find they cannot turn a profit. They either turn to other products or go out of business. Firms that adapt to the new have a better chance of surviving. The death of old firms through market forces is just as important a mechanism for improvement, indeed probably more important than profit. Failure is an integral part of improvement and progress in an industry and also for society.

With each innovation producers improve their competitive position. An improvement in marketability leads to a larger market share. It may even expand the market. An improvement in production lowers costs and therefore improves profits. The immediate beneficiaries are the producers who adopt the changes. But in time every producer adopts or is forced to adopt the methods that work best and any advantage from the change is given up.

When the whole market adopts the changes, then the beneficiaries are the consumers—in other words, society. Long- and medium-term it is the public that benefits from lower prices and better products. Eventually all the benefits of an innovation get passed on to society in the form of lower prices, greater availability, and a more desirable product.

So the process runs something like this. An innovation is created. It lowers costs, and improves productivity, time to market, taste, or some other important factor. Some producers adopt it because they see an advantage. These early adopters gain an advantage in the marketplace, market share, profits, sales, or some other important economic attribute. Some of the other producers adopt the change when they see that the early adopters are successful. Still others wait. Some wait to the bitter end before adopting it. Some go out of business. Sometimes the stronger companies buy those that are going out of business. Sometimes the weaker ones just fail because the market can handle demand with-out their resources. Eventually the whole industry adopts the innovation and the early adopters' advantage is lost. But the gain has been passed on to the consumer in the form of lower costs, better taste, or some other attribute.

I believe this process has been going on for millennia. One of the distinguishing characteristics of our age is that this process has been formalized. And we have sped up the process.

Cocoa has gone from being a rare and expensive product enjoyed by royalty to a universally consumed product. Its price has continually dropped. (Its price had to drop in order to be so widely consumed.) This has occurred not just in cocoa but in almost every commodity and continues to happen in manufactured goods as well as knowledge products. This is a strong indication that there is some universal process at work with built-in incentives.

By every measure cocoa and chocolate is a great business. It has almost universal market penetration, people consume it habitually, it is universally recognized, and everyone has tried it. People spend money on it every day without thinking about it. Yet by being so successful it has lost its financial glamour and mystery. Cocoa production is an economic commodity. An economic commodity is when something is virtually indistinguishable from one to the next. Since all producers have access to the same knowledge and it can be produced in quantity, much of the competition is based on business functions such as finance, marketing, and price. As a result, price and margins are constrained. Most significantly, the economic importance of commodities declines as they consume a decreasing percentage of the gross national product.

This is not to say that running a business involving an economic commodity cannot be profitable. The Hershey Foods Corporation does not grow cocoa but processes it and sells chocolate and cocoa throughout the world. It has a commanding presence in the industry with some of the best known products such as Hershey's Kisses, Hershey Chocolate Syrup, Kit Kat, and Hershey's chocolate bars. Hershey's is virtually synonymous with chocolate and has better margins than other manufacturers. In 2002 the Hershey Trust, owner of a controlling interest in the Hershey Corporation, put the company up for sale. The high bid was in excess of $12 billion, certainly a respectable sum, but this pales compared to the tens of billions of dollars that Qwest and AOL Time

Warner wrote off in 2002 and 2003. And it is a pittance compared to the trillions of dollars in market capitalization lost by telecommunication firms from the stock market's peak in 1999 to the end of 2002.

There are just a few companies left that mass-produce chocolate bars and syrup in the world today. But new companies are starting up all the time as high-end boutiques that offer specialty, gourmet cocoa products to those with more discriminating palates or more expensive chocolate addictions. Massive growth in cocoa consumption in developed countries is over, yet it can still be a good business providing jobs and profitability, not to mention great satisfaction to the makers and consumers alike.

The inevitable conclusion is that there is a very high knowledge content in cocoa and every agricultural product. A further conclusion is that the more knowledge invested into a product, the more it can be produced with the same resources and lower costs. When enough knowledge is invested it becomes an economic commodity.

Knowledge moves a product from being hi-tech and expensive to being a cheap and universally available commodity.

Inverse Effects

Almost every product becomes an economic commodity making it less expensive and more plentiful. The amount of time a typical person needs to work to pay for products therefore decreases over the years. The average person in the beginning of the twenty-first century needed to work fewer hours to purchase a car than an average person in the middle of the twentieth century needed to work. Products therefore cost less not just in dollar terms but in the amount of time a person must work to earn them. But this also implies that time becomes more valuable. An hour of time today buys many more products than an hour of time did ten, twenty, and thirty years ago, so time is more expensive. We should therefore not expect personal services or any experience that is heavily time dependent to decrease in price. In fact, prices for time-based products will increase. This includes education, especially higher education, hair and nail stylists, and mechanics. High-end shops in any of these categories continue to increase in price. Just price a haircut at a fancy hair salon or get your nails done in one of the new nail salons that are popping up all over the place to experience what I mean.

To get some perspective on the price of an economic commodity relative to time and capital, consider that the wholesale price of green (unroasted) coffee beans in January 2003 was about 60¢ a pound but the least expensive cup of coffee I could purchase at Starbucks was $1.30. A pound of coffee beans can make at least forty cups of coffee.

Extending the Model to Other Types of Business

In this knowledge model of an enterprise I designated six different categories of people based on their knowledge. There are (1) the entrepreneur, (2) those working under him managing a function such as department heads, and (3) those executing tasks in these departments. On the other side are (4) the substantive knowledge expert, (5) his functional assistants, and (6) laborers. We could easily break this down further: Entrepreneurial knowledge could be broken down into marketing, finance, and management skills, but that is not necessary for our purposes.

A manufacturing operation might have one entrepreneur, one department head for each entrepreneurial function, and several people under each department head. There might be several subject matter experts, such as engineers and production managers, each with many supervisors who in turn have many laborers. But consider a so-called knowledge-based company such as an accounting firm, a consulting firm, or an investment banking firm. An accounting firm has many subject matter experts (accountants and CPAs), a few people working under them, and few or no laborers or unskilled workers. There is one person running the firm, the managing partner who most likely is an accountant himself. The firm has an internal finance department and treasurer. If the firm is progressive it may have a marketing head who might not be an accountant.

Knowledge-based firms are characterized by the proportion of substantive knowledge experts to workers in the other five categories. There are many more substantive knowledge experts for each entrepreneurial expert. There are fewer department heads for each expert and there are no laborers to speak of. As an economy moves from an industrial economy to a post-industrial economy, manufacturing loses its importance and the number of people involved in manufacturing companies declines. The knowledge companies that replace them have fewer laborers and department heads and need many more experts. A society must train and educate more people to become experts and must create jobs for former laborers whose firms have shrunk. In the United States we have, so far, developed more knowledge workers in hi-tech industries, but have also developed more service jobs in fields such as retail. In 2002 the largest private employer in the country was Wal-Mart, with more than 1.3 million employees.

CHAPTER 3

DEATH AND BIRTH IN ECONOMICS

"Prices are too low! Every farmer should be able to earn a decent living; I am not saying an outstanding living but a decent living. And farm prices are now just too low." That was the message of Nick Parsons as he rode his farm's combine across Canada headed toward Ottawa, the capital of the nation, in the spring of 2000. Everywhere he went other farmers gathered and cheered him. The news was filled with stories of farmers losing their farms. Some farms had been in the family for more than a century, but despite the fact that husband and wife both worked day jobs to earn extra money, they couldn't make enough to support the farm.

Canada had been hit with a double whammy: low prices worldwide and the end of government farm subsidies. What was a tight situation had now become untenable. The situation in the United States was no better. Despite all the rhetoric of deregulating farming, in June 2000 President Clinton signed into law $7.1 billion of farm relief. This on top of $15 billion approved in 1998 and 1999. In 2002 farming deregulation was essentially abandoned in the United States as President Bush signed into law a massive farm subsidy bill providing close to $20 billion a year in welfare to farms, especially those growing major grain crops.

But the trend is in motion. The number of individuals involved in farming continues to decline and now is just less than 2%. There is no reason to believe the trend won't continue, meaning even fewer farmers in the future.

We can all sympathize with the plight of farmers who are about to lose their farms and everything they have spent their lives working for. But this is nothing new and these incidents will continue to occur in the future. There is little that any government can do about the low global prices of commodities that we have learned to grow efficiently in various regions of the world. There are no monopolies or cartels to save them. Subsidies only exacerbate the situation, dumping massive amounts of subsidized grain onto world markets and further forcing down prices.

The decline of farm prices is due to the success of farmers as a whole. It has been going on for more than a century and will continue. The forces driving this are larger than any government can control, except for short periods of time and even then only at enormous cost in terms of money and misuse of assets. But while some farms are forced to close, others are prospering. Pork and grain farmers are being decimated. But organic farming is a profitable new area to which many farms have adapted. Vineyards in North America are another profitable area. In each case, a major adaptation to new crops and new methods is required.

In 2002 wheat prices surged, almost doubling. One to two year surges in an agriculture product occur from time to time, allowing those who can get a crop out to prosper while those who can't face even worse times. But as farmers adjust or extreme weather patterns return to the more familiar, prices continue their long-term decline. Price surges are short-term phenomena that can obscure the long-term trend.

Those feeling comfortable with the old ways may believe they have a right to continue doing the same things their ancestors did and earn a decent living. They may find that those rights are not recognized by nature, economies, or consumers.

The plight is not just suffered by farmers. If it were this book would be of interest to just a small fraction of the population. The same is happening in manufacturing and for that matter in every industry. Manufacturing employs just 14% of the population compared to 50% early in the twentieth century. Many industries, especially the older manufacturing industries, have excess capacity even in boom times. We have two choices. We can fight these realities and suffer the consequences or we can recognize what is happening and adapt our actions and our policies to conform and take advantage of the situation.

Unemployment

If you follow this thinking into the future, you could conclude that unemployment will steadily increase. After all if we can manufacture and create the same number of physical goods with fewer and fewer people as we become better and more efficient, where will all the people who were formerly involved in manufacturing or service, or farming, go? Just that point of view was meticulously argued by Jeremy Rifkin in *The End of Work*, published in 1995.

Yet in the year 2000, the issue that government policy makers were most concerned about in the United States was not unemployment but too much employment. As ludicrous as it sounds, Federal Reserve Chairman Alan Greenspan had constantly voiced his concern that the economy was becoming overheated. One indicator often pointed to was the unemployment rate, which hovered around or below 4%. The fed was nudging up interest rates to try and "cool off" the economy and bring unemployment up (despite the fact that in Ireland the unemployment rate was 1.5% with little or no inflation).

Even in 2002 in the midst of a recession, unemployment was less than 6%. While no unemployment is good for workers or the economy in the short-term, the point is that improving efficiencies plus greater imports did not lead to 20% average unemployment as simple arithmetic might have predicted.

How could that be? If we are getting so good at doing more with fewer people, how could we have had relatively little unemployment? Well, the story is not uniform. While the United States, Ireland, Great Britain, and other nations were experiencing robust economies and falling unemployment rates, other nations such as France lagged and still experienced high unemployment rates.

How do some countries react when faced with the notion of declining employment in an industry? Some nations have carried out extreme measures to deal with it. The French government initiated a law in the mid-1990s that workers at major corporations could not work beyond a certain hour of the evening. Government inspectors would police the buildings and if employees were found working late their companies would be fined. The thinking was linear and well meaning. By limiting the amount of work that each worker could do the corporation would be forced to hire more people and therefore ameliorate unemployment. To some extent this kind of thinking is being challenged and reversed today in the European Union.

The thinking among unions was similar earlier in the twentieth century. Limit the workweek and work year so more people could work. Other solutions have been feather bedding, forcing employers to hire more workers than needed, or creating hundreds of job categories and then limiting what workers in each category could and could not do.

The end result was not higher employment but stagnation and lower employment as whole industries failed. The march toward improvement and greater efficiency cannot be stopped. Even those industries where these types of regulations were strongest, such as steel and automobile manufacturing, have given in to some kinds of efficiencies and fewer employed workers.

It has not just been the unions. Management has also sought government regulation to protect it from "unfair and destructive" competition. So how is it that we found ourselves in a situation where the fed was worried about too much employment? Well, as anyone who hasn't been asleep over the last few years knows, whole new industries developed. And they developed in those nations where deregulation was taking place and there was the greatest flux of both people and ideas.

Unemployment cannot be dealt with by restricting work or productivity. Just the opposite! It is best dealt with by encouraging ongoing improvement in quality and productivity and allowing those companies who can't keep up to fail. Short-term, of course, this seems to lead to unemployment, but long-term it creates greater wealth not just for the successful companies but society as a whole. With higher quality and lower prices, consumers have additional income to spend on new services, products, and experiences. Opportunities are thus created for entrepreneurs to create the new economic products and hire more people, leading to greater employment.

It is interesting to trace just how these new industries developed. One point of departure is Japanese consumer electronics. Before Japan became a powerhouse in electronics, a stereo system cost several hundred dollars. A really good one cost a thousand dollars or more. And some were pretty delicate. What is sometimes forgotten today is that in the 1950s the expression "made in Japan" was synonymous with poor quality, low-tech items such as the little bamboo umbrellas that were placed in mai-tais and other exotic cocktails.

But Japan absorbed a great deal of useful knowledge such as industrial engineering, quality control, and management of people in key industries. By the 1970s they were producing great stereos, the equivalent of anything else the world had to offer. Soon they were bringing the price down and improving quality. The stereos were no longer delicate but in fact quite robust.

One good example is Sony's Walkman. When first introduced it was small, weighed about a pound, and cost several hundred dollars. But soon other manufacturers such as Panasonic and AIWA brought out their own models. The prices kept dropping to much less than a hundred dollars. Anyone could afford a Walkman. The small original Walkman seemed large and bulky compared to later models. In effect, they commoditized their product over a period of eighteen months to two years. This is exactly the opposite strategy that other manufacturers were following. When Japanese industry next went after the semiconductor market, they successfully took over the market for memory chips and improved quality while lowering prices.

Then other companies began to study quality and related methods. One method that was adopted was the quick commoditization of a product. Look at one of the most successful products of the 1990s—the personal computer. If I had told you in the late 1970s that you would soon have a computer on your desk that had the power of a mainframe of five years earlier, you might have been excited. But if I had told you that almost everyone would have one and most people would want a more powerful one every few years, you might have looked at me like I was an eccentric whose feet weren't firmly planted on the earth. Why would anyone want a more powerful computer when you could do spreadsheets, word processing, games, and other fun things on your existing computer?

Intel and Microsoft, with their respective contributions of microprocessors and software, have effectively commoditized the computer. In fact they commoditized each new generation of computer every two years. A two-year-old computer has almost no residual value. Yet this commoditization of computers, a process that took cocoa several hundred years to accomplish, has not hampered employment in the industry. In fact it has dramatically increased it. Having a computer on every desk has done many remarkable things. It has meant that many people have access to computers. It has led to new ideas being generated. And it has created whole new applications that no one was thinking of even five years ago. Whole new markets have opened up.

In fact the very process of commoditizing the product, which one might think results in unemployment, is actually responsible for more employment. By lowering costs and making products more available a dynamic environment is created. When more people have access, a larger market is generated with greater financial incentives for innovation. Additional creativity is focused on new uses.

This hinges on the ability to create new products with new compelling uses. For physical goods that rely on reselling the same "perfected" product, the relative importance and relative profitability will decline. There are only so many razors, toothpastes, soaps, and other such items you can sell to the world. These products are declining in importance specifically because they have been mastered or perfected. While it may bring frowns from those involved in these industries, for humanity it is a good thing. That is not to say, however, that you cannot run a very profitable business in a mature market. You can! But the relative importance and relative size of that industry will decline over time.

As an example consider that in good years Apple, a company no longer vying for a major share of the personal computer market but has instead become a niche player, had higher profitability than Colgate-Palmolive, one of the largest consumer products companies. And Apple's profits are of course dwarfed by Intel, Microsoft, and other leaders in the technology industry. Colgate-Palmolive is one of the best run companies anywhere and has some of the best-known consumer brands such as Colgate toothpaste and Palmolive soap. Yet their profits —not their market valuation, but actual profits, the kind measured by honest accountants—have at times been exceeded by Apple. Apple's earnings, however, have been erratic while Colgate-Palmolive has seen a steady rise during the last eighteen years. When run well, old businesses, as evidenced by Colgate-Palmolive, can be quite prosperous. In fact Colgate-Palmolive had a better return to investors than General Electric and other well-known high fliers during the bull market of the 1990s. But soap, toothpaste, and related products will continue to decline over time as a percentage of the gross national product.

Long-Term Trend

The long-term trend is inevitable improvement in any industry. A new industry will at first employ more and more people until a certain level is reached. After that, fewer and fewer people are required to provide the same or an increasing level of customer gratification. The number of people employed in farming will continue to decrease, as will the number of people in manufacturing and traditional service areas.

Let me add a caveat. This trend is not continuous or straight. The economic environment is not continuous. There are boom times, recessions, and times of modest growth. There are times when improvements do not seem to be passed on to the consumer. And then there are times when all the improvements seem to go to consumers, and companies can't hold on to any profit. At times the trends we are discussing may not be evident but the factors underlying it are. Long-term we can notice the changes but in some periods the trend may be overwhelmed by turbulence in the economy.

Companies that prosper in shrinking industries will be those that invest in providing more for less, continually adding value over time. As an industry matures some companies may experience significant growth while others die. We have seen this in retailing where some of the major old-line retailing names such as Gimbel's and Abraham & Strauss disappeared while new ones such as Target and Wal-Mart sprung up doing business in new ways and offering more for less. Companies that want to survive will need to constantly ask certain questions such as the following: What does the customer want? What will the customer want? What may the customer want? What can I provide that the customer may not even know he wants?

Population Growth

There is another factor to consider: population growth. The most generally accepted notion of the twentieth century had been that population would continue to grow exponentially. A prediction made in the middle of the twentieth century had us so packed in on the planet by the early part of the twenty-first century that we would hardly be able to move without butting up against our neighbor. However, when nations reach a certain level of affluence and development, it appears that population growth levels off. It may even stop—and in some cases the population may voluntarily decline. In nature we have many cases where populations control themselves at levels below what the environment could sustain.

Italy has the lowest birthrate in Europe and it is projected that at existing levels its population will cease growing and even decline in the next few decades. Of course predictions of this kind are risky, even if based on mathematical models of existing trends. The next decade could see a generation of Italians falling in love with the idea of a big family. But as material affluence becomes a global phenomenon we are looking at a decrease in the rate of growth of the global population. A stabilization of the global population in the twenty-first century is now a real possibility.

A stable or declining global population could be one of the most significant of economic events. It could change whole spending patterns and result in very different investment strategies.

Malthus

One well-known economist of the eighteenth century, Thomas Malthus, made the observation that human population growth was capable of growing exponentially while the food supply was destined to increase linearly. He therefore forecast periods of misery that the poor would experience especially hard. This was a result of population temporarily outstripping food supply and then being brought back into equilibrium by hard times, resulting in a lower birthrate and a higher death rate. Some isolated periods of drought or famine in parts of the world seemed to play into that hypothesis. On the whole, however, we have not seen population declines due to starvation, such as predicted by Malthus and others who have forecast some kind of ecological disaster.

In fairness to Malthus, his observations and predictions have been factors in providing incentives to help slow down the growth of populations. Even people who have never read his work have been influenced by his ideas. The development of new methods of birth control and the shift away from seeing life's purpose as having children may owe some credit to his work and his dire predictions.

Respecting Malthus's intellectual work, however, our conclusion of future outcomes is, at this point in time, very different than his. Even if population continues to grow, we have the ability to increase food production even faster. Every manufacturer I talk to, even during a strong economy, feels he has the ability to quickly increase production on short notice. Generally the problem in both agriculture and manufacturing is not that we can't produce enough but that we can produce more than required.

Should population stabilize while our ability to increase the production and distribution of food and goods continue their bristling pace, the world would enter an economic realm without precedence. Even with population continuing to increase, our conquest of material needs is outstripping the needs of the human race. We are entering a time qualitatively different than the recent past. Old issues will disappear and new issues will become paramount.

Several things threaten this potential and might even render it obsolete. A major ecological disaster, a dirty war leaving parts of the earth ravaged, a shortage of some critical item, an astronomical accident (such as we witnessed when an asteroid struck the planet Jupiter), would put us back decades or centuries or more. On a more mundane level a successful cartel or inane government regulations, agreements among government, or a mismanagement of money supply might put up temporary roadblocks.

I would expect that some of these things or some combination of these would occur from time to time and cause some disruption. When they do occur they will become a subject of global concern and the world's intelligence will be summoned to deal with it. New areas of profitability and business opportunity will arise for each stumbling block. The long-term trends are in motion and have enormous consequences for the people of the earth.

Cyclical Unemployment

There are some potential structural problems. Large unemployment is a real possibility in future decades, especially during economic slowdowns. In order to insure future employment we need to keep investing and encouraging investment in new economic products, whatever they may be. Since we have no idea what the products or services of the future may be we are using the term "economic product" to denote any service, product, or experience for which people will pay money.

We do not limit the idea of investing just to capital. Time, particularly the time of people with entrepreneurial and substantive knowledge, is a key investment activity. Investment can take place in an established corporation or through the vehicle of a start-up company. Investments can also occur in the nonprofit sector and these also create jobs.

All that needs to be done to produce large-scale unemployment are some of the major policies of the past. These include excessive regulation of markets, creation of government sanctioned monopolies, and large bureaucracies that were fostered specifically to overcome unemployment. Any policy that limits the creation of new enterprises or the entrance of new technology or ideas into an old field will automatically lead to unemployment. Regulation is necessary and useful but it must be done in such a way that barriers to entry are not significantly increased. It should be noted that allowing the number of organizations in an industry to drop too low also increases the barriers to entry.

As the production of older economic products are mastered fewer resources are needed. Those resources must be free to shift into new uses. This means that failure and shifts of all kinds must be allowed. Disposable income freed up by better efficiencies and better prices is constantly becoming available for new economic products. It is the entrepreneur's job to find new economic products to fill the needs of consumers and industry.

Governments have been so poor at creating new markets that it is not even a reasonable consideration to allow them to do it. In fact, even successful older corporations have done a poor job of creating the future. Most often it is whole new enterprises. The older established semiconductor companies were essentially marginalized while new companies such as Intel became the leaders. General Electric and RCA were both massive failures in the computer business. Often the protagonists are outcasts from the older corporate world or those who just did not or would not fit in. It is doubtful that Steve Jobs, one of the founders of Apple, could have fit in at IBM. It was he and his partner who, working out of their garage, helped launch the microcomputer industry.

Since what the new economic products might be is totally unpredictable and speculative it becomes essential that governments refrain from creating regulations that hinder new technologies entering old industries. Governments must not create bureaucracies or regulations that slow down the death of economically obsolete businesses, business models, or organizational methods.

Governments need to focus their efforts not on the preservation of the old but on being midwives to the new. This means allowing and even encouraging less successful companies and less successful organizational forms to die so that new ones may take their place. Government and older corporations have a role in the development of the new. Government funding provided a critical stimulus for the computer and the Internet. But it was small upstart companies that successfully commercialized those industries. Corporations such as Hewlett-Packard and Intel have in turn made other newer corporations and technologies possible. Steve Wozniak, the other Apple founder, worked for Hewlett-Packard and developed much of the basic technology there. When he left to found his own firm, HP management was supportive—not angry. Silicon Valley managers have often spent time at one of these two giant firms.

There is nothing more inhumane than artificially keeping people in a failing environment. Few wish to leave voluntarily but with a healthy economy each person has a much better chance of finding better employment in a firm with a future.

Survival Skills

Certainly good marketing, finance, and management skills are important for corporate survival. But organizations that wish to survive must also learn to recognize when change becomes inevitable. Adapting and changing the way of doing business has become a necessary survival skill. Adaptation and change, however, need to occur within some framework. Adaptation and change must be done against a backdrop of long-term trends and cycles and a realization that some aspects of business will not change. Every forty years or so we have a bull market in stocks and some unlikely ideas are brought forward as signaling a whole new way of doing business. In the last go around with dot-com mania, profits became superfluous and credit standards disappeared. But this was not adaptation. This was intoxication. And this was not new. There was a similar period of excess in the 1960s when people could raise millions of dollars on Wall Street with nothing more than a concept or a vague notion of a business plan. And the roaring '20s also had their twenty-year-old millionaires who happened to be at the right place at the right time. But both periods were followed by heavy hangovers.

Caveats

We are looking toward a time when everyone in the developed world, perhaps even everyone in the money economy, can be fed, clothed, and bathed with a small portion of our resources. Naturally such a statement presents a positive and optimistic vision. But there are problems, issues, and potential drawbacks that should be kept in mind. Among these are pollution, health, and inequitable distribution of wealth. But among the most serious is the fact that billions of people on other continents such as Africa and Asia are having difficulty with much more basic issues of survival and health. Floods in Mozambique in the year 2000 left millions of people homeless. I was struck by a televised image of a woman being pulled off her roof into a rescue helicopter. As she was being pulled up, the bulk of her valued possessions, which were in a plastic bag, slipped from her hand. While still on the hoist she struggled to go back for her possessions but was pulled into the helicopter.

That scene made me very grateful to be living in the developed world. Not because I have so many possessions, but because anything I have is easily replaced, except for its sentimental value. Our bounty of goods means that most basic items are easily replenished. The real value of abundance is the freedom it provides. Having material abundance allows us to care less about goods and more about values and how we live our lives.

The economic difference between the wealthy or developed nations and the poorer or developing nations is startling. It presents some of the most significant challenges for humanity in the twenty-first century. There are indigenous societies in the world with very highly developed cultures and value systems. They represent part of the real wealth of humanity. Yet for the most part, when they encounter the physical abundance provided by our economic system, they want that as well. Often their approach to wealth destroys part of their own culture as they acclimate and assimilate the material blessings of the productive economy. Biological and cultural diversity are part of our common heritage and wealth. I for one hope we can preserve as much of it as possible. Yet our productive affluence directly and indirectly threatens both. Preserving each will be part of our challenge.

Consequences

How will the world and our society shift as material wealth starts being taken for granted? There are several models that might give us a clue. One was developed by psychologist Abraham Maslow. Dr. Maslow stated that humans have a hierarchy of needs. Initially their desires and attention are drawn to physical survival. Adequate food, shelter, and clothing are paramount. Once those are met security becomes a prime concern. Next is love and affiliation.

Finally when all the prior needs are met, the desire for self-actualization comes to the fore. This is the need to create, to express, to investigate for the sake of knowledge and the need for personal development. According to Dr. Maslow this need is never satisfied. Our collective mastery of the production of physical goods now allows our society to move its emphasis to other areas.

The Science of Improvement

But how is it that we can improve our control over physical production so much better now than before, at least in the developed world? At the core of accelerated progress over the last forty years is The New Management. And at the core of The New Management is MetaKnowledge.

CHAPTER 4

THE NEW MANAGEMENT

Back to the Future

Flash back to the early twentieth century. AT&T, a young monopoly, had established a research lab called, appropriately enough, the Bell Laboratories, after the inventor of the telephone, Alexander Graham Bell. AT&T had a problem, a problem of uniformity. They advertised that each phone was just like the last. Yet the more they tried to make the phones alike, the worse the results. They asked a young physicist at the laboratory, Walter Shewhart, to find a solution.

Shewhart worked on the problem and developed profound insights into quality and uniformity. He developed powerful tools for obtaining maximum economic results. Like other tools, however, they were useless or harmful if applied without understanding. The body of work that Shewhart was to create sparked a revolution of unfathomable magnitude. In his own lifetime many of his ideas and tools were adopted into AT&T's manufacturing and service areas. The result was a level of quality that the rest of the world only dreamed of achieving.

For years Americans traveling abroad were struck by the huge differences in quality between the American phone system and what was available anywhere else. Those born more recently may find it hard to believe that the difference was so huge. Let us call the success of AT&T from 1930 to 1960 Exhibit A for The New Management.

Shewhart published a book in 1931 called *Economic Control of Quality of Manufactured Product*. In 1938 he was invited by W. Edwards Deming, chairman of the department of mathematics at The Graduate School, U.S. Department of Agriculture (USDA), to give a series of lectures in Washington, D.C. Deming, who held a PhD in mathematical physics from Yale University, was a friend of Shewhart. Deming was to become Shewhart's most famous disciple.

Fascinated by Shewhart's work, Deming became the editor for the written version of Shewhart's Washington lectures. The manuscript was titled *Statistical Method from the Viewpoint of Quality Control,* and it was to be Shewhart's second book. This book contains a wealth of understanding still largely unappreciated by the world at large.

At the start of World War II, America found herself scandalously unprepared. The quality of American military goods was terrible when compared to the Germans. In response, the Department of War launched a crash course in quality control. Among the instructors was W. Edward Deming. Deming and others taught hundreds of engineers and managers who, in turn, taught thousands of others the methodology and tools of quality control. The result was a dramatic improvement in quality and production throughout North America.

Records uncovered in the 1990s showed that the Japanese had predicted the United States would have been able to produce a certain amount of war materials to fight a two-front war in a nine-year period. Using the theory and methods taught by Deming and Shewhart, the United States in fact produced twice that amount in three and a half years. We were producing at a rate about six times greater than what Japanese intelligence thought was possible. An incredible result by any standard! Even more impressive, this increased production was done using a less experienced workforce. Tens of thousands of women replaced the experienced, male dominated workforce who were redeployed for combat. This quality and production improvement was so visible that for decades after the Japanese surrendered it was said that, "Production won the war." Let us call this Exhibit B for The New Management.

After the war, America began to abandon most of what she had learned about quality and productivity. There was no need for it. The war was over. Things were just too good and demand exceeded supply. GIs returned to the workforce. Most received no training in quality. Managers accustomed to traditional thinking viewed quality as difficult and failed to appreciate its meaning and its importance. Any North American firm that could produce could profit. There was overwhelming demand as GIs coming back home needed to start a family. Any method, *with or without theory,* seemed to work.

Across the ocean Japan found herself in just the opposite situation. She was in dire straits. Japan had a well-earned reputation for making shoddy consumer goods. This reputation, earned before the war, was lived up to after the war as well. To make matters worse, her traditional markets in the Far East had been stripped away after the war.

After the war, Japanese industry started to receive some of the same management training that Americans had received during the war. The management and industrial engineering courses that were developed by the U.S. government throughout the war were instituted in Japan by the United States occupation forces under General Douglas MacArthur.

In addition, on their own, Japanese industrial leaders began to feel that knowledge of the new field of quality control would be very helpful. They began preparing a course for national distribution. As it happened, one person working for the occupation forces was the statistician W. Edwards Deming.

In 1950 Deming delivered a full-week seminar directed at the same level of management he had addressed in the United States during the war. These were plant managers, engineers, and middle managers. He realized that unless he did something different in Japan, the results would not last, just as they had not lasted in the United States. He insisted on addressing top management. At the now famous lecture in August 1950, the top business executives attended, representing approximately 85% of the capital of Japan, to hear him talk about their responsibilities.

What happened afterward was the most spectacular economic revival in the history of humankind. Japan gathered steam and became an industrial powerhouse while the United States seemed to be in a downward spiral. In the late 1950s and early 1960s Japan began to export more and more. Gradually, almost imperceptibly, Japan began to take over industries. Then it seemed to become a tide and finally a rout. Radios, televisions, consumer electronics, motorcycles, cameras, optics, watches, and other industries came under Japanese control. By the early 1980s Japan was dominating industry after industry. Cars and semiconductors seemed the next inevitable conquest for the Japanese juggernaut. Just the rumor of a Japanese firm competing in a new industry brought fear into the hearts of the executives of that industry. Call this Exhibit C for The New Management.

At the same time this was happening the quality of American manufactured products was plummeting. By the 1970s many consumers joked that "Ford" was an acronym for "Found On Road Dead" or "Fix Or Repair Daily." In the 1970s and '80s it was becoming sadly evident to American consumers that American manufacturers could not compete on the basis of price or quality. The Japanese, it was believed, had some magic ingredient that American companies did not seem able to replicate. To add insult to injury, Japanese companies began taking over failing American factories and making them successes, producing higher quality at much lower costs.

Then another twist of fortune occurred. Starting in 1980 a revolution in the thinking of major American companies took place. Whereas in the 1980s we had to restrain the number of cars imported into the United States, today American cars compete with Japanese cars and the cars of any nation on both quality and price. A stream of new products, new innovations, and new designs seemingly slowed down the penetration of Japanese cars into the U.S. market and stopped the flow of red ink in the financial statements of domestic producers.

In the 1980s the last American motorcycle manufacturer, Harley-Davidson, needed government protection, was forced to lay off one-third of its people, and looked to a new German engine for hope. In 2002 Harley-Davidson controlled close to 60% of the market for large motorcycles. Plant capacity had expanded 20–30% each year and the company still could not satisfy demand. Today the company is economically robust, and not only its bikes but many other products bearing the Harley-Davidson logo are in hot demand.

In the 1980s the American semiconductor and computer industries were threatened by Japanese companies and the Japanese government–sponsored fifth-generation research project was to have provided the next generation of computers to the world market. Today the fifth-generation project has disappeared, while the American semiconductor and computer industries are robust. American brands such as Dell, Compaq, IBM, Sun, and Apple are global players. The Microsoft Windows/Intel Microprocessor (sometimes called Wintel) combination is dominating microcomputers worldwide.

What happened? American industries were on the ropes as Japan charged forward. American executives visited Japan to learn the Japanese "secret." Some were told to visit Deming. Serendipitously, when NBC aired a documentary called *If Japan Can, Why Can't We?* in 1980, American management discovered Deming. The last part of the documentary contains footage of an eccentric, elderly consultant and professor. He is taped talking about what he had taught in Japan thirty years before. Many people found that to be the most interesting part of the show.

The next day his phone was ringing off the hook. He soon became a consultant to Ford and General Motors. He lectured, taught, and was in such demand that his schedule was booked three years in advance. Joseph M. Juran, another quality expert with ties to Shewhart, was also rediscovered.

As a result North American industry experienced a rebirth. Companies, even whole industries that were on their deathbeds, revived. In fact, in some cases, they redominated their industries. Let's call this Exhibit D for The New Management.

Here we have four distinct situations where certain principles and ideas caused a dramatic reversal in the fortunes of companies, whole industries, and even nations. In most of the cases it was the same people managing the companies before and after the change. What changed? What caused the profound transformation? It was a little knowledge. But in each case the successful companies were those that were able to adopt and implement a different way of thinking that led to a different way of managing.

Adopting and implementing is easier said than done. In order to change, the old preconceptions need to change. All too often managers, owners, and employees looking to improve are relying on their old beliefs, the very beliefs that got them into trouble, to somehow lead them out. Most often they are looking for quick bold action, new equipment or technology, or new employees as the keys to their success. While a successful transformation may include some or all of these, they are not the key. All the changes in the world without new beliefs and new knowledge won't be enough. Business history is littered with cases of managers who failed miserably in trying to bring about change. It is also filled with cases of companies that, upon reaching a certain level of success, regressed to their old ways only to fail again. A taste of success is often sufficient to induce old behaviors that lead back to failure. Why have some companies made such successful and seemingly effortless transformations while others floundered? These are interesting questions and we will return to them.

But first, just what is The New Management? The gist of The New Management can be distilled into three main principles.

Three Basic Underlying Principles

1. *An Intense Focus on Customers.* In The New Management the purpose of a company is to improve the lives of its customers. This translates into an intense focus on not just satisfying the customer but going beyond satisfaction to develop loyal customers. It is essential to understand the needs and desires of customers so as to organize and manage the company to best fulfill them. This is external quality.

Quality as used here is different than the common notion of quality. Quality in common use often refers to luxury or high-priced features. Since there are so many manufacturing examples around we'll use a service industry example. Nordstrom stores sell higher-quality merchandise to a clientele with substantial income. Wal-Mart, on the other hand, sells more common items to everyone. Regular Wal-Mart shoppers have a lower average income than regular Nordstrom shoppers. Does that mean that Nordstrom has quality while Wal-Mart does not? Absolutely not! The technical term for this distinction is "grade." Nordstrom may carry a higher grade of clothing than Wal-Mart. But both can and should have quality.

External quality here refers to the perception and needs of the customer. Does the store carry the items the customer needs or wants? Are they well priced? Is the store well organized, accessible, and well stocked? Are the salespeople helpful without being pushy? Are they knowledgeable? All these questions refer to quality from the point of view of those customers who frequent that store. And all these questions are applicable to both chains, indeed to all stores.

2. *An Intense Focus on How Economic Products Are Created.* Successful management requires a company to maintain a high level of quality and efficiency. There are various ways of delivering the economic product that fulfills the customer's needs. The company that can deliver that product efficiently and at a lower cost has a distinct advantage. It turns out that the company with the better internal quality and systems is also more flexible and better able to innovate and adapt to changes in the environment. So the second aspect is to design, create, and improve internal systems so that quality and efficiency are a natural product of

the system and not something that has to be inspected or reworked after the economic product is created. This is internal quality.

Picking up on the prior retail example, internal quality refers to the ability of the internal systems to stock the shelves, train and hire people, and assure that an adequate stock of undamaged product is available to customers on a continual basis. Internal quality refers to the systems and their capabilities in all types of organizations. This means both the hard systems that account for the flow of goods to the shelves and the soft systems such as decision making and hiring.

3. *A Commitment to Constant Improvement, Innovation, and Revolution.* Constantly improve, constantly innovate, and constantly revolutionize what you do and how you do it. Your internal systems and your customer's experience need to be constantly monitored, improved, and innovated. Satisfied customers are good but loyal customers are better. Resting upon your laurels is not allowed for long in The New Management. Innovation means putting yourself out of business in some areas by creating new economic products or ways of doing business. Revolution means creating new industries.

Benefits of External Quality

Certainly the first principle seems reasonable enough. Yet few companies practice it. Those that do experience great success. It is easy and natural to put the company first, ahead of customers. Common sense can get in the way. In order to meet a profit goal, a company may instinctively react by raising prices or lowering costs in some way that negatively affects the customer's perception. But inevitably when you put the customer second the company suffers. I should point out that this principle does not call for unreasonable action, such as working for nothing. Loyal customers want your company to succeed. They understand the company needs to charge a reasonable fee to stay in business and to prosper. It is in their best interest to see that the company is successful and continues to be in business so that they may continue to receive your economic product.

The benefits to the customer are evident enough. The customer's life is improved and enhanced with a high level of quality and with products, services, and experiences that meet his or her needs. As the company brings out new economic products, the customer's life is further enhanced.

But what are the benefits to the company in behaving so magnanimously, in giving so much? There are many significant benefits. As long as customers have the right and the ability to switch vendors, loyal customers become an asset that is just as powerful as any machine, logo, or employee. The company gains the following:

1. Higher sales from a steady core of customers.
2. Lower sales costs. The customer is so happy with her experience that she keeps coming back. She doesn't have to be resold again and again. A recent study estimated that the cost of obtaining a new customer is six to seven times greater than the cost of keeping an existing customer. This doesn't tell the full story, however, since loyal customers help bring in new customers.
3. Lower marketing costs. As customers tell others about their experiences the company's reputation is enhanced. This makes advertising and marketing dollars more effective. Happy and unhappy customers talk. Generally an unhappy customer tells twenty or more people of his bad experience. A happy customer will tell about eight people.
4. Sales are more predictable since a steady core of customers keeps coming back for more.
5. The company operates at a higher sales level with higher capacity utilization providing more employment and therefore greater security for its managers and workers.
6. Greatly increased profits.
7. The improved reputation and name recognition means that the climate for future sales is better. In other words sales growth increases and future sales are enhanced.

In most businesses where there are recurrent sales the company makes little or no profit on the first purchase. It costs money to acquire a customer. If the customer has to be instructed on the use of the product it may be a while before a specific customer becomes profitable. Should a customer purchase once and not return the company loses. If the customer keeps coming back you have a business. If the customer keeps coming back enthusiastically you have a very profitable business.

This is drastically different from the way many companies were operating (and many still do) twenty years ago. In The New Management you are not entering into a *transaction* with a customer. From the point of view of profit and successful management a single transaction is almost insignificant. You are entering into a *relationship* with the customer and that makes all the difference in the world.

Loyal customers are the source of profits. By taking care of the customer you are taking care of the company, its employees, and its shareholders. By giving you get. The source of profits is loyal customers.

Benefits of Internal Quality

And what are the benefits from improving internal systems? Doesn't it raise costs when you improve systems to produce better internal quality? The usual answer is yes, but it is worth it. Here The New Management radically departs from the old.

There may be an initial outlay and redirection of resources devoted to improvement. But if properly done, that is to say with the proper knowledge (MetaKnowledge), the payback is immense and almost immediate. Better internal quality and better systems lead to less waste and lower cost. And this usually occurs quickly. When done right, internal quality costs less.

Among the ways costs are lowered is less rework, fewer returns from customers, less waste of material, less waste of labor, more efficient use of capital, and much less space required for inventory, returns, and rejects.

The benefits of high internal quality are:

1. Better external quality with all the benefits we mentioned on page 43.
2. Much less rework.
3. Less waste in all areas such as labor, capital, materials, and managerial time.
4. As a result of points two and three, much lower costs of production.
5. This means higher profit.
6. And much greater capacity with the same or fewer resources.

The source of profits is internal quality.

The Double Helix of Quality

Notice that from the external point of view the source of profit is loyal customers. From the internal point of view the source of profit is quality operations, efficiency, and less waste. Which is right? Of course, they are both right. The idea is to have both great external or perceived quality and great internal quality.

By doing so you create a double source of improvement, a double source of success. Consider it to be like two arms of an upward spiraling helix. Each is producing significant benefits for the customer and the company. External quality produces higher sales, lower sales and marketing costs, and therefore higher profits. Internal quality leads to less waste, greater efficiency, lower costs of production and delivery, and therefore higher profit. You are achieving increased profits from two sources.

And there is a strong interactive effect. Together they lead to a change in state. Higher perceived quality leads to greater sales. Greater internal quality boosts capacity. Typically in the first year that a company commits to The New Management, capacity increases from 35% to 50%. Why is this so? Simple. There is less waste of all kinds, from people's time to material, space, and capital. More sellable product is produced with fewer resources. Your people don't have to spend time chasing down waste, defects, and complaints.

Consider what happens when a company, in one year, produces and sells 135–150% of what it did in prior years, with exactly the same resources. Same people, same plant, same resources. (Those who wish to see a graphical presentation of these principles can turn to page 253, in Appendix A.)

Of course, it's the same plant, people, and economic product—but it isn't the same at all. The attitude is different, the way things are being done is different, and the design may have changed. There are probably hundreds of changes, some small, some not so small. And the results have no bearing on prior results. Profitability soars. A company can go from losing money or breaking even to becoming the profit leader in its industry.

Companies that were on the brink of bankruptcy have become the leaders in the industry upon adopting The New Management. In the midst of Harley-Davidson's worst years in the 1980s, they wholeheartedly committed themselves to quality and the principles of The New Management. The result was dominance in their industry. Intel sent hundreds of people to Deming's seminars in the 1980s when they were having terrible problems with Japanese competition. In a magazine interview, their CEO, Craig Bartlett, refers to the cycle of continuous improvement, which he called Plan, Do, Check, Act, as being central to their way of doing business. Their successful adaptation of New Management principles allowed them to reemerge as the largest semiconductor company in the world and allowed them to dominate the microprocessors market.

Commitment to Improvement

And why seek improvement? Why not leave well enough alone, especially if you are doing well? One very compelling reason is to improve your chances of staying in business tomorrow. If you don't do it someone else will. This becomes especially true as more companies around the globe embrace this principle. But there is perhaps another more compelling reason. Magic! You have no idea how good you can become. Listen to this quote of Pete Peterson, former chairman of Ford Motor Company.

> . . . continuous improvement to me is one of the most powerful thoughts that someone can keep in his or her mind. I can remember back at the beginning of the eighties it was very, very difficult to see just how you could lay down a plan that would resolve the difficulties that the Ford Motor Company faced. And then if you implemented that plan, why you would have a solution. There was no visible solution.
>
> If you follow . . . [these] . . . ideas you will see a progressive improvement in your efforts and the results of your efforts that will be far beyond anything you can anticipate or analytically forecast beforehand.

But where do you apply continuous improvement, on internal or external quality? It's applied to both. Each area requires different tools. For external quality we need to get constant feedback from customers. Customer surveys, consumer studies on both customers and non-customers, are required. These need not be formal. There are many ways of obtaining additional data but one must be cognizant of the scientific and statistical principles we discuss in this book to keep from making gross and harmful simplifications. Some companies have found that there is a wealth of information to be gathered from customers who are not paying their invoices or are asking for credits. If there is a particular area of customer concern, it should be addressed. What about non-customers—why aren't they buying? Using this feedback the economic product can be modified and improved. When new designs and new offerings are completed they will have the benefit of customer input. The goal is improved customer satisfaction. Internal quality needs to be constantly improved also. The larger and more complex your systems are, the more room there is for improvement. There isn't a factory, office, studio, or any kind of working environment that cannot be improved.

The processes of creating and delivering the economic product must be examined continually and improved upon. Improvement means lessening the problems in the process; cutting down the time, complexity, or number of steps involved; lowering costs; and bringing the process under control.

In his 1939 book *Statistical Method from the Viewpoint of Quality Control*, Dr. Shewhart compared the old way of doing business with the new. In the old way, a product was designed, then built, then inspected in linear fashion. First design, then build, then inspect. He proposed turning the steps into a loop forming a continuous circle. The inspection would serve as feedback for the design and the production phase. In effect these would be constantly improved based on feedback from the inspection process. In his words: "The three steps constitute a dynamic scientific process of acquiring knowledge. From this viewpoint, it might be better to show them as forming a sort of spiral gradually approaching a circular path which would represent the idealized case . . ."

When Dr. Deming introduced these ideas into Japan in the 1950s and again into the United States in the 1980s he added a fourth step. His four steps were initially Plan, Do, Check, Act. Later these were slightly modified to Plan, Do, Study, Act. In any case the basic idea has remained the same. Gather data that is used to modify the process, its specifications, and design on a continual basis.

There is no way of knowing just how successful you can become when you enter the path of continual improvement. But I need to add a caveat here: Continual improvement is not about change—it is about a certain kind of change. I have seen the idea of continual improvement often perverted to mean change of any kind. Change without stability can lead to chaos. Improper adjustments to a system have a special name. We call them tampering. Most changes made without Meta-Knowledge, indeed most adjustments, are either tampering or they produce no positive effect. Continual improvement as we use the term here means improvement to a system that has been brought into control. There are several steps along the path to control.

The Hierarchy of Control

A company can be in business yet have chaotic operations. An office or plant can appear wild. Supplies and materials are not readily at hand, equipment doesn't work, and people are uncooperative. It is difficult to achieve anything. This is a state of chaos.[2]

A turnaround artist walking into a failing business will most likely find the company's operations to be in a chaotic condition. Should this persist for long the operations will take on a very different complexion. The phones will cease ringing, the equipment will cease to work, and all noise will stop as well. This is called death.

There is an alternative. The turnaround artist can begin to rationalize the operation. He will ask questions, investigate and identify the major sources of problems. Then he will work to eliminate them. With a few changes the operation will become smoother and productivity will improve. But there will be regular intermittent periods when everything seems to fall apart again. This is a state of near-chaos.

In many industries near-chaos is sufficient for survival. But if the managers want better results they must continue to examine and improve processes and systems. They must continue to get feedback from people involved in the process and use their senses, most notably vision, constantly to improve. Data need to be collected. This is visual control. Perhaps a better name would be sensory control since the eyes,

---

[2] Here I use the term "chaos" in the ordinary sense of the word, meaning disorderly and out of control. I am not referring to any concepts from the new science of Chaos that we discuss later in the book.

ears, and other senses are used to direct the inquiries and improvement efforts.

But as major problems, the low-hanging fruit, are eliminated, more exact data becomes necessary. Now we can start to measure our systems and use numbers to guide our efforts. This is numerical control. Ideally when numerical control is begun, visual control is not abandoned. Numerical control is a supplement to visual control that continues forever. But now numbers supplement your efforts and allow you to detect subtleties that your senses could not. Once the very big problems are alleviated, smaller and subtler issues need to be addressed and this requires more data, more analysis, and more theory.

While numerical control is a big advance it can create problems. It becomes tempting for an enthusiastic but uninformed manager to set numerical targets or goals that are just beyond the system. He may have no understanding of variation. Any system will have variation—it will have good days and bad days, ups and downs. When the system has an up day the manager is ecstatic and hands out praise. But when the system has a down day, week, or month, the manager may scold or look for scapegoats. But the variations themselves are mostly due to chance; they are a natural occurrence of the system. As a result the person who gets caught on the bad day is being punished for a chance occurrence of the system. The person who gets the praise for the good day is the beneficiary of the roll of the dice. And this kind of arbitrary action, based on ignorance, prevents the team and the company from truly excelling.[3]

For numerical control to work it must be accompanied by some statistical understanding or knowledge of variation. The next step is statistical control. Achieving statistical control is quite difficult. This is a major achievement. Once achieved, the next step is continual improvement.

Continual improvement allows a system that has been brought into the highest state of control to continue to improve. A system in control can improve faster and better than a system that is not. In some situations, however, achieving statistical control is not likely to occur in the necessary time frame. In these cases continual improvement must begin

---

[3] This is extensively covered in my earlier book, *Dr. Deming: The American Who Taught the Japanese About Quality*, chapters 4 and 5.

before statistical control can be achieved. But I have found that a system must at least be in a state of visual control for continual improvement to be effective and pay off. Prior to that, major improvement efforts should be directed at achieving some level of control.

Summary

We have made a case through four global examples that The New Management is a powerful, state-of-the-art path toward excellence. It makes other management systems obsolete and allows us to enter a state of accelerated material abundance.

We have also distilled the essence of The New Management into three principles: focus on customers (external quality); focus on internal systems (internal quality); and continual improvement, innovation, and revolution.

The New Management allows a company to better serve the marketplace by adapting to the needs of the customer and improving its delivery system. Central to the success of the first two principles is the ability to learn and improve. But learning is neither simple, obvious, nor direct. Improvement is not based on common sense. In fact much of improvement is counterintuitive.

Let me use an example to illustrate. If you know what happened this year you can accurately predict what will happen next year. Right? Absolutely wrong! This is confusing information with knowledge. Information tells you what happened. Knowledge, however, is about prediction; it is about the future. Knowledge concerns our ability to predict into the future.

The New York Mets won the National League championship in 2000. Therefore one could have predicted they would win the championship in 2001 as well. Most people can see through this kind of performance-based prediction as verging on the ridiculous, especially people from outside New York, such as those in Atlanta or Arizona. And by 2002, the Mets found themselves in last place.

Few people would place much reliability on predicting next year's baseball championship based on this year's results. Yet people routinely predict the performance of people, companies, and farms based on the same illogic.

Management is about prediction. All the decisions that managers make impact the future, not last year's results. The New Management implicitly relies on prediction, and many of the tools that were developed for it are tools of prediction. Dr. Shewhart, who developed the underlying theory for The New Management, literally changed the world for the better. He is best remembered for the tools of quality control, all of which help mangers control a system and predict its future results. But he felt that his main contribution to mankind was his work on knowledge and prediction. His work is one of the main roots of MetaKnowledge.

CHAPTER 5

MOVING FROM AN EXACT WORLD TO A PROBABILISTIC WORLD

If one of us were shooting at a mark and failed to hit the bull's-eye, and some one asked you why, we should likely give as our excuse, CHANCE. Had some one asked the same question of one of our earliest known ancestors, he might have attributed his lack of success to the dictates of fate or to the will of the gods. I am inclined to think that in many ways one of these excuses is just about as good as another.

—WALTER SHEWHART

In *The Lexus and the Olive Tree*, a popular book on globalization, the author, Thomas L. Friedman, cites a farmer using the latest technology to gain a productivity edge. Sensors built into his machinery detect with great precision the amount of crop being harvested. The equipment has a link to a global navigation satellite so that location can be precisely determined. The technology provides information on the "exact" amount of grain harvested in every square yard of the farm. This information is then stored in a computer. Presumably by knowing last year's productivity for each square yard, the farmer can vary inputs to make the best use of his most productive terrain, thereby increasing his yield and lowering his costs. The equipment, purchased at great expense, also allows him to vary inputs, such as water and fertilizer, also down to the square yard, when planting. Technology is billed as the answer to increased productivity.

This is nothing new. Technology has been used by many economists and lay people alike to explain almost all productivity differences. Many people believe that technology automatically leads to higher productivity. And that only technology improves productivity. But this is nonsense. Without having seen this farmer's equipment I will make a bold statement: He has wasted his money. He will see no measurable improvement in productivity or in the cost to run his farm. But he will have a large bill for the equipment.

Suppose we had a conversation with this farmer. It might run something like this:

Us: *Now that you have all this information about last year's yields on your farm, down to the square yard, how are you going to use it?*

Farmer: *It's obvious. Certain parts of my farm are more productive than others. I will feed the more productive parts, using my resources more intelligently. The more productive parts will get more fertilizer, increasing their yield further.*

The argument sounds pretty convincing. But there are serious flaws involved.

Us: *All your data are from last year. We have several questions. How do you know that last year's conditions will be "exactly" duplicated next year? How do you know that adding more fertilizer or water will improve the yield of any part of your farm? Just because it happened to produce more last year, how can you infer that that parcel of land is inherently more productive? Even if it happens to be more productive, how do you know that adding even more water or more fertilizer will make it even more so?*

Farmer: *That's the problem with you non-farmers, consultants, and intellectuals. You take something that is really very simple and make it very complex. I know because I have years of farming experience.*

Despite his protests our farmer is trying to be a scientist. He is making predictions about the future. There is a major difference between knowledge and information. At its most basic level information is just data. Information as it is commonly used also implies something more complex than pure data. But knowledge is something else again. Knowledge is the ability to take data and information and make predictions. Knowledge is useful if it helps us make better decisions. Decisions affect the future, not the past. Knowledge is about the future.[4]

[4] Predictions can be about the past if we infer about the past using data that are not currently available to us. In this case our predictions about the past can only be confirmed or disconfirmed when new evidence is discovered. Even when used to predict the past, knowledge is about the future, i.e., predicting that yet undisclosed evidence will confirm our hypothesis about the past.

There are two kinds of statistical studies: enumerative and analytical. An enumerative study gives you all the numbers about what happened. Financial statements for instance are enumerative; they tell you what happened. It is a common mistake to believe that an enumerative study, especially one with lots of numbers that have been statistically gathered, will tell you the future. The census tells you about our population in the past. An analytical study is conceptually very different. The intent of an analytical study is to predict beyond what you can currently measure.

Prediction requires a model or a theory of how the world works. Everyone's model of the world has presuppositions or assumptions on the nature of reality. These presuppositions underlie our thinking and our knowledge. These presuppositions make up an important part of this farmer's metaknowledge and need to be questioned and examined.

Assumptions on the Nature of Reality

Our farmer's beliefs only make sense with an exact model of the world. An exact model is often referred to as a deterministic model. It relates variables, which are items over which we have some control, to some kind of desired result over which we have no direct control. The exact model is a great advancement over what preceded it. Before any kind of rational or scientific method, humans may have had a magical or religious model. One wished or prayed for some desired outcome. While one need not give up wishing or praying, the rational or scientific model attempts to understand cause and effect and the relationship between them. In early scientific models this relationship was exact, meaning that changing one or several variables was believed to result in a change that could be predicted exactly.

Since scientific thinking is associated with mathematics it is natural to infer mathematical relationships in nature. For instance, we all believe that addition holds in nature. We assume this is so and take it for granted. As obvious as it seems, does $1 + 1 = 2$ in the physical world?

Suppose I take one mud ball in one hand and one mud ball in the other. I then bring them together. What do I get? I get one large mud ball. Here $1 + 1 = 1$. Now, if I don't smack them together in my hands, but instead just place them on the table and count them, $1 + 1$ does equal 2. But even here there are some problems. What if the mud balls are of different sizes? We might have one that is 2 ounces and one that is 1 pound. When we count them we still have two mud balls, indicating two discrete objects. Suppose that instead of mud balls we have pies. One is a 12-inch pie and one a 3-inch pie. We cut each pie in half, so now we have four half-pies. Then I take one half from the 12-inch pie and one half from the 3-inch pie and place them together. Now I have two halves together. $1/2 + 1/2$ is supposed to equal 1. But do we really have one pie? I think if you tried to sell that off as one pie you would be laughed at or sued pretty quickly.

The point is that mathematical law doesn't hold in the physical world. It is valid only under certain conditions. And then it is an approximation. In fact, developing and refining physical theory is to some extent about determining the conditions under which some kind of mathematical model is valid or useful.

One of the most successful applications of mathematics to the real world is geometry. Euclid of Alexandria was one of the most influential thinkers of all time. Anyone who has taken a course in geometry has been exposed to his work. He didn't invent geometry. In all likelihood, geometry developed over hundreds of years, perhaps millennia. It was used by the Egyptians. Certain rules of geometry that we take for granted must have been painstakingly researched. But Euclid developed geometry into an axiomatic system. Given his axioms and logical method all the theories of geometry could be derived. Axiomatic geometry as we learned it is an exact science. It deals with exact relationships and exact results. And it is perfect. It provides a complete explanation of geometry that we used to think was perfect.

Is geometry a branch of mathematics or is it a science? It is both. It is a branch of mathematics that has been very successfully applied in the world. For years there was no clear distinction between mathematics and science. But that changed when around 1850 three different mathematicians independently dropped Euclid's fifth postulate and discovered non-Euclidian geometry. Suddenly, one of the most successful sets of laws describing a fundamental aspect of reality with thousands of years of verification was no longer unique. A postulate that everyone knew was self-evident and true was shown to be just an assumption. In some cases it was not true. In Euclidian geometry the sum of the angles of a triangle always equaled 180 degrees. In non-Euclidian geometry the sum could be less than or more than 180 degrees.

Now we had two kinds of geometry that differed by one axiom but made very different predictions. It would be difficult to overestimate the effect this has had on our thinking in the West. While philosophers had often talked about the difference between our knowledge and the "real" world, now this difference became explicit and obvious for all to see.

Instead of being a self-evident truth, geometry was shown to be a theory, a map. It was useful to explain reality, but it was not reality. It was an approximation, albeit a very successful one. And it only applied when the surface was flat. When the curvature of the earth or space was large enough it broke down. The analogy between theory and maps is best enumerated by Lewis Carroll in the following passage.

"What a useful thing a pocket-map is!" I remarked.

"That's another thing we've learned from your Nation," said Mein Herr, "Map-making, But we've carried it much further than you. What do you consider the largest map that would be really useful?"

"About six inches to the mile."

"Only six inches!" exclaimed Mein Herr. "We very soon got to six yards to the mile. Then we tried a hundred yards to the mile. And then came the grandest idea of all! We actually made a map of the country, on the scale of a mile to the mile!"

"Have you used it much?" I enquired.

"It has never been spread out, yet," said Mein Herr. "The farmers objected: they said it would cover the whole country, and shut out the sunlight! So we now use the country itself, as its own map, and I assure you it does nearly as well."[5]

For a map to be useful it has to be small. It has to be less than the object being mapped and has to leave out much detail that isn't useful for the purpose at hand. Similarly any theory must leave out much detail.

Knowledge is like a map. It helps us understand, it helps us predict, it helps us survive. But knowledge is not reality. The map is not the territory and the name is not the named thing. This principle was made famous by Alfred Korzybski and introduced to many by Gregory Bate-

---

[5] *Sylvie and Bruno Concluded* by Lewis Carroll, page 265. Mercury House edition of *The Complete Sylvie and Bruno.*

son. When you picture a coconut there is no coconut in your head. Likewise when you call out the word "coconut."

But if knowledge is like a map, is it possible that any single map may be insufficient and that often you need more than one map? We use a road map for driving. But if we are going from door to door we may need a map with more detail. If we are backpacking instead of driving we need a very different kind of map. If we are drilling for oil we need an even more exotic type of map. In fact there are a variety of maps for different purposes. Has Euclidian geometry been made obsolete? Not at all. It is still used today to build houses and buildings, and it does a superlative job. In *The Emperor's New Mind*, Roger Penrose places all scientific theory into one of three categories, depending on how well they have worked over time. Only a few theories are placed in his highest category that he calls superb, and Euclidian geometry is one of those. But if we are building roads or flying planes Euclidian geometry just won't do. We need a different kind of geometry in those cases.

Two Models: Perceptual and Scientific

The analogy of knowledge as a map is useful even in more subtle areas. Let me give an example. Look around you. You see various items and some people in your environment. You hear sounds and words. You touch your desk or chair or floor and it appears to be totally solid. You see colors all around you. You make out words from sounds and derive meaning from the words. This world, this reality is accessible through your senses. But the scientific model of the physical world developed over the last four hundred years says that there is no color in nature. There are only various frequencies of electromagnetic radiation. Those that the eye can perceive we call light. Of those that we can perceive there are different frequencies that the mind and eye interpret as different colors. Color by itself does not exist outside of our minds.

We could arbitrarily designate a particular frequency range of the electromagnetic spectrum as a certain color, say blue. Then we could say that blue exists in nature, but this is just a labeling of a frequency range. The experience of blue does not exist in nature, just a frequency that has been arbitrarily labeled. What frequency is blue varies from person to person and undoubtedly there are different experiences of blue. I can look at a color with only one eye and I experience it a little differently with the other eye. Further, what we see as blue is not just dependent on the wavelength of light. There is a more complex relationship involving what is in the background and other factors.

Solidity also does not exist in nature. Matter is composed of molecules that are just atoms bonded together. But these atoms in turn are made up of minute particles with most of the matter being concentrated in a tiny packet in the center made up of protons and neutrons. The outer edge of the atom is composed of an even smaller packet of matter called an electron that is rotating at immense speeds around the nucleus. The vast majority of the atom is emptiness.

In fact, according to this view, our scientific view of reality, our everyday perception of reality is just an illusion created by our mind. It is an illusion, however, that is useful and has survival value. But on the other hand you might easily claim that the world you live in, the world of perception, is the real world and the physical model is merely an abstraction. Which one is the real world?

For many who hold a rational view of reality, the reality is the scientific model. From this vantage everything that happens in our perception can be or eventually will be explained through the scientific view. Many things that we perceive are shown to be false. But an equally good case could be made that who we are, the "I" or we in a sentence, is the person who lives in the world of perception. The person who feels, sees, hears, smells, and tastes. That world of the senses is what we experience on a daily basis.

Rather than claim either one as being more real or valid, we can consider each of these to be a useful map that allows us to live and deal with reality. Both have survival value. Neither is more real or more valid. For certain purposes it is useful to consider the scientific model a better picture of the "real" world. But for other purposes such as art and music, feeling and consciousness, the world of perception is more "real."

Which to Use

From the point of view of Western science and most of Western philosophy our personal perceptive world would be called subjective reality. Our attempts to develop a scientific understanding of the physical world correspond roughly to objective reality. In business both subjective and objective reality are important. Dealing with people effectively requires that we deal from and respect the perceptual world. But our actions and decisions are informed and molded by some rational exterior model that most of us would like to call objective or scientific.

One of the worst comments you could make about a person's actions is to call them irrational or unscientific. Most people are sold on the idea of applying "scientific" principles to their business. But a change has come over the principles themselves. In many areas exact principles are inadequate, counterproductive, meaningless, or just wrong.

The Exact World Meets Chance and Variation

In its simplest form an exact model would call for exact relationships, few variables, and smooth and continuous relationships between variables and results. But you rarely get such conditions even in an approximate sense. Exact relationships do not exist in nature, or else we have not found them. In fact, one of the most constant characteristics of our world is variation. Virtually anything you can think of has variation: the time it takes to walk to your neighbor's house, the amount of gas you use on a trip, the temperature at noon. One area with the closest claim to exactness is in the celestial bodies such as the Sun, Moon, and planets. Our theories allow us to predict with great accuracy sunrises, sunsets, eclipses, and the motion of the planets. But even here there is going to be variation. Your clock will not register the "exact" same time for a sunrise or sunset as will the "official" clock. Even if you were to use the "official" clock there would be variation, although it might be measured in seconds or tenths of a second.

In order to deal with this variation, science has increasingly turned to statistics, which is based on probability and the idea of chance. And this has been incredibly successful. Virtually every branch of science has taken on a statistical view with great results. One example of the value of statistics is in the area of life and death. Nobody has any idea when he or someone else will die. The factors are immense and immeasurable. Yet when we consider the whole population of a region or a nation we find that we can establish mortality tables that help us predict the death rate in any given year. Indeed the average deaths per year do not vary much over time. Death, while totally unpredictable on an individual level, lends itself to statistical analysis, interpretation, and most importantly stable predictions when large parts of the population are involved. But it is not doctors or nurses or any healthcare professionals who use the information and make the predictions. It is statistically trained professionals, actuaries, who make the predictions about death in a population. And the insurance companies that employ them have made a lot of money because of their predictions.

We find the same laws hold in areas that are seemingly unrelated. Radioactive decay, for instance. In a given amount of radioactive material individual atoms decay to create the radioactivity. We have no ability to predict which atoms will decay, yet we can predict with great accuracy the number of atoms decaying in any period of time.

Statistical thinking becomes necessary when the number of variables or factors becomes too large to allow for any kind of meaningful computation. But in certain areas such as mortality tables or radioactive decay there are no alternatives. In these cases an exact or deterministic model borders on being meaningless.

In order to make sense of this world and be able to predict, statistical thinking becomes indispensable. Many people, including eminent scientists, want to hold on to the notion that the "underlying reality" (increasingly it is becoming questionable whether this expression has any meaning) is exact or deterministic but just too complex for us to handle with our current state of knowledge. Some have given in to the idea that we will never know things exactly but the universe might still be exact in some sense. Most notable is Dr. Einstein, who commented that he could not believe that God would play dice with the Universe. I believe there is ample evidence to indicate that the Universe is not exact. And holding on to a notion that cannot be demonstrated is futile and counterproductive. Most serious thinkers have reconciled themselves to living in a world where chance, probability, and statistics play a necessary and pivotal role.

A statistical world is, by its very nature, very different from an exact world. Let us examine our farmer's efforts to improve the productivity of his farm. He now has all this information. He knows how much each square yard of his farm yielded. He knows what the farm produced last year. But his interest is in what the farm will produce next year with the changes he plans to make. And there is the rub.

Undoubtedly different parts of the farm produced more than others. But is that meaningful or were the differences due to chance? If you took the exact same measurements under substantially the same conditions, would you get the same result? Of course on a farm you could not possibly even roughly re-create the same circumstances. The weather and microclimate are always different. But that question has been asked and put to the test in an industrial setting where we could pretty well duplicate substantially the same circumstances. What was discovered is that the results do not stay the same. In fact, it was discovered that the more effort put into creating substantially the same conditions, the worse things got. That was the problem that Dr. Shewhart was asked to work on in the 1920s at the Bell Laboratories.

Variation

Variation is everywhere. Anyone who honestly looks at the world experiences variation. This law is so powerful that when someone claims there is no variation in his data, his numbers must automatically become suspect. In almost all cases it is because the numbers have been tampered with. People tamper with data all the time. Scientists throw out data that don't agree with their theory. The lowest and highest numbers are often discarded. And some of this is justified. But if you examine the uncensored data you invariably find lots of variation, some of which leaves people uncomfortable. Yet by denying variation you are leaving out important information.

Two Kinds of Variation

Dr. Shewhart discovered that there are several kinds of variation. Even when you have what appear to be substantially the same conditions in a controlled environment such as an industrial setting there are two kinds of variation. One kind tends to be larger and unpredictable. It comes and it goes. He called these assignable causes of variation. A cause could be assigned to these and in most cases the causes could be eliminated. By systematically identifying assignable causes, hunting them down, and eliminating them at their root, variation could be lessened, costs lowered, and quality improved. What you are left with is natural variation inherent and characteristic of the system. This we call common causes. But how do you distinguish an assignable cause from common causes of variation? One of Shewhart's great contributions was to devise some simple methods to identify the existence of assignable causes. He developed a deceptively simple tool, the control chart (for an example of a control chart see Appendix B on page 259), which in more than seventy years of use has time and again shown its effectiveness. The simplicity of the control chart is both a blessing and a curse. While it is relatively easy to use, its simplicity leads many people to believe that they fully understand it when in fact they do not. As a result its significance is often misinterpreted and its power misused or neglected.

Once the assignable causes are eliminated the variation becomes truly random. It approximates the variation one would get by drawing normally numbered chips from a bowl. This is true random variation. In Shewhart's terminology you have eliminated all the nonrandom variation. Now the process becomes predictable in a statistical sense. The variation has a kind of predictability to it. With elimination of assignable causes, a state of "statistical control" is attained. Constant improvement really begins once statistical control is achieved. What is done before control is achieved should have a strong bias toward bringing about control.

Attaining statistical control is a great achievement. Statistical control does not readily occur in nature. Once the effort to eliminate assignable causes ceases, the state of statistical control will soon cease as well. In virtually every situation one encounters where an intense effort to eliminate assignable causes is absent, assignable causes will exist in abundance along with common causes. This is true even though the circumstances from moment to moment appear to be essentially the same.

Our farmer is looking at data that are affected by common causes, assignable causes, and all the variations that exist when conditions are essentially not the same. Indeed they are not even approximately the same from year to year or from month to month. He certainly has no control over weather. Nor does he have control over assignable or common causes of variation. How could he possibly infer that the differences in productivity are due to the soil or those aspects that are unique to the farm? Nothing that he has applied to his farm is uniform. Among the many causes of variation, consider these: The seeds vary in quality and other characteristics. They, by themselves, can produce significant differences in the yield. The water, the fertilizer, all the inputs have significant variation. What about weather factors such as wind, temperature, humidity, and rainfall? These also vary greatly over the farm and they will vary in a different way next year.

And now we come to the key issue. Is the farmer's investment in all this equipment to improve his farm's productivity justified? Will he be able to adjust his inputs in a way that will improve his productivity? If you go back in a couple of years and ask, in all probability he will say that of course it was worth the investment. It produced better results. It is nearly impossible for people to break with their cherished assumptions. The philosopher Hegel said that when theory and data clash, so much the worse for the data. But if you were to compare the farmer's productivity with other farmers who didn't make the adjustments you would not find any significant improvement.

We live in a probabilistic world, like it or not, and must think differently to manage effectively. A given farm's results, and indeed all farmers' results, will vary significantly from year to year. And in comparing results, we must ask if the results are better in a statistically significant way. If the farmer is making changes based on one year's results, or even several years without proper analysis, in all probability his results will be worse not better. And when one factors the cost of the equipment involved in this futile exercise his financial results will be very much worse.

When there is variation of any kind that you do not control your results will vary from year to year and there may be no significance in those differences. One part could be the best one year and the worst the next if it is totally due to chance or factors that are beyond anyone's control. You need to have a method to determine if something is due to chance or not. And you need to be able to eliminate all causes of variation except common causes.

What can you infer from one data point? Not very much. In fact, you could easily be misled. You might make things worse. Making predictions based on one year's results is total lunacy. Agricultural predictions, and in fact any case where assignable causes are present, require careful observation over time. A crop, method, or technology must prove its value over many years. To determine the qualities and productivity of a given piece of the farm can only be done with careful observation over years.

Implications for Management

Let's go back to an industrial setting for a moment. Are there any implications for management? Clearly the answer is yes. Many managers rate all kinds of things. Managers and workers are rated from best to worst. At GE the bottom 10% of managers are booted. But is their performance due to chance or other factors? Anyone who has worked in a corporation knows that a performance review is highly subjective and dependent on how well you get along with your boss. Performance means performance in pleasing the boss. But let's assume for the moment that there are objective measures and that these are the main ones used in rating managers. As long as there is variation in the world, it is very likely that the performance differences are at the very least partially due to chance.

Does that mean that all of it is due to chance? Absolutely not! Some differences are due to performance or ability. But how do you know it is due to performance and not chance? Without a method for determining whether differences are due to chance or performance, you are playing roulette with major decisions. And the cost can be tremendous. Why is the bottom 10% booted? Why is 10% the magic number? Why not 15%, 20%, or 5%? Unless you have some statistical basis for this you are just guessing and guessing can be very expensive.

Thinking statistically, we can make two kinds of mistakes. We can assume that the differences are due to some real or inherent factor when in fact they are due to chance. This is called a Type 1 mistake. This is the mistake that is most commonly made in business today. It is made because most managers assume an exact world when all scientific thinking has acknowledged the need for statistical thinking. We are using eighteenth-century thinking to try and manage in the twenty-first century.

But there is another mistake being made in business as well. We could assume that the differences are due to chance when in fact they are due to some real or inherent factor. These are called Type 2 mistakes. In Type 1 kinds of mistakes, we act when we should not act. In Type 2 kinds of mistakes, we fail to act when we should. A typical Type 2 kind of mistake is to assume that all the problems and crises are outside of your control. Therefore nothing is done about them but firefighting or taking care of them as they arise.

For some things, of course, you don't need any kind of sophisticated or statistical tool to know there are real differences. If you compared a Major League hitter with a sixth-grader, you could confidently predict differences in future results. But much of the time things are not so clear-cut. They may appear to be obvious but further investigation might show a very large chance factor. And here is where you need some statistical tools to help you determine the difference. One indicator that is often necessary is time. If a difference persists over five or six periods you can become more confident that it is real.

And now we come to a question similar to the one contemplated by our farmer. What can you infer from a point of data, in this case one year's crop yields? In most cases the answer is not very much. If the differences are due to chance or causes outside your control then next year's results may bear no resemblance to this year's results. They could be just the opposite.

The best-case scenario would be when the process you are dealing with is in statistical control. In this case only common causes would be present. The system behaves predictably in a statistical sense. Assignable causes of variation, on the other hand, enter and leave the system in an unpredictable fashion. They can give your process or system a schizophrenic character. When assignable causes are present a process behaves one way. When absent it can behave differently. You can be operating quite smoothly three days of the week and then all of a sudden there are problems galore and your whole company seems to be in chaos. These are indications of the presence of assignable causes.

One of my clients, a printing firm, was experiencing significant problems on some days. Other days things went smoothly. When we started to examine the incoming ink we found that there were significant differences from batch to batch. The viscosity, density, pH, and hue varied considerably. The ink was out of control. Once we addressed that the operations became smoother, but we still had a large task ahead of us to track down other sources of variation. How sensitive is a process? Does it make any difference whether you put a tea bag into a cup filled with hot water or pour hot water over a tea bag already in a cup? Most of us would say it makes no difference, and for most purposes it doesn't seem to matter much. But there are differences. Place a tea bag in a cup and pour hot water over it and the bag will float at the top of the cup. Place a tea bag into a cup filled with hot water and the bag tends to stay at the bottom of the cup. For some very sensitive processes that can be a big difference. If one person does it one way while another person does it the other way, the difference might be large enough to introduce an assignable cause of variation.

When there are several assignable causes analysis is virtually impossible. The best course of action is to systematically eliminate assignable causes. This leads to an almost magical improvement in quality and the performance of your company. In an industrial setting, assignable causes can be eliminated. On a farm, of course, that is impossible. But farmers and managers both need to know they can't make quick judgments just because they have more information.

I was recently struck by what I learned about GE's Six Sigma program. This is the pride of GE and has been credited with improving GE quality and saving the company billions of dollars. But I was struck when I learned that one of the issues at the company is that the variation in their processes has not changed much. Their Six Sigma program focuses on process improvement, which is great. It is important and definitely helps. But it is not enough. If that is all you do, your process will remain unstable. Assignable causes will continue to creep into your process leading to intermittent periods of chaos. Quality will suffer and you will leave your customer frustrated. Thinking based on exact science rather than probability is seventy years behind the times and insufficient for the modern world. But our managers, including our political leaders, are sorely lacking in this kind of thinking and fail to appreciate its significance.

CHAPTER 6

HOW DO WE KNOW?

Have you ever been driving a car when the navigator found a street that wasn't on the map? In my case I heard the person say, "But that can't be, it's not on the map." Maybe it couldn't be, but it was. This little story is not just about physical maps, however. It's about the maps we all have inside our heads; the stories, legends, and beliefs that we hold about the world at large.

A certain element of uncertainty is associated with belief. In talking about others' beliefs we can all appreciate that a belief may not be totally accurate or true. But what about knowledge? When someone says, "I believe that . . ." or "I believe this to be true," there is a recognition of some uncertainty and an openness to alternatives is implied. But using the phrase, "I know . . ." implies much greater certainty. We know based on personal experience but we also know based on some collective and formalized body of knowledge like history or science. The historical record tells us what happened. Scientific experiments help to confirm or deny hypotheses. The historical record, however, is often suspect and certainly open to different interpretations. That leaves scientific knowledge as being generally recognized as the most reliable.

Scientific Proof

But here is a fact that many people will find hard to swallow: "SCIENCE NEVER PROVES ANYTHING." I took this wording and the large caps from the renowned anthropologist Gregory Bateson's book, *Mind and Nature.* I could have just as easily quoted Einstein, Carl Jung, or any one of many eminent scientists and philosophers who have spent a great deal of time thinking about this.

Let me clarify what I mean by prove. Proof is a mathematical expression. It implies certainty and no fear of contradiction at some future time. It is inexorably tied to Euclid's formulation of plane geometry and Aristotle's logic. From a given set of axioms or presuppositions, we use rules of logic to derive or prove a proposition or theory. Once it is proved, it is proved for all time. You cannot disprove it sometime in the future. What you can do, however, is change the axioms and derive or prove different propositions. You can also change the logic used to prove or disprove a proposition. This leads to different inferences even with the same beginning axioms.

Given the very strong relationship between mathematics and science, especially the hard sciences such as physics and chemistry, it is easy to fall into the trap of assuming that you can prove a scientific proposition about the world, so let's examine this more closely.

A mathematical proof would take the following form:

Prove that if A then F.

Step 1	If A then B.	This is Axiom 1.
Step 2	If B then C.	This is Axiom 2.
Step 3	If C then E.	This is a prior theorem.
Step 4	If E then F.	This is another prior theorem.
Step 5	Therefore, if A then F.	This is one of our rules of logic.

If you have been trained in this kind of thinking, it is natural to try to apply it to the real world. A problem develops, however, when you try to find the equivalent of an axiom. In mathematics an axiom is a starting point, it is assumed. But if your starting point in science is an assumption then your whole intellectual structure comes into question if the assumption turns out to be incorrect. Even the word "assumption" implies an arbitrary quality to it. In the past some scientists and philosophers relied on the notion that some things were just self-evident. These self-evident truths could play the role of being axioms. But what is self-evident to one may not be self-evident to another. What is self-evident in one period may not be self-evident in another. Consider some of the things that were found to be self-evident in the past: The world is flat; the earth does not move and is the center of the universe; disease is caused by sin. The list of things that were evident and obvious to people in the past that we now find ludicrous is endless. Euclid's fifth postulate was considered obvious, but could not be proved. It turned out not to be self-evident. Despite the best efforts of some very prominent minds to find some self-evident scientific truths, we have been forced to admit that the label of self-evident is subjective based on the person, the culture, and the time.

A Special Example of Self-Evident Truth

One very well-known attempt at deriving a self-evident starting point was by one of the founders of modern scientific thinking. In René Descartes's famous tract on his Method, he attempted the skeptic's method of doubting everything. Eventually he came to a proposition that seemed beyond doubt. "I think therefore I am." But even with this he had to admit the possibility that he might be deceived. His famous maxim relating thinking to being was not the ultimate step in his method but the penultimate. He needed to go one step further— and that step was faith. He had faith that his god would not deceive him. For our purposes here I take faith to be logically equivalent to making an assumption or starting with an axiom. I realize that psychologically and otherwise faith is quite different, but from the point of view of rationally understanding the basis of our knowledge they are equivalent.

If there are no self-evident truths, at least with respect to empirical knowledge, then the next best approach is to test our propositions experimentally. If we wanted to verify an empirical statement of the form "If A then F," then we could create condition A and observe if F occurred or not. Examples of statements of this form are "Germs cause disease," or more specifically, "Bacteria X causes disease Y." Another example is "Our model of the solar system predicts that the Sun will rise over Setauket Harbor at 6:31 A.M. on a given day." This kind of proof or verification would be inductive as opposed to the mathematical method of deduction.

Suppose you set up an experiment to test one of these propositions, and find that indeed when you establish A you observe condition

F. How many times must you observe this relationship to hold in order to prove that A causes F, or microbe X causes disease Y? Certainly few would agree that observing it just once would constitute a proof. Even after a few successes few would call this a proof. But what if you observed it 1,000 times? From our rules of logic, the answer is no matter how many times you observed the relationship to hold you could not prove it. It is always possible that the next trial might fail and disprove or at least cast doubt on the proposition in question. Our strength in the belief of the proposition increases with time and we may rely on it to predict, but it is still not proven.

We have many examples where there were no counterexamples for long periods of time and then all of a sudden one was found. We have had some cases with thousands of years of confirmation. For example, the sum of the angles of a triangle totals 180 degrees, according to Euclidian geometry. For millennia we had no record of anyone finding any evidence to contradict that. But as soon as non-Euclidian geometry was developed, which allowed for triangles to have more or less than 180 degrees, we found such examples.

Reality and Beliefs

Here is one of the really strange things about human knowledge: When our ideas or theories change the data change. The data change in several ways. For one, we now have justification and an idea of where to look for the new data. Secondly, the experimental data is interpreted differently. Thirdly, the numbers themselves can change. Different experiments are run but varying data emerge from the same experiments.

In Chapter 2 I recounted how my lab grade was lowered by my physics professor because I reported all the data I observed. My lab partner received a higher grade because he deleted the data points that did not agree with the expected results. Like it or not, science is a social phenomenon and therefore subject to social forces.

A lesson for business people is that no matter how convinced you are that your current way of doing business or delivering your economic product is optimal, you need to keep an open mind. A different approach might turn out to be much more effective, yet as long as you are tied to the old ideas it can be very difficult to find application of the new in your enterprise. A certain amount of experimentation with new methods and new ideas in a company is a very healthy sign. Without it a company can find itself totally unable to move when there is a significant change in the environment or a strong new competitor.

Disproving a Theory

If no amount of confirmation "proves" a statement, how many counterexamples do we need to disprove a particular theory? Einstein is quoted as saying that no amount of empirical verification could ever prove one of his theories, but just one counterexample would disprove it. This kind of statement is not unusual in physics. But in physics, to a large extent, we are looking for universal laws that hold throughout time and throughout the universe. In this case it is true that one counterexample proves that the relationship does not always hold and therefore disproves the theory.

But the situation becomes a bit trickier when the relationship is not assumed to be universal or there is more than one factor at work. Suppose instead of just A causing F, you need A and B and C and D and E. If any one of these is missing, then F doesn't occur regardless of how many of the other factors are present. You may not even know of the existence of some factors. They may be a part of the environment that hasn't been identified. In this case, when A occurs you will sometimes have F and sometimes you won't. But you cannot then say that A does not cause F. By itself A doesn't cause F, but A is necessary for F to occur and in a sense is a cause.

So the situation rapidly becomes more complicated. Suppose that you have tested the proposition A causes F tens of thousands of times in the laboratory. Never once did you find a contradiction. Clearly your confidence in this proposition is becoming quite strong. But what allows you to then infer that same level of confidence to a different environment and a different set of conditions? Could you even strongly infer that with substantially the same conditions but at a different time your confidence would be justified? While we would all like to say yes to some of these statements, experience has taught us that such strong statements often aren't justified.

Around 1972 an author named Immanuel Velikovsky put forth a strange theory that our planetary system was not always ordered the way we see it now. Specifically, Venus was in a different place at some point in the past. But the solar system now appears to us to be stable, operating under laws and relationships that have been thoroughly observed and investigated. For Venus to have changed its orbit the solar system would have to display nonperiodic or chaotic[6] behavior. While some parts of the general population found the idea intriguing and compelling, the idea seemed to feed into the hands of those who had an interest in astrology. Some very well-known scientists felt a need to refute that assertion. A full-page spread in *The New York Times* with the signatures of many prominent scientists was published. They concluded that " 'We know' that the solar system is absolutely stable and we have scientific knowledge that refutes the claims of Velikovsky, so you are wasting your time."[7]

What allowed them to have such confidence in such an absolute statement? A prominent scientist named Mitchell J. Feigenbaum, an expert in the new Chaos Theory, concluded that, other than as a result of undue confidence based on ignorance, there was nothing that one could know with such certainty about the past stability of the solar system. Indeed the theoretical work on Chaos Theory done in the last few decades casts great doubt on the assertion that the solar system has been absolutely stable. A few isolated objects do display chaotic behavior and over a larger time frame, large parts of the solar system may very well display chaotic behavior, at least according to our newer understanding of Chaos Theory.

I believe that the confidence in making these great assertions about the level and strength of our knowledge comes from the mistaken notion that empirical science is mathematics. While the two are intricately intertwined historically and conceptually, they are not the same.

But why not agree on a definition of proof for empirical data in a given field? Suppose all the practitioners in a field get together and agree that with a certain amount of verification followed by a favorable peer review process, we agree to use the word "proof" for the proposition in question. Then we can say "proved" with a fair amount of rigor. The problem is that words have particular denoted meanings and connota-

---

[6] Here chaotic is not the common usage of the term implying total unpredictability, but refers to the new science of Chaos or dynamic nonlinear systems.

[7] Comments by Mitchell J. Feigenbaum during a panel discussion on *The Impact of Chaos on Science and Society*, in Grebogi and York.

tions. While the specialist may understand that the denoted meaning of proof is an agreed upon procedure, the word "proof" has the connotation of being as absolute as a mathematical proof. And it is not only the lay public that begins to believe that once proved there are no refutations. Many practitioners as well fall into that trap. In other words, using the word "proof" under these circumstances is inherently dishonest.

The Universe as a Clock

One view of the relationship of science to mathematics is that the universe is a large clock. All we need to do is "discover" the gears and their relationship to one another and we will be able to predict with certainty. Unfortunately even if that were true, we have discovered that mathematical models that are not linear can display chaotic or unpredictable behavior. One of the characteristics of these chaotic models is that they are very sensitive to initial conditions. That is to say that with slight differences in the initial conditions, the differences in some cases being so small that they cannot be measured, two almost identical starts soon lead to very different results for the model. This is sometimes referred to as the butterfly effect, which implies that the flapping of the wings of a butterfly could result in a change in weather on some other part of the globe at some future time.

What this says is that when a model used to predict a physical system is nonlinear, its ability to predict is limited to the short-term. In the case of weather, the current thinking is that a model cannot accurately predict weather beyond three days.

So even if the world were like a large clock there would still be great uncertainty. The clock model is useful in certain fields, such as mechanics and geometry. This is especially true over the short-term. But the clock-like model of the world and our knowledge of it break down in such areas as quantum mechanics. They break down with complex systems such as we find in modern enterprises. They also break down over longer time periods and where there are several variables.

I believe that a better model of our knowledge of the empirical world is not to assume that the world is a big clock or inherently predictable. It is possible that the world is irrational and unpredictable, but we have developed models that are very effective in allowing us to predict and survive in certain areas and certain ranges of conditions. We need to keep in mind, however, that our theories are maps and there are differences between our maps and the world or the data we are mapping.

The clock model, or any model of that nature, can be helpful. We should use it as long as it is proving useful and fruitful. If it leads to better results, use it. But results need to be measured, tabulated, and analyzed with some appreciation for variation and a sense of humility. Once the clock model fails you need to go on to something else. Unfortunately too many business people keep sticking to their clock models well after the feedback from the universe tells them it should be abandoned or at least questioned.

Some may find these few paragraphs to be fairly pessimistic, but they are probably accurate and certainly rely on fewer assumptions than do other systems. It also helps us maintain a certain level of humility with respect to what we do know, respect for what we do not know, and gratitude toward those theories that are successful and help us improve our lives. It is the assumption that we "know" things that we really do not that leads to much grief and loss in business and life in general.

Let me make this idea more intuitive. We have an expression: Seeing is believing. But our seeing is based on visible light, which represents a fraction of the available electromagnetic spectrum. We would see the world much differently if, for instance, our eyes could register X-rays instead of or in addition to visible light. How much different would our world be if we saw radio waves or microwaves—both of which, like light, are electromagnetic radiations? Even in the small range of radiation that our eyes do detect, which we call visible light, we only see a small range.

Telescopes have taught us that there are some very big and distant objects in the heavens that our naked eye cannot see. A microscope gives us a very different view of this world, with whole ecosystems of living creatures, animals, and plants at different scales. One of the first people to look through a microscope observed that creatures too small to be observed by the human eye had even smaller creatures attached to their surface. And he speculated these in turn had even smaller creatures preying on those that, in turn, carried even smaller creatures and so on down to who knows where. Our use of more powerful microscopes has essentially confirmed this insight. The world around us is teeming with life and matter that we do not see. Almost any surface that appears smooth to the naked eye appears rough under an electron microscope.

The same can be said about our hearing. We hear sound vibrations of a certain frequency and volume. Dogs' hearing is much more sensitive than ours but even dogs are hearing just a fraction of the noise around them. The same could be said about smell, taste, and touch.

So what we experience through our senses, what we see, hear, feel, smell, and taste, is a minute part of what is occurring around us. But our senses clearly have great survival value in the world that we have evolved in. If conditions were different it would be reasonable to infer that our senses would have evolved differently as well. But our senses have developed only within a small range of available data, and we are blind and deaf to most of what is going on around us.

Let me reiterate that although this may seem very theoretical to some people, it has some very practical and important consequences in industry. Consider the practice of establishing specifications. In an example from my prior book, Barbara Lawton, a statistician, was involved in developing a sophisticated process in our nuclear weapons program. The most sophisticated methods were used to develop specifications for suppliers. But as a government sponsored program, everything had to be purchased on the basis of lowest price. If a new supplier came along and offered to supply an item, he had to be used if his price was lower. But even though all the new suppliers manufactured to specifications and met them all, every time a new supplier was used the process would be thrown way off and additional specifications had to be developed.

Even specifications developed with the most sophisticated methods and tools are incomplete. All the specifications in the world are not sufficient to establish that two products made in different processes are identical for use in a complex process. Specifications that we establish are based on past experiences and past circumstances. It is a mistake to assume that they are reality or that they are a complete picture of reality.

Often the picture we have inside our heads of how a process should run or what happens in an environment that we manage, own, or control has nothing to do with what actually occurs. Or it may differ by a small amount, but that amount is significant enough to lead to different results. Small differences, even invisible differences, can lead to different outcomes.

Nor is this awareness limited to manufacturing operations. Any service industry, such as a temporary employment agency, is processing something on a repetitive basis. In effect they are manufacturing some forms or information. Wherever you have complexity in your process, there will be unseen factors that greatly affect it. It is management's job to try to understand these factors and control them. Management needs to make those things that are invisible to the senses visible to the mind. But this can only happen if the mind is open to possibilities other than "If it can't be seen it isn't real."

Testing a Proposition: The Necessity of Falsification

But this brings us to another related point. How can we have any confidence at all in the validity and usefulness of an empirical proposition? This is of course distinct from a mathematical or philosophical proposition. The most well-reasoned argument with the subtlest and most profound mathematics must be tested if it is a statement about the world. There must be outcomes that would provide additional verification and help bolster our belief in it. Even more important, there must be some possible outcomes that would disprove the proposition or cast additional doubt on its usefulness. These would lead to its modification or rejection. In other words, testing a proposition demands that it be falsifiable. This is even more important than verification. Indeed verification is meaningless if there exists no possibility of showing the proposition to be false.

This is of extra importance in those fields where an idea will be used without further confirmation in the future. That is the case in most fields of thought. Once an idea gains some standing we use it all the time. Rarely can we test it after we start using it. What we are proposing here is greater rigor when making statements about what we know. We need to be aware of the limitations of our knowledge, otherwise we are more likely to make errors that result in financial loss or physical injury to people.

It is not unusual to hear of theories that make predictions but all the outcomes are within the acceptable range of likelihood for that theory. No matter what the outcome, the theory is confirmed. Is this knowledge? This is as useful as discussing the required number of angels that fill the head of a pin.

Let me give one example. In market economics a theory that gained some popularity and fame was the Random Walk Hypothesis. This theory stated that the price movements in the financial markets, especially the stock market, were random and therefore totally unpredictable from one day to the next. Trends, according to this hypothesis, do not exist; they are strictly due to chance, are of no significance, and cannot be used to predict the future direction of the market. Whenever a chart was brought up that seemed to indicate that prices had trended up or down, the argument was raised that chance allowed for any combination of events. You could flip a two-headed coin 100 times and get 100 heads, or 4 heads out of 5 tries 20 times. In fact any combination is possible. This was an attempt to apply probability to the financial markets, and as such was laudable. But by having no way of being falsifiable, its value as empirical knowledge was negated. That it was not subject to falsification under any circumstances should have been a red flag.

Ironically, Shewhart confronted the same problem decades earlier but handled it very differently. Since a random process could, in theory at least, create any outcome, how do you distinguish whether a process is random or not? At what point does a certain outcome become so improbable that a signal must be raised before someone checks to see if something other than randomness is at work? Sure, any outcome is theoretically possible, but if you are getting highly improbable outcomes on a regular basis the odds that the markets are random is so unlikely that the theory itself becomes worthless.

Shewhart started solving this by looking at what men in the field do. While any outcome was possible, it would be irresponsible for a scientist to assume randomness of a coin if he flipped ten heads in a row. Sure, if you stopped the process and it turned out you could find nothing causing "nonrandom" behavior you would have lost some time and perhaps some money. But if you allowed the process to continue and it was indeed nonrandom, there is a loss associated with that as well.

So Shewhart ran some empirical tests to determine at what point one should decide the process was nonrandom so that the sum of these two kinds of losses would be minimized. He found a consistent pattern: Almost always when control limits were breached, a nonrandom or assignable cause could be found.

If our underlying theories are based on probability they lead to a different treatment for occurrences. Individual events by themselves give little information but must be considered with respect to a much larger picture. On the other hand our belief in our statistical theories is in turn probable only. They need to be subjected to as much rigor as an exact theory but with statistical thinking as an aid.

The Normal Distribution

A fascinating outcome of Dr. Shewhart's work is that after removing all the nonrandom causes—the assignable causes in a system—a state of statistical control is achieved. Many people, including many statisticians, expected that the process would be distributed according to the normal distribution. That was certainly the hope and the expectation. In Shewhart's own words, "Some of the earliest attempts to characterize a state of statistical control were inspired by the belief that there existed a special form of frequency function f and it was early argued that the normal law characterized such a state. When the normal law was found to be inadequate, then generalized functional forms were tried. Today, however, all hopes of finding a unique functional form f are blasted."[8]

These few sentences have some fascinating implications. Scientists and academic statisticians habitually assume a normal distribution and then make calculations based on these assumptions. But what Shewhart's work showed was that in the real world a random process doesn't exist except under extremely controlled conditions. Achieving a state of statistical control is a great achievement of man. Processes found in nature are filled with nonrandom causes. But even when all the nonrandom causes are removed the resulting process does not display a normal distribution. In fact no generalized mathematical forms could adequately fit all the resulting distributions.

When an idea gains general acceptance it is used in all kinds of circumstances to justify all kinds of decisions. Sometimes these decisions are harmless but many times they are not. Even small mistakes can lead to large calamities. If you believe at all in the scientific method and the use of scientific principles to help order our lives then you must believe that any fundamentally mistaken notion that is used repeatedly very likely makes things worse. If you don't believe in the validity of scientific thinking then it is unlikely you would have read this far.

[8] *Statistical Method from the Viewpoint of Quality Control* by Walter Shewhart, page 12.

There are two well-used modes of thought that have limited use in the real world. One is linear equations. Unfortunately the world is not linear—there are few straight lines. But until recently we did not have the tools to deal with nonlinearity. Even now it is still difficult and sometimes impossible. Nonlinearity does not bring the neat and precise answers we are used to with linearity. We have used linearity because in large measure we have had the tools to solve them, but that is an insufficient reason to rely on any tool.

The other problematic idea is the assumption of a normal distribution in every circumstance. Dr. Shewhart's work and the seventy years of practice by many people since he first published make it highly improbable that you are even looking at a single population when you initially confront most sets of data. We will discuss this further in subsequent chapters.

If science, and I mean this in the general sense of our knowledge of the world around us, proves nothing, then our knowledge of the world around us, strictly speaking, is a belief about the world. This is not to put this on the same level of belief as all the other beliefs we have or are forced to make with limited information. Scientific knowledge is made up of beliefs, but beliefs with greater rigor associated with them.

The testing, the peer review, and all the other mechanisms give our scientific beliefs a particular conservatism that can be both their strength and their drawback. We cannot use the word "prove." Instead words like "verification" and "confirm" are much more appropriate. As a statement gains greater verification over time, our level of belief in it rises to the point that we feel confident using it to predict within areas where it has been tested. We can extrapolate to areas where it has not specifically been tested with a lower degree of belief. Our degree of belief must remain of a general character with nonspecific words such as weak, mild, and strong degree of belief. Our degree of belief can never be assigned a specific number or level of confidence.

This is a consequence of the fact that we never "know" what lies outside our tested domain. And since the world at large is not in statistical control there is no chance of assigning any kind of probability to our knowledge or our ignorance. We can only estimate in the most general sense. Using some kind of numerical measure of the probability of our knowledge being accurate or false is not justified by either theory or experience. To do so would be completely misleading.

But now I want to add one large inference that I believe is justified by my experience. We can categorize knowledge into three broad categories. First is that which we know. This means we have some evidence and sufficient history to have been able to consistently predict outcomes. Second is the unknown but knowable. Here we don't know the information or the relationship, but we can get it. It might require some work but it is knowable. So, the first category is finite, the second infinite and therefore larger than the first. The third category is the unknown and unknowable. There are many things that you can never know. You may not have the resources or time or even the method to find out. This category is infinite also. But it is a larger infinity than the second category in the same sense that both irrational numbers and rational numbers in mathematics are infinite, but we can mathematically prove that the infinity of irrational numbers is larger than the infinity of rational numbers; the unknowable is larger than the knowable. The unknowable is more densely packed in our world—there is just more of it.

Rather than feel a sense of pessimism from this insight I feel a sense of exhilaration. We are, each of us, like surfers riding a huge wave in a seemingly infinite ocean. But our knowledge, like our surfboard, keeps us moving above water and dry, but only if we are diligent, respectful, and humble about what we know and what we don't know.

CHAPTER 7

MULTIPLE POPULATIONS AND THRESHOLDS

"To make a sale ask a closing question seven times. Keep asking for the order until you get it." These instructions were given to many salespeople throughout the 1960s, '70s, and '80s. Even today some people still hear this. Sales trainers wrote books and made recordings that promised the listener great results with these techniques. Apparently it worked—at least for some.

An Alternative Selling Model

Today many sales trainers advocate a consultative approach to selling. Current methods advocate taking the customer's point of view, not selling her anything she really doesn't need. Instead of forcing sales down her throat, develop a long-term relationship with the customer. The relationship is emphasized over the transaction. Despite the boisterous protestations by advocates of the beat-them-over-the-head approach, a better way was discovered.

Becoming a Belief

One incorrect assumption is the notion that all data is normally distributed. People take data and compute the mean, the standard deviations, and other statistical variables that only have meaning under certain conditions. A normal distribution really involves two key assumptions: one, our data comes from a single population with just one peak; two, that population is normally distributed. Based on these assumptions, decisions are made that impact people's lives, yet both assumptions, according to the empirical work done by Dr. Shewhart, are probably . wrong.

Two Populations or One?

Let me explain what I mean by a single population. Suppose we calculate the average height of a group of potential customers, and it turns out to be 5 feet 5 inches. Average height is important because to achieve profitability our product must be usable by the largest number of people possible. Let's say it's a car and we need to design interior space. However, when the car is built it doesn't sell. In our post-failure investigation we find that the population in question consists of two tribes, each with the same number of people, living side by side. One, the Watusi, has an average height of 6 feet 6 inches and adults are between 5 feet 11 inches and 7 feet 2 inches. The other tribe, the pygmies, has an average height of 4 feet 4 inches and adults are between 3 feet 10 inches and 5 feet 3 inches. There are no drivers of the calculated average height in the combined, or general, population.

We can compute statistics such as the average, the range, and the standard deviation for any group of numbers. But what do they mean? Do they have any real use when the numbers are distributed this way with two distinct populations? In this case the distribution has two peaks. One is at 6 feet 6 inches and the other at 4 feet 4 inches. We assumed that there were more people of the average height of 5 feet 5 inches because we assumed a single population. But instead the average was just a number representing the average of two very different groups (or populations in statistical jargon). We can compute all the statistics we want based on these assumptions but they lead to faulty conclusions when the underlying assumptions are incorrect. And more importantly, knowing the existence of two populations would have helped focus our analysis and decision making along much more fruitful lines. One ubiquitous example is the existence of men and women in the population. Being cognizant of this difference allows for clothing designs with different fits. Rather than designing a pair of pants that doesn't fit either sex well, two different types of clothes are designed giving each sex a better fit. Another very well-known example of a two-peaked distribution is the death rate. The number of deaths by age for the population has two peaks: one around birth and the second in old age.

Are Customers a Single Population?

It is tempting to categorize all our customers into a single population. Some companies assume price is the critical criterion that drives customer purchasing. How do managers come to this conclusion? Well, they had several pushy and boisterous customers, perhaps trained in the beat-them-over-the-head approach, call and threaten to take their business elsewhere if they didn't get a better price. These few customers left a big impression on the manager. From there it was a simple but incorrect inference that all customers were driven by price—the cheaper the better. This is faulty on several fronts. First, they are inferring something about the larger population of customers based on a small sample. That sample was not randomly generated and therefore is not representative of the whole customer base. Other customers with other criteria may never complain, or if they do it is much less dramatic. They may voice their concern to a customer service rep who fails to pass it along because the complaint was so mild mannered. A second, equally wrong assumption is that your customers all fit into one population—they value price first and it is just a question of degree. The old bell-shaped curve is invoked in the mind of the manager.

More likely, however, customers are not a single population. When one of my clients actually did a customer survey, few if any mentioned price. Instead, reliable delivery and being given timely notification when delivery schedules could not be met were much more important to customers. There were some customers who valued price first and foremost, but the client was stunned to find that these constituted a very small group. His customer base was made up of several populations and we were able to devise different strategies to reach each group based on its needs.

A more sophisticated breakdown of the marketplace was delineated by Geoffrey A. Moore in his book *Crossing the Chasm*. Moore breaks down the market for technology products into several categories: Innovators, Early Adopters, Early Majority, Late Majority, and Laggards. Instead of a single population, there are five. And some of these relate to others. He maintains that in order to successfully sell a technology product, Innovators and Early Adopters have to be sold to first. When you have successfully sold to them your marketing must change and focus on the Early Majority. If you treat the market as a common mass you will be unsuccessful.

Companies that recognize differences among their customers can identify their most profitable customers and provide them additional services, helping to keep them satisfied and thereby raising profitability. But a company also needs to be cognizant of the Innovators and Early Adopters who, while not as profitable, are a harbinger of things to come. If they leave they may not directly impact profits much, but it may be a signal to other customers that they have found something better, and it may just be a matter of time before the others follow.

A Single Population Stock Market?

Another example of an assumption of a single distribution is the Random Walk Hypothesis for financial markets mentioned in Chapter 6. In business school I read an article investigating the rate of return of the stock market. The author gathered data from various periods of time. His data fell into about seven different categories, each with its own peak. He then went on to state he was confident that if more data were taken all the intermediate points would be filled in and the result would be one large normal distribution.

I was stunned by the article. It was evident that no matter how the data fell out nothing would cast doubt on his assumption of normality. And further, he assumed additional data would justify his belief of normally distributed stock prices. At the time I read the article I didn't have the arguments to refute it. (That was just as well since if I had written a well-thought-out and documented paper refuting that and other articles I read in business school I would have been failed. As it is, I got into enough trouble verbally arguing against what was presented.)

Seven different populations of stock market returns suggest quite strongly seven different states of the equities markets. Traders talk about bull markets and bear markets. In the popular press, a bull market is a market trading up and a bear market is one trading down. I recently encountered a definition of a bear market stating that it is when the market index trades 20% below the peak. With this kind of definition you are sure to lose money trading. A good trader will distinguish between three markets. In addition to the up and down market, he recognizes the existence of a trading market. A trading market has up days and down days, but looked at over the time frame relevant to the trader it is really moving in a range. The trading rules for each of these markets is different. In a trading market, for instance, you buy low and sell high. In a true bull market you buy high and sell higher.

But the article suggests to me that there may be seven different states for equity markets. From my own experience, I would call these a trading market, an up-trending market, a down-trending market, a bull market, a bear market, panic buying, and panic selling. A trending market moves up or down but not as strongly as a bull or bear market. It is basically a trading market with a bias. A panic market, on the other hand, seems to be unstoppable in either direction. If there were distinct markets it would be a gross assumption, probably incorrect, to suggest that a bear market is just a bull market in a different direction. There might be very different relationships between stocks in each of these markets. Yet the popular descriptors used in the securities markets assume that the characteristics are the same in all markets. The beta of a stock is supposed to be a measure of its risk relative to the general market. A high beta stock will move more than the market and is therefore riskier. But if a bull market is distinctly different than a bear, the beta of a stock might be nothing more than the average over different markets. You could not assume that beta over the next two years would have any relevance to the stock.

Incidentally if this notion of seven different kinds of stock markets has some validity and usefulness, we cannot automatically extend it to other markets such as commodity markets.

Beyond Financial Markets

The notion that things are not evenly distributed, but that we have distinct classes, categories, and states with relatively sharp differentiation is not limited to financial markets. The application is much wider. Essentially the universe is lumpy. It is not evenly distributed in almost any respect. Just think in terms of galaxies in space. Matter is not evenly distributed among the stars but instead tends to be clumped in large bodies of stars or galaxies. Galaxies in turn tend to group together.

In between the galaxies and the groups of galaxies are vast stretches of space with little significant matter.

Even more, fluid matter such as air and water, at least on Earth, is not uniform. The oceans have currents and different distributions of temperature, life, and matter throughout. As does the atmosphere. We have tornadoes and storms with their own characteristics, yet a few hundred feet away stable and dry conditions exist. If you are in a storm and you extrapolate that the whole world is in a storm you will be wrong. You can take the average temperature of a storm area and a surrounding calm area, but what does that average mean?

People often use the law of large numbers to justify the assumption of a normal distribution. But the law of large numbers is a mathematical law, not a physically demonstrated relationship. There are different versions of the law, each with different requirements before it can be proven mathematically. There are several problems with applying the law of large numbers empirically. First, it is a mathematical law about the relationship of many distributions when they are combined. Second, there is no clear-cut method to determine how many distributions or how much data are required before you approach normality. And third, one needs to remember that it is a mathematical law that may not apply in many physical cases.

Threshold

One thing that creates different states and therefore different populations is a threshold. A threshold is any point that, once exceeded, leads to completely different behavior. Examples of thresholds are all around us. Heating 1 gram of water requires 1 calorie of heat to raise the temperature 1 degree centigrade. It requires 100 calories to heat water from just above freezing to the boiling point, or threshold, of 100 degrees centigrade (212 degrees Fahrenheit). Now, heating it further does not give you hotter water—a change of state occurs. At this point an additional 560 calories of energy are required to convert 1 gram of water to steam. It takes more energy to convert water into steam than it does to raise the temperature from just above freezing to the boiling point. In fact, it takes more than five times as much energy.

Other thresholds in nature include the breaking point of a rope and the velocity required for a rocket to escape the earth's gravitational pull. If the velocity is below escape velocity, the rocket will fall back to earth; above escape velocity, it successfully leaves the earth's gravitational pull. A cliff represents a threshold. Climbing a cliff requires a lot of energy, work, and skill. Once on the cliff the difference between safety and death is just a few inches. Another example of a threshold is getting that big sale.

Thresholds are often hard to cross but once crossed they result in a significant qualitative difference. If you have some ice in your drink during the summer, the beverage stays cold, pretty much at the same temperature with even just a small bit of ice left. Once the ice melts, however, the temperature of the drink quickly rises. Notice that clumps of snow remain after a heavy snowfall even when the temperature reaches more than 40 degrees Fahrenheit (well above the melting point of snow), for a day or two.

Crossing one threshold in a complex system may alter the whole system. Venus is closer to the sun than we are. We can easily calculate how much additional solar energy reaches its surface due to its proximity to the sun. It's an easy linear calculation to extrapolate how much hotter Venus should be than the earth. It should be about 80 degrees Fahrenheit warmer, or about 160 degrees Fahrenheit; hot, but certainly capable of sustaining water and biological life. This is a straightforward, linear conclusion that today may seem simplistic. But in the middle and latter part of the twentieth century, that was the best guess of many prominent scientists. Venus was believed by many to be a much better candidate for biological life than Mars.

But later in the twentieth century satellite probes sent into the planet's atmosphere revealed a very different environment. The temperature at the surface of the planet turned out to be 600 to 800 degrees Fahrenheit or more. This is too hot for water and too hot for life. How could there be such a discrepancy between the model and reality? A more complex computer model of the earth used for weather prediction was run to see what would happen on Earth if the Sun's luminosity was increased enough to heat the planet by another 80 degrees. The model predicted a surface temperature on Earth similar to what actually exists on Venus. Once the temperature threshold was crossed, enough carbon dioxide was released to change the properties of the atmosphere. Instead of allowing excess heat to escape, the atmosphere trapped most of the heat forcing the surface temperature to climb dramatically. At a certain point the atmosphere jumped to a different state.

We rarely know beforehand how a system will react once a threshold is crossed. Predictions of very complex systems based on mathematical models are sophisticated guesses. But the existence of thresholds teaches us that the results of our actions may be much more severe than we can currently predict. The existence of thresholds should at the very least give us a measure of humility. Thresholds and discontinuous jumps in state are part of a group of ideas popularly called Chaos Theory.

Here the term "Chaos" is very different from the common understanding of chaos. The common language definition of chaos is "a state of utter confusion completely wanting in order, sequence, organization or predictable operations."[9] But modern Chaos Theory refers to several lines of explorations being pursued by mathematicians and scientists. The author James Gleick conveniently grouped and discussed several of these phenomena in his book *Chaos*. Nonlinear dynamics and sensitivity to initial conditions are two phenomena often labeled as Chaos Theory. Jumps in state caused by breaching thresholds is part of Chaos Theory as well. It would be appropriate to say that the atmosphere of Venus behaved chaotically, in the scientific sense of the word.

Other Markets

After observing markets over many years it seems to me that many markets have thresholds that once reached and breached result in different behavior. You may have a period of stability where the price seems unaffected by supply pressures, yet once the threshold is reached prices start to jump, either up or down. One example is the petroleum market. In the mid- and late 1990s oil seemed to be abundant. Gasoline prices were at historic lows when adjusted for cost of living. The fuel-efficient automobile fell out of favor. Consumers started toying with larger cars like coming home to an old lover. Automobile manufacturers responded by building bigger and faster cars and trucks. Bigger houses came into vogue again. Energy consumption picked up again

---

[9] *The Impact of Non-Linear Dynamics and Chaos on Cardiology and Medicine* by Leon Glass.

and all the while the price of energy seemed to be unaffected. Then at a certain point when excess capacity shrank to a manageable level, OPEC was able to reexert its presence. Crude petroleum, which had been selling at around $10–12 dollars a barrel, shot up in price in a few months to more than $25 a barrel. A threshold was reached and breached, and the resulting price increase was not linear but more like a jump to a different state.

We witnessed the same thing in reverse in the mid-1980s. At that time Americans and the world were concerned about fuel efficiency. Fuel efficient cars were in demand and the large American automobile had been all but pronounced dead. The higher prices had also induced more and deeper exploration and new sources were discovered. Petroleum, which had been trading at more than $20 a barrel, after some fits and starts declined to the mid-teens. The market does not behave the same when crossing the threshold on the upside as on the downside (the scientific term for this is hysteresis). But it is as if there were two main states in the current petroleum market: relative tightness and relative glut. The in-between state is relatively short-lived and unstable.

One well-known threshold is the break-even point of a company. A company above break-even can survive. A company well above thrives. There are two break-even points a company must breach: the profit break-even point and the cash flow break-even point. A company that goes well beyond break-even reaches a different level of prosperity. But companies that go below their break-even points, either because of a sales decline or cost increase, are no fun to work in. And companies that stay below it for any length of time disappear. Of the two, cash flow break-even is more important for survival than profit break-even. These thresholds serve to cull companies. The difference between being below breakeven and above it may be just a few percentage points difference in sales or costs, but the outcome couldn't be more different. It is just a few percentage points difference that determines success or failure.

A world with significant thresholds is very different from one without. Thresholds break things up into categories, creating multiple classes and deterring the existence of single populations. Thresholds create unevenness, lumpiness, and distributions that are not smooth.

CHAPTER 8

LEVERAGE

A concept complementary to threshold is leverage. Leverage refers to anything that magnifies your efforts.

Mechanical Leverage: Simple Machines

The term "leverage" originally referred to the seven simple machines categorized by the ancient Greek scientist Archimedes. These are simple machines like levers, pulleys, inclines, wheels, gears, etc. Each of these machines allows humans to do things they could not do otherwise. Inclines, levers, and wheels allowed the ancient Egyptians to move massive stones, which made the building of the pyramids possible. When using a lever the force exerted is multiplied, allowing you to move a much heavier object than you could otherwise. A seesaw is a lever: If you sit very close to the center of a seesaw someone much smaller than you can make you rise and fall at will using her own weight. A force of 10 pounds on the end of the seesaw can move 50 pounds, if those 50 pounds are close enough to the center, or axis. In this case we would say the leverage is 50 to 10, or 5 to 1, or just 5. Whatever force we exert is multiplied by the leverage factor, in this case five.

Tools

Tools are another form of leverage. They multiply the effects of our efforts or allow us to do things that we could not do unaided. Some tools, such as a screwdriver, a rolling pin, or a sewing needle, employ one or more kinds of mechanical leverage. When twisting, a screwdriver is a kind of gear, with the handle being larger than the tip. Because of this, the force you exert on the handle is multiplied at the tip. It can also be used as a lever. A sewing needle and a rolling pin also have leverage aspects to them. The critical function of each is not its leverage but what it allows us to do that is impossible to do otherwise. They extend our abilities. Tool use is not unique to humans. Chimpanzees use stalks to reach into an anthill and pull out ants for consumption. Crows use a similar technique to pull beetles out of rotting tree trunks. We, of course, have taken tool making and usage to a much more sophisticated level. A strong case can be made that sophisticated tool making is the single most distinguishing characteristic of human beings.

Energy-Aided Leverage

A third type of mechanical leverage occurs when we add an outside source of energy to our machine to increase our results even further. This is energy-aided leverage. The outside source can be a steam engine, an electrical motor, gasoline or diesel engine, waterpower, or some other source. The results are modern tools such as cars, cranes, tractors, power saws, jigsaws, and other powered items. Consider that an Olympic-caliber athlete can run the marathon, 26 miles, at about 12 to 13 miles an hour. This is a human operating without mechanical leverage. Cyclists competing in the Tour de France travel about 125 miles in a day and average more than 25 miles an hour. They ride at this pace for more than 20 days and cover more than 2,500 miles. This is an example of people operating with mechanical leverage. But of course, we can go faster and farther still. In a car one can easily travel at 60 or 70 miles an hour for 5 hours or more covering 300 to 500 miles in a day. On a plane we could cover 2,500 miles in a few hours and wouldn't even have to train or work up a sweat. These last two are examples of mechanical energy-aided leverage. As you can see, with each higher level of leverage there is a marked increase in speed and distance.

The high standard of living and material abundance in industrial societies is in part due to leverage. By herself, a farmer can work a few acres of land. With a tractor, a farmer can till hundreds of acres and produce enough food to feed hundreds of people. One person can operate a crane and lift steel beams, allowing us to construct buildings that dwarf the pyramids. A pyramid took decades to build; a modern skyscraper can be up in months.

Commercial Leverage

But the idea of leverage extends well beyond the physical manipulation of matter. We have leverage in commerce as well. Traditionally two kinds are mentioned in business literature: financial leverage and operating leverage. Financial leverage means taking on debt to increase your return. Suppose your business regularly and predictably provides a return of 10% on capital invested. With equity of $1,000,000, your return is $100,000. But if you could borrow an additional $1,000,000 at 5% and invest that in your business at the same rate, your return is increased. Your return is now $200,000 (10% of $2,000,000) less the $50,000 in interest (5% of $1,000,000), or $150,000. This is a 15% return on your $1,000,000 of equity capital. You have leveraged your own capital with debt to increase your return by 50%, from $100,000 to $150,000.

There is a downside to financial leverage. If you fail to earn the expected 10% or if interest rates rise, your return will decrease and may even be smaller than without leverage. When financial leverage works against you it becomes negative leverage.[10]

The second type of commercial leverage is operating leverage. This refers to the number of people working for the company. If 100 people work for the company and each produces more than her salary and related expenses, then each is adding to the profitability of the organization. If sales happen to tumble and you can't fully employ all your people, then profits are adversely affected in a multiplicative way. The easiest thing to cut when sales decline is people. Most leases and equipment purchases are long-term investments with substantial penalties for early termination, but there are few such constraints for early termi-

---

[10] Suppose your operating return drops to 5% of invested capital and interest rates increase to 11%. Unleveraged, you would have earned $50,000 on $1,000,000 of capital (5% of $1,000,000). With leverage, however, your return is now $100,000 (5% of $2,000,000) minus $110,000 of interest expenses (11% of $1,000,000) for a loss of $10,000, or minus 1%.

nation of employment due to management error, at least in the United States. As a result recessions and sales slowdowns lead to layoffs and unemployment from mediocre companies. Workers share in the downside of these businesses, but do not share in the upside.

There is a third form of commercial leverage. This is capitalization. Suppose your company earns $400,000 a year. From the earnings and cash flow of the business, you have access to several hundred thousand dollars to expand or acquire other companies. But if the stock market values your company at 20 times earnings, your company is worth $8 million and you have a currency, your stock, that you can use to expand. If the stock market values your company at 100 times earnings, the stock of your company is worth $40 million. We have seen the stock market value companies that were making little or no money—or even losing money—at billions of dollars. This only happens under certain market conditions, but when it does it creates huge leverage. We saw this in the late 1990s with telecommunication and Internet companies being valued at hundreds of billions of dollars. In some cases the companies weren't even profitable.

There are additional forms of leverage as well.

Organizational Leverage

When we enter into an association, or organization, with someone, especially if she has different and complementary abilities (knowledge and skills) to ours, we also have the potential for leverage. Because your skills are complementary the two of you are able to do things that neither one could do alone. This is not the same as division of labor, where one person could do the work but by breaking it up you become more efficient. When people combine into well-thought-out teams or organizations, their different skills allow them to do things that none of them can do on their own. An example would be combining a promoter with an engineer. The engineer may design the neatest product in the world, but it is of limited value if it isn't developed, promoted, marketed, and sold. The promoter with a mediocre product or no product can't do much either. Put them together, however, and a very useful product can be sold in large numbers, and the two can develop a lucrative business.

Knowledge Leverage

Knowledge can be leverage. A little story demonstrates this. A steamboat was laid up and despite the best efforts of its owners could not be made to run. The owners had called in several mechanics, each of whom was confounded by the problem. The company was losing literally boatloads of money as its prime asset was tied up and not functioning. They decided to call a highly regarded consulting engineer. He came into the engine room, walked around, and tapped on some pipes. He left and fifteen minutes later walked back in with a new valve. He replaced the old valve, started up the engine, and it worked perfectly.

A couple of days later they received his bill. It was for $5,000. Miffed and dismayed they asked for a breakdown. The next day the breakdown arrived. It read: New valve . . . 96¢. For knowing where to tap . . . $4,999.04. Without knowledge nothing happened. With the right knowledge the company was able to operate.

Replication

Replication is a form of knowledge leverage that multiplies the results of your efforts. An early form of replication was simple broadcasting, such as having a meeting and addressing several people at once. The ancient Greek amphitheaters allowed thousands of people to observe the same theatrical performance. The written word is another form of replication, as it allows the words of one person to be read by many people at different times. One major form of replication that changed the modern world was the development of the printing press. This allowed for the quick duplication of books and manuscripts. With the printing press, a person's words could be read by thousands of people at once.

Broadcasting, film, records, tapes, CDs, and floppy discs are all forms of replication. A performer can sing only to a finite number of people. When she stops, her performance is over. Prior to the advent of records audiences had to wait for her to personally perform to enjoy her singing. But recordings and broadcasting changed that. With a record, CD, audiotape, video, or film, people all over the globe could appreciate her performance. Just as important, she personally did not have to do anything further once the recording was completed. Her voice could be heard endless times by any number of people without her having to prepare or exert herself. She need not even be alive to be heard and appreciated. This allows for an incredible leveraging of knowledge, in this case musical knowledge.

Making the recording is one form of replication. But the actual record or CD, the recording vehicle, can be indefinitely duplicated. Hundreds, thousands, even millions of copies can be made easily once the original is made. Here we really have two kinds of replications. We have the making of a single recording that replicates the voice and the performance of the singer. This can be played at will. But we also have a process to rapidly replicate the record, tape, or CD. We are replicating the replicating instrument. The large-scale manufacturing of recordings can be said to be meta to the recording. It is a meta-replication, a second level of replication.

System Replication

It is not just products that can be replicated. Whole systems can be duplicated. Each McDonald's restaurant has a system for efficiently making hamburgers. The company not only sells hamburgers, but a whole system for making hamburgers—it sells McDonald's franchises. McDonald's has two main products: hamburgers and its hamburger replication system. This gives it additional leverage. From the point of view of the company, McDonald's gets additional financial leverage. The franchise owners provide additional capital and manage the store while the company earns royalties and fees. The franchise owner gets a whole business system with demonstrable success.

In order for franchising to work, indeed in order for replication to work, the results in one area have to be transferable into a different area. This is an interesting phenomenon that needs to be appreciated in commerce. The success of global products and franchises indicates strongly that people's needs, tastes, and desires are similar throughout the world. The success of global franchising indicates that people's ability to run a business is transferable across boundaries, into different languages and cultures. And the inference is that once you find a formula that works well in a local market, there is a good chance of transferring that, perhaps with some modifications, to many other local markets.

This gives me some confidence in the proposition that many exceptional managerial methods are transferable as well. Once you learn how to accomplish something, that knowledge and skill can be taught to someone else who will get similar results in other parts of the world. The major effort is in development or learning how to do it right. How well a business will work can't be determined or analyzed ahead of time. It has to be tried and refined. But once all the kinks have been worked out it can be replicated many times over.

In the case of McDonald's, the very idea of stamping out a system to produce a food item can be transferred to other foods. The McDonald's model has been transferred to other foods like pizza and tacos. Whereas a single restaurant is a hamburger replication system, and a company is a system for replicating restaurants (for replicating replication systems!), or a second-order replication, lifting the idea and applying it to other foods or other products is a third-order replication. We are now replicating (franchise concept) a system for replicating (franchise) a food replication system (restaurant).

The power in this is that improvements can be made and tested at very little cost. If the system is pretty much the same from one restaurant to another, then making a change in a few restaurants and testing it is incredibly powerful. If the change works it can be quickly implemented systemwide. If it fails, however, the costs are spread out over so many outlets that it is negligible.

Universal Application

While a McDonald's might work in many locales, we should not assume that it would work everywhere. One example is India. Could you successfully sell hamburgers in a culture where cows are considered sacred? I suspect not. But the franchising concept with a different food might do very well there.

Just how closely should you copy the initial system? The initial franchising philosophy called for the franchise owner to exactly duplicate the model. Any deviations from the model could jeopardize the franchise. But today some franchises allow owners to make adjustments to the local market. Some even encourage it. These are adjustments, not radical changes.

Wal-Mart stores are replications. One Wal-Mart store is very much like another. The formula seems to work in many different environments. But the system is too big and carries too many items to be an exact clone. It needs to be managed. Each store manager has much more authority and flexibility than a manager of a McDonald's. She requires much more training if the stores are to replicate the Wal-Mart culture, prices, efficiency, and service. In this case the replication, while still being heavily dependent on mimicking the model store in layout, design, and rules, also relies heavily on the people running it to replicate culture. This is not an exact copy but a higher order replication.

What applies to stores that are owned or aligned by a single corporation can also apply in some degree to independently owned stores. The best examples are the ubiquitous Chinese restaurants that dot the landscape in North America and throughout the world. You can walk into any of them and get wonton soup, hot-and-sour soup, egg rolls, chicken chow mein, beef with broccoli, or any one of a number of other dishes that appear on virtually all the menus of all Chinese restaurants. While the stores are independently owned, the similarity from restaurant to restaurant is striking. A cooking method that has a very long history—wok cooking—has been perfected over centuries and forms the basis for most of these restaurants.

This demonstrates that replication can be done outside of a corporate system. But the stores need some kind of mechanism to quickly distribute useful innovations to other stores. This highlights the notion that management ideas and improvement to these ideas are transferable across and into very different systems. This point is one that makes continual improvement very powerful for whole societies, not just individual companies.

All forms of leverage are used in abundance in wealthy societies. There is a strong correlation between the gross domestic product of a nation and the number of installed phones. Farmers use tractors, construction workers use cranes, commuters use cars, buses, and planes. Corporations use operating and financial leverage, and capitalization helps companies grow. Books, telephones, radios, and televisions extend the conversations of people across time and space. Leverage makes a society wealthy and it also accounts for some individuals being more financially successful than others.

Consider some occupations. An unskilled worker has little leverage and earns little. A skilled worker with knowledge leverage earns more. Very skilled professionals, such as doctors, lawyers, computer programmers, and managers, earn still more. But a lawyer working on her own has only knowledge leverage. If she joins a successful partnership she also adds organizational leverage. If that partnership grows and hires additional lawyers, she then has operating leverage as well. A partner in a successful law firm earns more than an associate. The partner enjoys the fruits of operating leverage since she shares in the profits of the firm. In a sense the associates work for the partners.

A successful insurance salesperson has financial leverage. Thousands of dollars of premium control millions of dollars of insurance. A trader with a large firm has organizational leverage—and lots of financial leverage. Each one of his trades may involve millions of dollars of which little or none is his. If he is also a partner he has operating leverage as well. In good years he can make much more than a partner in a law firm where there is little financial leverage or a doctor in a practice where there is no financial leverage, limited operating leverage, and no replication leverage.

The wealthiest people use many forms of leverage to create wealth. Bill Gates used replication (software sold on floppies or CDs) of general purpose software for computers (knowledge tools and knowledge leverage) that were available to virtually everyone in the developed world. He employed many people (operating leverage) to write the code. When he started the company his partner, Paul Allen, had many of the people skills that made the business possible (organizational leverage), which Bill Gates lacked. His company went public. As successful as his company was it was the stock market valuation of his share of the company (capitalization) that boosted his personal wealth into the stratosphere. He employed replication, knowledge, knowledge tools, organizational leverage, and capitalization. Of course in order for leverage to work, there must be great execution and strategy. If you fail you are no better off, perhaps even worse off.

Substitution of Leverage

It is easy to ignore some forms of leverage. Many observers of the economic scene seem to think that leverage only comes from economies of scale, that is to say bigness. But bigness can be as much a curse as a blessing. A small company can make use of other kinds of leverage to effectively meet a big company on its own turf. Other management writers relate productivity increases exclusively to technology and computers, or what I have categorized as knowledge tools. This is simplistic and often incorrect.

When the personal computer was introduced many proponents envisioned a dramatic improvement in productivity because of it. Yet most economists claim they cannot measure any increase in productivity as a result of the ubiquity of the personal computer. Prior to the introduction of the personal computer, managers had their letters typed by their secretary, a typing pool, or someone in the company who was proficient in letter writing and typing. The typist might have been able to type sixty words a minute error-free. The manager would dictate a letter in a few minutes and then get back on the phone, performing a skill at which he was particularly adept. Let's assume his unique skill was selling. Because he had a competent partner whose skills complemented his own, each could spend a great deal of their time focusing on those tasks at which they excelled. Each could be highly productive as a result of this organizational leverage.

When the word processor was introduced that should have made the typing pool more efficient. For the typist who could type sixty words a minute error-free, and where there were few mass mailings, there was some marginal improvement. What word processors did was make it possible for much less skilled typists to get letters out the door. Now someone who could type forty words a minute and who made several mistakes a page could quickly and easily edit and correct his letters and print them.

Eventually, typing pools were eliminated. Now each manager had a PC on his desk. Even though he could only type twenty words a minute he could get his letters out after reviewing and editing them several times. In one sense this was progress. But it also meant that he now had to spend more of his time each day typing and editing, something at which he was relatively inept. He spent less of his time performing those tasks at which he was excellent or unique. The same could be said of the typist, who now may have been shunted off to perform an entirely different function. Here one kind of leverage (knowledge tool) was substituted for another (organizational leverage). Whether there was a net productivity improvement is unclear.

Dan Sullivan of the Strategic Coach advises entrepreneurs on making the best and most productive use of their efforts. He believes what each of us does can be separated into four categories: incompetent,

competent, excellent, and unique. Many entrepreneurs spend a fair amount of time doing things they are not particularly talented at. This leaves much less time available for those things they do that are unique and add the most value to their enterprises. While his system is geared toward entrepreneurs who can control what they do, it seems to me that his ideas have relevance in managing larger corporations as well. When a management decision forces more people to spend time doing things they are marginally good or even incompetent at, instead of things they are great at, it has to impact negatively on the effectiveness of the individual and ultimately the company. A good manager should have an idea of where individuals excel and try to manage so each spends more of his or her time and effort in those areas.

The PC and Small Business

The personal computer did allow small companies, even one-person operations, to compete against larger firms. A one-person operation was now able to analyze data and send out letters well enough to be in business, something that was impossible prior to the advent of the PC. At around the same time that the PC was introduced, we witnessed a mass creation of small firms as many individuals and small groups went off on their own—often to compete against their former employers.

While all the forms of leverage, such as mechanical, energy-aided, and knowledge, are important, most of these can be purchased in the marketplace. By themselves they don't instill an advantage. Central to success is organizational leverage—putting together a great organization that performs its specific niche in the economic ecology well. This can't be purchased; it relies on several forms of knowledge. This is management. Great organizations smoothly integrate technology and other forms of leverage into fulfilling their mission within their strategy.

Merger Activity

Over the last twenty years we have witnessed a huge merger game as many established companies were bought or merged with others. The rationale often given for the mergers was the benefits of size and economies due to bigness. This is one of those ideas that cannot be verified each time it is applied, yet it was used to justify and influence major social and economic decisions. But very few of these mergers have been as successful as they were first made out to be. In many cases the mergers were outright failures. One of the most obvious examples at this writing is the merger of Chrysler with Daimler-Benz, the maker of the Mercedes-Benz.

There is an overriding financial force acting as an impetus to mergers. And that is the stock market. When stocks trade at high multiples (when there is high capitalization leverage) there is an impetus to buy other companies. An example is the merger of AOL and Time Warner. Technically AOL bought Time Warner. The high stock valuation of AOL and the lure of having the stock market value the combined company equally high made that purchase possible.

With a high price to earnings ratio, companies have a currency, their stock, that they can use to buy other companies. If the purchase price of the acquired company is at a lower multiple to earnings, the acquiring company is in effect buying earnings at less than what the stock market is paying for earnings. This is a kind of arbitrage that further bolsters the stock of the acquiring company. For instance, if a company whose stock trades at twenty times earnings buys another company at ten times earnings and pays for it with its stock, the purchased company is instantly valued by the equity markets at twice what the company paid, making it an instant winner.

On the other hand, when stocks trade at relatively low price earnings multiples, the cash market for companies may value businesses at higher prices than the stock market. A division might fetch more cash than it would be worth if it were sold for stock. Companies then have a financial incentive to sell off divisions for cash. That cash can be used, among other things, to buy a company's own stock at an attractive price. There is a broad threshold of stock valuations that once crossed leads to very different, indeed, just the opposite kind of behavior. When the stock market valuation is high relative to the cash market there is a strong financial incentive to merge and conglomerate. When the stock market valuation is low relative to the cash market there is a strong incentive to behave in just the opposite manner and sell off non-core businesses.

Here, as with other thresholds, a linear change in one variable (stock market valuation) leads to a change in state. The resulting change is an economic state with very different characteristics. Thresholds combined with leverage reinforce cycles and help create very different economic environments. Leverage properly employed produces wealth for society and we all gain by that. But thresholds in combination with leverage, especially economic leverage, produce large inequalities of income and wealth. One person may become much wealthier than another not because he is necessarily smarter or more knowledgeable in substantive knowledge, but because of better use of leverage.

CHAPTER 9

EXPONENTIAL GROWTH

There are two additional concepts closely related to leverage and thresholds. One is what I call cumulative benefit, the other is compounded growth.

Cumulative Benefit

Once something is up and running it becomes significantly easier to maintain. Ideally it is self-sustaining once started. The biggest input of energy and effort is in the beginning. After that it requires much less energy to run, yet it produces benefits such as profits. One example of cumulative benefit can be found in residential real estate. It might require a fair amount of work and capital to acquire a rental property, but once purchased and developed, if it was a good purchase, it is fairly routine to run and maintain. This allows a person or corporation to build up a real-estate portfolio. The tricky part is the development of the property or the astute purchase, often made with a significant amount of borrowed funds or financial leverage. But running each property can be routine and is often outsourced.

Another example refers to the replication examples of the prior chapter. When a company with many similar units, such as a Pizza Hut or Wal-Mart, is growing, it is opening new stores with regularity. A great deal of research goes into opening a new store. The local market needs to be researched, a site has to be found, lease terms agreed to, people hired for each new location, and so on. It might take three or more years of work with no income being generated from that location before a store is opened. The effort might fail and all you would have to show for those years of effort is plenty of documents (although you now know that the area is inappropriate, something you didn't know before). A new store needs to be promoted and closely managed. Once successfully up and running, it has momentum. Running an ongoing store is very different than setting one up. For the managers who actually run the store, there are numerous problems, challenges, and emergencies they need to deal with, but on a different level of replication, for a different level of management, that store can take care of itself. It should have its own systems to train associates and managers. If the corporation has well-established systems for training, human resources, and legal, all the day-to-day problems can be handled within a routine. So for the second order of replication, store openings are cumulative. After a store is opened and established, attention can be turned to opening another one. The income benefits from the opened store continue to accrue to the corporation.

The fact that things have a cumulative nature allows an economy to become richer and more prosperous over time. It is much more difficult to build roads and infrastructure than to maintain them. This is especially true if the initial construction had an economic rationale. If they are economically sound they generate revenues directly or indirectly through increased tax revenues that can and should be used to maintain the system. More planning and time is required to build a house than to maintain one, especially if properly built in the first place. However, if a structure or business entity is not maintained it will run down and eventually collapse. Some examples are some of the bridges and infrastructure of New York City that were allowed to go without maintenance for extended periods of time. As a result, the Williamsburg Bridge has required extensive work to bring it back up to par. Lanes were closed and its utility was greatly diminished while being renovated. The Golden Gate Bridge, on the other hand, receives constant maintenance and is in excellent condition.

Compounding

Whenever something grows by the same percentage each year we have compounded growth. But as we will see, the percentage growth makes a tremendous difference. Early in the history of Wal-Mart, when the company had just gone public, revenue per store was growing at 25% each year. The number of stores was also growing by 25% each year. This translated into sales growth for the company of 56% each year. No wonder the stock was zooming. Sam Walton, the largest single stockholder, became the richest man in the world. (Several of his heirs are among the ten richest people in the world today.) The compounded growth allowed Wal-Mart Corporation to quickly become a giant. Consumers obviously preferred the prices and services because they bought from the stores in ever-increasing amounts. Vast wealth was created as well, not just for the Waltons but for all the shareholders.

Early Experience with Compounded Growth

One of the early legends concerning exponential growth centers around King Shriram of India. According to ancient legend his grand vizier Sissa ben Dahir had introduced the game of chess to the kingdom and presented it to the king. The king wanted to reward his grand vizier and asked him what he wanted. The clever Sissa asked his king for one grain of wheat for the first square of the chess board, two for the second, four for the third, eight for the fourth, and so on, doubling the number of grains for each succeeding square until every one of the squares on the board was filled with the appropriate amount of grain. This seemed like a reasonable request to King Shriram and so he granted it to his grand vizier and ordered a bag of grain to be brought in, which he thought would be all that was needed to grant the request. But before the twentieth square was filled, the bag was exhausted. More bags were ordered. It soon became clear that all the bags in India could not fulfill the request—it would have taken 18,466,744,073,709,551,615 grains to do so. This is equivalent to 4 trillion bushels of wheat, or roughly 2,000 years of global wheat production.[11]

The king found himself deep in debt to his grand vizier and had to either face the incessant demands of his vizier or cut off his head. Legend has it that he cut off his head for tricking him. Rightfully so. Exponential growth is not just powerful, it is deceptive.

[11] *One Two Three . . . Infinity* by George Gamow, page 20.

Modern Compounded Growth

King Shriram was fooled by 100% compounded growth. Each square required a doubling of the number of grains, or 100% growth. But let's look at some smaller increases. One approximation used by financial planners is the rule of 72. This states that the amount of time it takes to double an investment can be approximated by dividing the interest rate into the number 72. An investment that returns 3% a year, with all the returns reinvested, will double in 24 years (72 / 3 = 24). If a twenty-year-old invested $10,000 in a 3% investment, it would double to $20,000 by the time he was forty-four. It would double again to $40,000 by the time he was sixty-eight. A 3% investment quadruples in 48 years.

A 6% investment doubles every 12 years (72 / 6 = 12). That same twenty-year-old would see his investment double to $20,000 when he was thirty-two, double again to $40,000 when he was forty-four, double again to $80,000 at fifty-six, and double one more time to $160,000 when he was sixty-eight. A 6% investment is four times larger than a 3% investment after 48 years.

A 12% investment doubles every 6 years. Over the same time period a $10,000 investment grows to $2,560,000. Now a doubling of the rate increases the total value of the investment by a factor of 16. Clearly, compounding at these higher interest rates has a dramatic and not necessarily obvious effect. The rule of 72 breaks down for higher interest rates, so I ran some calculations through a computer. A $10,000 investment at 18% becomes $28,000,000 after 48 years. As you can see, anyone obtaining these kinds of returns will do quite well financially. But what about someone paying these kinds of rates? Lenders have been floating credit cards with 18–24% interest rates. What happens to someone who falls behind on a load like this? In many cases they can never pay it back and end up becoming financial slaves.

There is a reason why civilized societies have usury laws. But in the rush to deregulate we have thrown out many good regulations that had stood the test of time. When the rates of inflation were 12–15% it made sense to borrow at high rates. The payback on the loans was made with dollars that had lost value over time. Americans became used to borrowing at these rates. But we have not had a real inflationary bias for close to two decades. The high corporate and inter-bank interest rates of the 1990s were artificially induced by Federal Reserve monetary policy. But even though these base lending rates have declined at this writing, the rates to consumers have not come down appreciably. We have the worst of all possible worlds for borrowers: high rates and very low inflation coupled with a weak economic environment.

Should investors even care? After all, it seems that if someone is losing in this game someone is winning. Borrowers are paying high rates, but lenders are collecting these high returns. But such a situation is untenable in the long run. High interest rates are bad enough, but the amount of consumer debt continues to increase as lenders use modern marketing techniques to target borrowers. In some cases those borrowers are not likely to ever pay back the loans.

At some point when the borrowers find they just cannot handle the load and get swamped, the banks and other lenders will suffer too. Bank crises are a normal, almost predictable part of an industrial economy. In the last two decades we had the savings and loan crisis and the third world loan crisis, both of which threatened the survival of lending institutions, many of which did disappear. Each case required action from the federal government. In other words—the taxpayers bailed out the lending institutions. But the taxpayers did not receive any warrants or additional incentives that an investment banking house would have collected for similar assistance.

What if you have no credit card debt? What if you are a net investor? Should you care about the numerous people who are swamped by credit card debt? The reality is that in an economy we are all tied together, especially over the full business cycle. If the borrowers have trouble, the economy and the banks will have trouble, and no one will be immune to what might happen.

Different Kinds of Compounded Growth

Compounded growth is a very powerful force. As a whole, the economy tends to grow about 3% a year over the business cycle. That may not sound like much but remember, this is a cumulative effect spanning hundreds of years. This kind of growth accounts for our wealth as a nation. I want to draw the distinction, however, between a corporation growing at 20% or 30% or more each year by providing an economic benefit to consumers and a transfer of income between economic entities at rates of 20–30%. If the corporation is providing a new service, such as more efficient distribution, customers benefit with better prices and perhaps a bigger selection. Of course some other businesses might be displaced, but that is part of societal change and growth and the displaced businesses need to reapply resources elsewhere. The growing company and its shareholders prosper due to their exponential penetration of the market. For society this is a positive development—customers, managers, and shareholders all win.

On the other hand, when one person gains at the expense of others—because of excessively high interest rates to borrowers who are in a bind or don't fully understand the consequences—there is no overall gain to society. When this happens to small groups of people it is merely unfortunate. If it were to occur to large segments of the population, it could have reverberations throughout the economy. Should large numbers of people become burdened with excessive debt at excessive interest rates and are unable to make major purchases, the economy could slow down. If large numbers of borrowers defaulted the lenders could find themselves in trouble. This is not a general condemnation of interest rates and lending. Money lending and credit are an important part of a developed economy. This is a condemnation of companies that break one of the fundamental rules of good management: They disrespect or try to take advantage of their customers so they may gain. An excessive price of any kind will come back to haunt a business as customers defect. But an excessive interest rate is more insidious as many borrowers are presently unaware of the true cost. That can change, however, as customers learn that cost—either the hard way, through their own experiences, or from others.

CHAPTER 10

THE LEARNING LADDER AND SUBJECTIVE REALITY

Just at this moment, somehow or other, they began to run.

Alice never could quite make out, in thinking it over afterwards, how it was that they began: all she remembers is, that they were running hand in hand, and the Queen went so fast that it was all she could do to keep up with her: and still the Queen kept crying "Faster! Faster!" but Alice felt she could not go faster, though she had no breath left to say so.

The most curious part of the thing was, that the trees and the other things round them never changed their places at all: however fast they went, they never seemed to pass anything. "I wonder if all the things move along with us?" thought poor puzzled Alice. And the Queen seemed to guess her thoughts, for she cried "Faster! Don't try to talk!"

. . . And they went so fast that at last they seemed to skim through the air, hardly touching the ground with their feet, till suddenly, just as Alice was getting quite exhausted, they stopped, and she found herself sitting on the ground, breathless and giddy.

The Queen propped her up against a tree, and said kindly, "You may rest a little, now."

Alice looked round her in great surprise. "Why, I do believe we've been under this tree the whole time! Everything's just as it was!"

"Of course it is," said the Queen. "What would you have it?"[12]

When the heliocentric theory of the solar system replaced the static theory of a flat Earth at the center there was an immediate change in all our thinking. Whereas before, the Earth and the people on it were

---

[12] *The Annotated Alice*, by Lewis Carroll, notes by Martin Gardner, pages 164–165.

quite still, all of a sudden we were all moving at tremendous speed. Furthermore we were accelerating as well! Yet with all this motion we were pretty much in the same place year after year. The Earth became round and on the other side of the planet people were standing upside-down to us. Why didn't they fall off? Gravity needed to be invented to explain why people didn't fly off the Earth. Our society learned a different way of thinking, but each of us also had to go through his or her own learning and accepting of these ideas. I remember as a child feeling uncomfortable that I might fly off the planet into space, and I witnessed a similar development when my young son asked me why people on the other side of the globe didn't fall off.

A human embryo develops through all the evolutionary stages of the species. It starts as a single cell—at one point it has gills before it develops lungs. The formal expression of this phenomenon is, "Ontogeny recapitulates phylogeny." In our learning we continue this evolution as each person must learn and often struggle with the ideas that our society has accepted.

And that begs the question, "How do we learn?" This is really two questions: How does a society learn and change its accepted theories or paradigms; and how does an individual learn. I believe the two questions are related.

The Learning Ladder

The learning ladder describes the steps involved in progressing from incompetence to competence. The steps are as follows:

1. Unconscious Incompetence
2. Conscious Incompetence
3. Conscious Competence
4. Unconscious Competence

Unconscious incompetence is pure ignorance, as we are unaware of our ignorance or incompetence. If ignorance is ever bliss—and that is a big if—it is at this point when we don't even know there is something to learn. Every generation refers to a point in time "before we lost our innocence." Before the loss of innocence the subject matter is outside our conscious awareness.

Then we become aware that there is something we don't know. This is conscious incompetence. If the issue or the subject is deemed important enough, we make a decision to learn it. Our initial attempts at learning are inevitably clumsy. We appear incompetent. Of course that is the reason we are attempting to master it. Any beginner must pass through this stage, where doing is uncomfortable and hard. Some will pass through it faster and easier than others. Some have a natural inclination for the subject matter or the skill.

As we progress, and with practice, we develop some competency. In a short time we become less clumsy and even appear satisfactory compared to rank beginners or ourselves when we started. When we first learned to drive a car there were many things to be aware of, many things to do at once: We had to watch out for other cars and pedestrians, put the car in gear, use our feet to start and stop. If we drove a stick shift we also had to coordinate the clutch with the gear shifting. What seemed impossible and overwhelming at first soon just required focus and concentration to accomplish. This is conscious competence.

Then with enough practice, many of the things that we found so difficult at first became automatic. They passed through our conscious awareness and were learned by our unconscious mind. The clumsiness disappeared. When we reach this point we don't even think about doing it. When the learning has passed to the unconscious, we have achieved a certain mastery. This is unconscious competence. Mastery is achieved when we can perform something with our unconscious mind—we just will it or we just do it.

Unconscious Action

How many items are you capable of manipulating consciously? Most people have difficulty doing two unfamiliar activities at once. Our conscious mind is capable of handling five to nine things at once, but our unconscious mind is capable of handling an unlimited number of functions. Walking involves the coordination of several large muscles just to maintain balance. It would be impossible for us to walk using only our conscious minds. Virtually everything that we have learned has passed to and now resides in our unconscious, which is capable of performing without assistance from the conscious mind.

Consider times you have been conversing while driving. If the conversation was engrossing, you became totally involved in it. After reaching your destination you realized you had no recollection of driving. Who did the driving? It was not your conscious mind! It was another part of your mind, and that part of the mind is different and operates through different rules than your conscious mind. For those versed in some form of psychology, the existence of the unconscious mind may seem old hat. Yet it is an important phenomenon completely neglected in business literature and in most commercial decisions. Many distinguished psychologists of the nineteenth century denied even the need to hypothesize the existence of anything other than our conscious minds. In *The Principles of Psychology*, the eminent American psychologist, physiologist, and philosopher William James asks, "Can States of Mind Be Unconscious?" He concludes in the negative.[13] Many very smart people labor under the same stubborn refusal. But among psychologists and anyone with any kind of psychological sophistication, such blind denial of mental functioning other than the conscious has outlived its usefulness.

Unconscious Mastery

Once something has been "mastered" by the unconscious, however, it does not stop there. Further work and practice deepen the understanding or the ability. Deeper mastery, perhaps we should call it real mastery, occurs in the unconscious. The fifth step could be called unconscious mastery. And this step can be never ending.

Most things we learn pass through the conscious mind. Some do not. Some build on skills already in the unconscious. An example is walking. Walking is an incredibly complex process requiring balance and the use of many muscles in a coordinated effort. It is something we do automatically and take for granted.

Just observe a toddler as she learns to walk. She tries, falls, tries again, falls, and keeps trying. At one point she gets it. She stands knowing she has mastered standing. She sways back and forth but keeps her balance. A big grin comes over her face. Then she takes that first step only to fall again. With further practice she learns to walk. Of course there is still

---

[13] *The Principles of Psychology, Volume One,* by William James. Dover Publications, pages 164–176.

more to learn, and the more she practices the better she gets. Each time she practices she is learning. But much of the learning is occurring unconsciously. Coordination of all the muscles involved and balance are becoming better. Her conscious mind is focused on doing the task and making sure she gets up after each fall. Her unconscious mind is busy making adjustments and learning with each trial and each error.

Skills

Running, skipping, and jumping are skills. Skills are extremely important in accomplishing almost anything. There is a distinction between skills and knowledge. The difference as we define it here is that skills are, for the most part, unconscious. It is very difficult to explain a skill. When someone says they just do it, they are not being deceptive. They are being honest. They cannot explain their skill. There will be exceptions to this, but for now let's go with this definition. Skills also often bypass the conscious mind when being learned. You can go out to shoot baskets to improve your accuracy. The conscious mind is only aware of the shooting. The unconscious mind does the learning. It coordinates the muscles to perform the exact timing and force exerted by the arms, wrists, and fingers. The shooter is consciously doing exactly the same thing when he misses or when he sinks a basket. But something is different: The wrist snapped just an instant too late; one finger had slightly more pressure. All these subtleties occurred and are compensated for in the unconscious.

Knowledge as Skill

Knowledge, too, passes into the unconscious and is often difficult to bring back into conscious awareness. We have to reverse the learning ladder to do so. I learned to multiply and divide fractions in grade school and it became second nature. When my daughter was learning fractions I was the parent designated to help. When I tried to explain to her how I obtained the answer, I found myself at a loss. All the in-between steps, all the explanations were so deeply embedded that at first I couldn't explain it. I struggled and bit by bit I was able to remember and derive the explanations I needed in order to make it clear to her why the steps I took automatically were the correct steps.

Anyone who has prepared a presentation knows just how difficult it can be to take something we know well and bring it out to explain to others. A one-hour presentation might take several hours of preparation. It might take several days. And much of that time is just making conscious what you know and do automatically. Teachers regularly have the learning process readily at hand. They become expert at teaching each step of the process.

Knowledge can become a skill or like a skill if it becomes embedded deeply enough in the unconscious. But it can be brought back out. A skill like walking is almost impossible to bring into some kind of conscious form. We often say that a skill cannot be taught. Strictly speaking, that is not totally correct. But the actual mastery of the skill comes from doing it repeatedly, not from studying or contemplating it.

Even though we have made a distinction between knowledge and skill it is important to note their similarities. Both knowledge and skill enter the unconscious. Sometimes knowledge can be recalled from the unconscious into the conscious. In the conscious mind we can examine it, listen to it, feel it out. We can change it and manipulate it with some ease. It is a different story for things that are left in the unconscious.

Imprinting

Most of us are influenced by what we see or hear or feel. Words have a big impact on us. But words are a relatively new addition to our mental functioning.[14] Most of the communication between people takes place through other channels, and most of this is unconscious. Much of what we believe (for instance our values, which shape our behavior) we have learned through messages that were given through channels other than the spoken word. What is really important is communicated by voice qualities and volume, postures, actions, and behaviors.

As children and apprentices we observed certain behavior. We were induced to act in certain ways. On the basis of these behaviors, we formed certain values and beliefs. Other values and lessons were stacked on top of these. Each of us has a set of beliefs about the world. Some are unique to us. Some are unique to our families or our cultures.

[14] See Chapter 12 for further elaboration of this point.

But for almost every belief we have, there are alternative beliefs that other people might consider just as good.

Stacking

Stacked that deeply in our minds, beliefs become very much like skills. And they are very difficult to bring to consciousness. A skill is close to impossible to change. Notice for example that someone who learns English as a second language initially speaks with an accent. Thirty years after living in this country, speaking English all day, she continues to speak with the same accent. Speech class may lessen the accent but won't eliminate it.

When a manager tries to change someone's behavior, generally she tries to reason with the person. But if behavior is dictated on the basis of beliefs that the person is not cognizant of, all the reasoning in the world is for naught.

Robert Dilts has done a great deal of work developing methods to help people change beliefs. He worked intensively with his mother, who had life-threatening cancer. After working with her for a week, examining her beliefs, questioning them, and using his methods, she became unable to accept the idea of her death from cancer. And all signs of cancer disappeared from her body.[15] His mother's sister and mother had both died of lung cancer and there was an almost dutiful acceptance of her own role as someone who would die from the same disease. But Dilts forced his mother to confront the possibility that in the future her own daughter would look at her as a role model and might succumb to the same disease because of that. That powerful experience of the consequences of her beliefs forced a shift in his mother. She was re-imprinted, and her condition quickly improved from that point onward.

Hierarchy of Beliefs

Dilts has proposed a structure to our beliefs. At the lowest level are our beliefs about the environment. Next are beliefs about our capabilities, then general beliefs. The next level is values, and the highest level is our

[15] *Changing Belief Systems with NLP* by Robert Dilts.

identity. The higher the level of belief the harder it is to change. In order to change beliefs at one level one must work at a higher level—at least at the next highest level.

His hierarchy of beliefs from highest to lowest is as follows:

1. Identity
2. Values
3. Beliefs
4. Capabilities
5. Environment

In his model, identity is the most difficult belief to change. In order to change identity one must work at an even higher level, or a spiritual level. Let me call that level the level of transcendent beliefs because it is the level that allows one to transcend personal identity.

Can our beliefs affect our health? There have been numerous studies showing that beliefs do affect our ability to heal and overcome disease. But it is not just the beliefs of the patient. What the doctors or nurses believe is also of great importance. Some experiments have shown that when a doctor gives a placebo to a patient and believes it is the "real" medicine, its effect is greater. Patients who received a placebo that the doctors thought was morphine had pain relief closer to that of patients who actually received the morphine without the doctors knowing what it was. Patients who received morphine that the doctors thought was a placebo had significantly less relief than those who received the morphine without the doctors knowing. This principle is implicitly recognized in current science. A drug cannot receive FDA approval unless it goes through a series of double-blind experiments where neither the doctors nor the patients know if they are receiving the drug or a placebo.

Beliefs in Society

In *The Structure of Scientific Revolutions,* Thomas S. Kuhn observed that in science, even after a new theory showed clear superiority over the old, there were many scientists who could not or did not change and adopt it. He had no explanation for that. I believe that one reason for this is the link that develops between a person's identity and his belief in the old theory.

Our beliefs often have more than just personal identification. They are sometimes tied to our identification with our tribe. Our need for tribal identity has not died out in modern society. It has simply become subtler. Scientists, doctors, and professionals receive some indoctrination into their tribes in order to be accepted as bona fide members. Is it just a coincidence that almost all doctors have terrible handwriting? I think not. In order to join the profession they must subscribe to a certain set of beliefs and rituals. As in most tribes, those beliefs are thought to be complete, a full expression of reality.

Tribal orientation forces one to have an intense distrust and dislike of anyone with a conflicting set of beliefs that challenge their own. This goes back not to our rational minds, but to a deeper level. A person with a different set of beliefs is labeled a barbarian of some kind. In many ancient languages the word for foreigner was "barbarian." In the church the outsider was a heretic. Medicine labels the heretic a quack. Scientists label nonbelievers as irrational, ignorant, or laymen.

Those ideas that entered our minds unconsciously and at the earliest dates, those that we identify with our parents and tribe, are the ones that are most deeply imprinted and least likely to be changed, regardless of how strongly they are attacked.

Corporations, of course, have their tribal nature as well. In all corporations, accepted members of the clan share some values. If your first corporate job lasts for ten years or more, you will very likely find yourself adrift if you leave for a different organization.

We absorb not just through words and formal instructions, but less formal means as well. The rituals of an organization, the habits, behaviors, and actions of its leaders, are broadcast throughout the organization and absorbed by its members. Many of these members internalize these values and principles. Some members are never able to change them. We are innately social and tribal creatures with an innate ability to learn to fit in. But our mechanisms for unconsciously fitting in are designed for fitting in to one place. It's the exceptional person who can override this programming and make a swift transition to a different setting.

Subjective Reality

In an earlier chapter, we contrasted the precise mathematical model of scientific reality with the sensory model of reality that we inhabit each day. Roughly speaking, the two have been called objective reality and subjective reality by philosophers. One of the prime questions asked by philosophers is, "Are individual subjective realities the same for each of us?" Do we have any assurance that when I make a statement like, "This shirt is red," the listener perceives red like I do and has the same understanding of the phrase as I do? When I encountered this question in philosophical works, most of the authors concluded yes, our understanding was similar enough since communication was occurring.

Unfortunately these writers never operated extensively in organizations where complex tasks had to be accomplished by teams of people. How many managers have had the experience of speaking to someone, thinking you were understood, only to find out days or weeks later that your understanding of the communication was a world apart from the person you spoke to? Miscommunication is an almost daily occurrence in business. We constantly deal with people whose way of processing issues seems totally foreign to our own. I and many others have concluded that subjective reality can be quite different from one person to the next.

CHAPTER 11

PSYCHOLOGICAL TYPES

After a certain point people are no longer motivated by money. They need to give input and have some impact on their environment. If they are asked for their opinions not only will they gladly give them but they will be motivated to contribute more.

This composite statement represents one of the major themes of the management revolution created by the rediscovery of quality during the 1980s. Intuitively many of us felt this to be a valid and powerful idea. We had been frustrated in our own organizations when we were kept in the dark about decisions that directly affected us. We had seen too many poor decisions made without consulting people on the line. Such decisions were unworkable from the start, and they were left to line managers to somehow "make it work." Input from workers could have led to large or small modifications that would have made the unworkable a snap. The success of organizations who took this to heart and brought their people into the decision-making process added further evidence of its validity. You can imagine our surprise, then, when greeted by a blank stare or annoyance from workers we had asked for input.

Does that mean people in the workplace don't wish to share their ideas and contribute? Does that mean workers don't want to impact their environment and be heard and respected? Of course not! Are the italicized statements at the start of this chapter true? Yes they are. Are they false? Yes they are. Well, which is it? It's both—it depends. It depends on which people. Any blanket statement about people or managing people has to be taken with a grain of salt for the simple reason that people are innately different. Some of these differences have been observed, categorized, and intensely studied.

Observers going back to antiquity have proposed the existence of different types of people with characteristic traits that divide them into categories. Hippocrates, the father of Western medicine, suggested different body types required different foods and prescriptions for health. Ancient Indian Āyur vedic medicine distinguishes between body types with different dietary needs. Theophrastus "described thirty typical characters in vivid and precise language."[16]

Jungian Psychology of the Conscious Mind

But the introduction of the idea of psychological types to the modern Western world and its subsequent development was provided by the eminent psychiatrist Carl Jung. Dr. Jung was a younger contemporary of Sigmund Freud. His work with patients led him to independently postulate the existence of the unconscious mind. Many of his conclusions were similar to Freud's and the two became very close, with Freud at one point adopting Jung. But fundamental disagreements led to an acrimonious split. In seeking to explain his differences with Freud and another of their contemporaries, Alfred Adler, Jung wrestled with the question of types. Different people responded differently to the world and even seemed to perceive and experience it differently.

In 1921 his book *Psychological Types* appeared. Dr. Jung observed that people had different ways of processing the world. His main distinction was between rational functions and irrational functions. By rational he implied what is reasonable and what "accords with reason."[17] But the irrational did not ". . . denote something contrary to reason but something beyond reason, something therefore, not grounded on reason. Elementary facts come into this category; the fact, for example, that the earth has a moon, that chlorine is an element."[18]

The rational functions are thinking and feeling. While the meaning of "thinking" may be clear, the word "feeling" is perhaps inadequate. The

[16] John G. Geier, from his introduction to William Moulton Marston's *Emotions of Normal People*, page iii, 1979.

[17] *Psychological Types* by Carl Jung, page 458.

[18] Ibid., 454.

word "feeling" in everyday speech can imply sensations, intuition, or emotions, among other meanings. But in this context, feeling refers more closely to values than sensations or emotions. A thinking person will tend to analyze and deconstruct; a feeling person will act based on his values. A feeling person who values harmony might pronounce a picture beautiful because to do otherwise would upset the people who own the picture. A thinking person would make a judgment based on some other criteria and might be indifferent or unaware of the effects his pronouncements have on the owners.

The irrational functions are intuition and sensation. "In intuition a content presents itself whole and complete, without our being able to explain or discover how this content came into existence."[19] Intuition may present itself as feeling, sense perception, or intellectual inference although it is neither of these. An intuitive person has hunches or insights that just seem to pop up. She knows something without knowing how.

Sensation is synonymous with perception, both internal and external. External sensation implies sense perception while internal implies our body senses such as balance or the sensing of our internal condition. A sensate, particularly an extroverted sensate, will have an extraordinarily developed sense for objective facts. Concrete experiences and sensations are the main reality of his life.[20]

The four basic psychological functions Jung postulated were Thinking, Feeling, Intuitive, and Sensate. Each of these is a way of approaching the world that to some extent is latent in all of us. But each of us has a preference, in many cases a very strong preference, toward one of the four. To many people, especially in youth, there seems to be a predisposition to one mode to the almost total exclusion of the others. As we grow we develop our preferred mode at the expense of the others. And the four functions are different enough that operating in one may make it very difficult to appreciate or communicate with someone who strongly operates in another mode. A thinking person, for instance, might have a lot of difficulty understanding or appreciating an intuitive person. He might even resort to calling him names and berating his abilities. Dr. Jung postulated that each of us has

[19] Ibid., 453.

[20] Ibid., 363.

one main function from which we operate and one auxiliary function that consciously influences us. If our main function were rational then our auxiliary function would be one of the two irrational functions, sensation or intuition. In addition, each of us has a particular attitude of consciousness—either introvert or extrovert.

Eight Jungian Types

There are three main axes in Dr. Jung's psychology of the conscious mind. One axis is Thinking–Feeling. You can be in a thinking mode or a feeling mode but you can't be both at once. The other two axes are Intuitive–Spontaneous and Introvert–Extrovert. From this scheme there are eight major types: Thinking Extrovert; Thinking Introvert; Feeling Extrovert; Feeling Introvert; Intuitive Extrovert; Intuitive Introvert; Sensate Extrovert; Sensate Introvert.

By itself this scheme offers considerable insight. Intractable conflicts with others transform into relief and clarity when we realize these are due to differences in our psychological makeup. Each of us approaches a problem differently due to inherent characteristics of our makeup. But our differences are not haphazard. We tend to cluster and will have great similarities with some people while having great differences with others. We will naturally get along better with those who share a similar outlook and this is heavily influenced by psychological type.

It is possible for someone to access more than one psychological function. Some people seem to have greater flexibility, allowing them access to more than one type. In Eastern psychology a developed person is considered to be one who has many personalities. Certainly from a business and human effectiveness point of view, being able to access more than one function leads to greater empathy with others. This enables and enhances the ability to communicate effectively with more people. As one climbs higher in an organization, psychological flexibility becomes more important.

Dr. Jung thought his Psychological Types were a framework for additional work. In his book he suggested that thinking could be further broken down into three categories, as people think in more than one way. One of his disciples, Isabel Myers, working with her daughter, further emphasized another axis that Jung had discussed: Judging–

Processing. This brought the basic number of types to sixteen. They developed the Myers-Briggs system along with corresponding tests to help place someone into one of sixteen types.

While people may not like being placed in a category, the insights gleaned from these concepts have made many managers more understanding and more effective. The first aim of any such system is to increase one's self-knowledge and self-awareness. The second aim is to help one understand the differences in personalities to allow greater appreciation and flexibility in dealing with others. The system is a guide and can easily be misused—or perhaps more accurately, overused. It can be used to try to explain everything, which is inappropriate in my opinion. But even here the system is useful. People who are high judgers or high J's (in the shorthand terminology) on the Judging–Processing axis will tend to take any theory in which they find value and apply it to every circumstance. In my experience high J's will place everything in one of the boxes in the theory. For many of them the map is the territory. This can be a very useful characteristic. Elementary school teachers, for instance, do not have to introduce their pupils to all the nuances of literature or numbers. They need to make sure that their students have a grasp of basic skills. For them being high J's is certainly not a drawback. It is probably a useful trait. On the other hand many students are disillusioned once they reach secondary school or high school, when they discover that what they had learned in earlier grades may be incomplete, representing a partial picture, a single point of view where there are many.

On the other side of the coin, someone who is a high P in the Judging–Processing axis might find it very difficult to make a commitment early in life or in some cases ever in life. They see many points of view, and several may be equally good. This can clearly be a drawback but once again in the right setting could be a great strength. A researcher for instance might very well need to be able to keep an open mind about an issue until all the data have been gathered and analyzed.

My experience with Myers-Briggs is that for about 40% of the people the type is extremely accurate. For another roughly 30% of people the type has approximate value. About 20% appear to be hybrids between two or more types. And there is some percentage of people, between 5% and 10%, that seem to show great flexibility among types. In my mind there is no doubt that there are many more than sixteen different types, but as it is Myers-Briggs is a useful approximation, a useful map.

Proper Distribution of Types

In many companies a few of the psychological types are overly represented in management. We tend to communicate best with people similar to us. So it is not surprising that some companies have similar psychological types in management positions. However there are significant drawbacks to having a few types overly represented. This leads to narrowness in points of view. Each type excels in certain areas and is least proficient in others. A well-rounded management team is healthier than one that is skewed to one type. The best accountants and salespeople, for instance, tend to be drawn from different types. Short-term thinking and long-term thinking need to be balanced in an organization and these two are best practiced by people with different profiles.

A successful management team needs balance and it is useful if the major psychological types are represented. But this of course creates problems since each type processes reality differently and may communicate differently as well. How then do you have a unified team? Balance is struck when the major psychological types are represented but share values and are unified about the vision and direction of the organization.

Some Benefits of the Theory

Many people will not like the idea of placing people into profiles or types. I can certainly sympathize with those who feel this is typecasting. But our personal preferences can be biases that keep us from accepting important innovations. What is most important is how useful this knowledge is. Does it lead to better decisions and better organizations? People who understand it have found it revolutionary in the impact it has on their interactions with others. It has led to the formation of more functional teams. I think it would also help in picking a marriage partner. There can be a strong unconscious attraction to someone with a different, almost opposite psychological makeup. The differences can lead to a kind of completion. But there would also necessarily be a fair amount of dissension in such a relationship. Knowledge of types would at least give you some understanding of what to expect.

Psychological types also render some other systems of psychology and their one-therapy-fits-all approach obsolete. You would expect psychoanalytically trained people to completely dismiss the whole idea. While many psychologists consider Freud to be the founder of modern psychological theory and analysis he has had almost no influence in management circles. Jung's influence, on the other hand, has been immense and continues to grow.

But perhaps some of the best indications of this theory's usefulness are the many other systems now available for determining people's types. Most designate four main types like Myers-Briggs, but with different categories and different ways of determining the categories. Each has its own followers and detractors and its own special uses.

Type and Job Performance

How important is type in job performance? Most companies hire on the basis of an existing skill set without any attempt to measure or determine type. Yet the most avid users of type systems would argue that the person's mental makeup is more important for success on the job than skill levels or past experience. You can always teach skill and people will get experience, but you cannot readily change a person's personality and innate abilities.

Determining Type

Each system of typology has tests that can be administered to help determine type. But after gaining some familiarity and experience with Myers-Briggs I have found it possible to do a pretty quick evaluation after spending just a few minutes talking with a person. Many of the tests ask people to choose among certain answers and since people have their own self-image they will claim that they respond in a given way. But an objective observer can quickly identify that a person behaves differently than how he claims to behave. As a result an objective evaluation of a person can be more useful than a self-administered rating system or test.

Type Distributions and Averages

Whether you use Dr. Jung's scheme or one of the many others that have been developed since, major insights can be garnered. If we combine this psychological knowledge with the statistical knowledge of prior chapters we must question whether the characteristics of people vary smoothly or are discontinuous. Most of the time when experts talk about the differences inherent in people in the general population, there is an underlying assumption that the differences are distributed smoothly. In other words, it is assumed that the differences are from what statisticians would call a single population. There would be one peak and the differences climb smoothly. But as I have pointed out, this is an assumption that often turns out to be incorrect. The Jungian scheme points quite strongly to the existence of categories.

Any single characteristic of the general population need not be smoothly distributed. There may be several statistical groupings. A population in general usage is any group of people. But a statistical population must meet certain criteria. We could have a group of beetles and a group of ants. We could combine these two groups into a group of insects. In the ordinary sense of the word, we have a population of insects. But in the statistical sense, when we measure some important characteristic, such as length, weight, or food consumed, we really have two statistical populations. In other words, the weight distribution would show two very distinct groups or populations with one being generally larger than the other although there may be some overlap.

It is believed that each psychological type represents a certain percentage of the population with some stability. In the Myers-Briggs scheme, for instance, it is believed that a particular type, INTP, represents about 1–2% of the population. This type is sometimes called the theoretician because the people tend to excel in intellectual pursuits and have great mental concentration.

Can we then expect that INTPs will represent about 1% of the population of each organization? The answer of course is absolutely not! This type, like most others, will be attracted to organizations that make better use of their innate abilities. You will find them more concentrated in some organizations and virtually nonexistent in others.

Now we can address the problem we started the chapter with. Do all people want to contribute to the organizations? Whether it is because of innate predisposition, their upbringing, or their training in the organization, not everyone wants to make a contribution. Some people just want to be told what to do. Some want to be told with an explanation. Some want to contribute passively, and some get a great thrill when they have a chance to contribute their knowledge and their opinions, particularly as it relates to their work environment. Some people will find it intolerable not to have input, but most of these will have already left a static organization.

A manager has to approach each situation with openness and freshness. By providing an opportunity for input, she will find some people respond and some don't. Some will take time before they buy in and some never will. But you cannot assume that behavior will be uniform across the board or that all people are motivated by the same thing.

Religion and Psychological Type

Psychological types apply to all humans. Each type will be represented in each culture, in each country, and in each religion. If you examine each of the great religions you will find that each has splintered into a number of different sects, philosophies, or points of view. Christianity has a group of Protestant branches. The Catholic church has had and still does have considerable dissension: There are many points of view about Christ's message. The same can be said about Buddhism, Islam, Hinduism, or Judaism. Each has its hawks; each its pacifists. Each has those who emphasize ritual or tradition and those who discard ritual and tradition.

The Buddha is reputed to have said there are 64,000 ways to enlightenment, which implies there are that many psychological types. Regardless of the number of types, similar types get along better, agree more, and understand one another better. The hawks of Christianity and Islam have much in common. Those who emphasize nonviolence, regardless of religion, have more in common with one another than the myriad of others of their same faith.

Good Management, Great Management

A good manager needs to know something about the innate ability of his people and their psychological types. A great manager, however, relates to each person as a unique individual with talents and traits like no one else in the world. Each person is unique and different, a marvel unto himself. To treat them otherwise is to do them a disservice. Indeed no two people are alike and the potential of each is unknown. But knowledge of psychological types is a useful map that can help you coach your people concerning their strengths and weaknesses. It can provide insights that might take years or decades or might never come otherwise. It can help your people grow in ways that are most beneficial to them and the organization. It can also point out areas where each will need extra work if he is to become proficient as a manager. Much pain and trial and error can be avoided with a good psychological map. Properly used it can help foster wisdom in both you and your people.

CHAPTER 12

LANGUAGE, MATHEMATICS, AND MULTIPLE INTELLIGENCES

A great organization creates extraordinary results with ordinary people. People's efforts are magnified in a good system but severely hampered by a bad system. Two fundamental types of actions can be taken to affect results: You may either work in the system or on it. Those who work on the system, the managers, have a disproportionate effect on the results. Intelligence is certainly a prized commodity for everyone but especially for those managers who have the greatest impact on the system. This brings up a fundamental and important question.

What is intelligence? Someone might say intelligence is the ability to learn. Another person might give a very different answer. Is there even something we can call Intelligence? The response of social scientists in the early part of the twentieth century was to devise a uniformly administered test. Of course, everyone who took the test generated a result expressed as a number—an IQ, or intelligence quotient—and that number was his intelligence.

This definition was well promoted and gained broad acceptance by the general public. But is that a useful measure of anything? There are numerous problems with IQ. Different IQ tests give different results. The results are not even consistent. A person could score lower than someone else on one IQ test but higher on a different test.

Problems with IQ as a Measure of Intelligence

Perhaps most damaging to the value of IQ is that it is not a very good predictor of much of anything. If intelligence is an important factor in life then a measure of intelligence should be a reasonable predictor of success in life or a given field. But the only thing IQ seems to be good at is predicting how well one might do in an academic environment—and even there it is highly flawed. One stunning example of IQ's irrelevance is *Time* magazine's man of the century, Albert Einstein. Einstein didn't speak a word until he was three years old and was considered to be slow for most of his life. Yet most of us would consider him to have been one of the most intelligent men to have ever lived.

Inherent Problem of IQ

There is something inherently and fundamentally wrong with IQ. Suppose you asked me to tell you where I was on the planet and I told you I was at 41 degrees latitude. Would that tell you much? It would narrow down my possible locations. I might be in Chicago or New York; Madrid, Spain; Naples, Italy; or Anshan, China.

The surface of the earth is two-dimensional, which means I need at least two numbers to adequately locate someone's position. In fact if I tell you I am at 41 degrees latitude and 73 degrees longitude, there is a third number missing. That is time. If you look for me at that location a year from now, you are not likely to find me.

A branch of mathematics called linear algebra deals with dimensions. One of the basic laws from this branch of mathematics is that to adequately describe a point in space you need as many numbers as there are dimensions. We are all familiar with spatial dimensions. An object has height, width, and depth. At least three numbers are required to locate a point in space. But the world is fleeting and constantly changing. Locating a point in space also requires some reference to time. While time is not a dimension of space, it is another important dimension mathematically and descriptively speaking.

We need not limit ourselves to three or four dimensions in describing complex phenomena. Mathematically there is no limit to the number of useful dimensions. If a quality requires sixteen numbers to usefully describe it, then we should use sixteen numbers. We could always derive a formula to create a new single number. For instance, we could take the width of an object and add it to the height and the depth to get a single number. But such a number conveys much less information. In most applications the single number would be inadequate.

The Case for Multiple Intelligences

What I am suggesting is that intelligence is a multidimensional phenomenon. How many dimensions might be required to get a useful description? How many dimensions of intelligence are there? In his groundbreaking book, *Frames of Mind*, Howard Gardner presents a strong case for considering the existence of seven different kinds of intelligence. There are other researchers in the field who have identified many more than seven kinds of intelligence. Some have put the number at more than one hundred. They are probably correct from a purely descriptive point of view. But to consider intelligence and its impact on human society, the idea of seven major intelligences is quite useful.

Gardner established several criteria that an ability needed to satisfy before it could be considered an intelligence. One is a respect and valuation for that kind of intelligence across many cultures. For instance, the ability to recognize faces is clearly an important skill and would be a candidate for being included as an intelligence. However, by itself that ability has little special valuation in human cultures. Another one of his criteria, which is critical, is the ability for an intelligence to disappear without affecting the other intelligences or for it to exist in isolation. That is to say, some kind of brain damage could destroy one of the intelligences without affecting the others. Or correspondingly, the existence of idiot savants who are capable of operating at very high levels in one intelligence while lacking even the most basic ability in other intelligences is also evidence that an intelligence may exist independently.

Using these and other criteria, the seven intelligences that Gardner identifies are linguistic, musical, logical-mathematical, spatial, bodily kinesthetic, interpersonal, and intrapersonal. Bodily kinesthetic refers to the ability to move the body. Certain athletes or dancers are sometimes referred to as geniuses in their ability to accomplish feats that the rest of us think are impossible. Interpersonal refers to the ability to relate to others. Intrapersonal refers to the intelligence of being in touch with yourself.

Two of these intelligences, linguistic and logical-mathematical, are the ones associated with IQ. Yet in Gardner's system there are at least five other major intelligences. One might object that the other five are not really intelligences but are significant abilities. But then one can say that linguistic and logical-mathematical are also nothing more than significant abilities. All seven meet the pre-established criteria for intelligence. If you arbitrarily neglect one or more as a dimension of intelligence, you can rightfully neglect all. There is nothing wrong in calling the other intelligences abilities, but then we need to call all seven of them abilities. To be fair and consistent we would need to say we have linguistic abilities and mathematical and logical abilities.

Smart but Stupid

How useful is a theory of multiple intelligences? I remember reading a management article in the 1970s claiming that it was possible for someone to be too intelligent for business. The article cited several examples of individuals with high IQs who would say or do things that made them hated or disliked by others. The article concluded that it was possible to be too intelligent for your own good, at least in business. Among the examples cited by the author was one high-IQ individual who was brutally blunt with people who couldn't keep up with him. Most of us would readily label such behavior as downright stupid. And that leaves us with the inconsistency that someone who is very smart is really very stupid.

On the other hand, if we recognize that there are different kinds of intelligence that to some extent are independent of one another, then it is quite natural to assert that someone may be very intelligent in one area but not particularly gifted in another. Business being primarily a cooperative endeavor, where one must solicit the assistance of others in order to be successful, requires a very heavy emphasis on interpersonal intelligence. And with this model of intelligence it becomes possible to talk of someone as being very intelligent and not intelligent at the same time.

One of the problems with an inaccurate theory is that it leads to inaccurate or even stupid conclusions. If one really believes that smart people are not good at business then by inference business is a place for the mediocre. That kind of belief is not only damaging to business, it is damaging to all of society. This is an example of a presupposition. Presuppositions are suppositions that are so readily accepted as to be beyond question, yet they significantly influence our actions. They may be conscious or unconscious. They are in the realm of metaknowledge.

For most people the presupposition that there is but one intelligence and either you have it or you don't has never been questioned. Many presuppositions are not accessible to us because they are unconscious. That makes them difficult to address. But revolutionary changes can result from changes of presuppositions.

The Value of Multiple Intelligences

On some level many excellent managers implicitly recognize the multi-dimensional nature of intelligence. The enlightened manager knows that promoting someone who is skilled in his craft to a supervisory or managerial level is one of the most difficult of transitions. Management is not about being a great technician. Qualities and abilities that make for a great worker are insufficient to make a good manager. Sure there are overlap areas important to both. The ability to arrive on time, to be conscientious, and some degree of loyalty are essential for both. But by and large the skills of management involve whole new areas that are largely independent of the skills that make for a good worker. As a result that person needs to get extensive training and coaching to successfully make the transition.

Despite the usefulness, even the necessity, of the theory of multiple intelligences, there is a deep-seated bias to the idea of a single intelligence that is determined by linguistic and mathematical ability. I asked myself why this should be so and why it is so deep rooted.

The Importance of Language and Mathematics to the Human Race

It seems to me a very plausible explanation lies in the possibility that these two intelligences are the newest in our evolution and have given humans an advantage over other species. As an example consider musical intelligence. It is clear that certain people have an ability to create and play music that the rest of us can only marvel at. Music is universally valued in all cultures. Two recent articles in the *Journal of Science* report that the unshakable and indescribable desire to sing and rejoice is not only a universal feature of all societies known to anthropology but is deeply embedded in the human brain and is far more ancient than previously believed. It may very well be much older than the human race itself.

The articles examine the music created by birds and humpback whales. While whales have a musical range of seven octaves and could in fact create music very different than our own, their compositions follow patterns and progressions very much like our own. They sing in key. They mix percussive and pure tones in a way found in much of Western symphonic music.

Spatial intelligence is another example. Surprisingly most scientists think with words only and have a great deal of difficulty visualizing.[21] But the ability to visualize can be developed to an astounding extent. The inventor Nikola Tesla "could project before his eyes a picture complete in every detail, of every part of the machine." [22] Tesla's pictures were more vivid than any blueprints, and he could build his complex machines without drawings. Further, he claimed to be able to test his devices spatially, in his mind's eye as well.

Many creative people in the arts, sciences, and mathematics have a highly developed spatial intelligence. Dr. Einstein stated that his thinking process didn't involve words at all. Central to spatial intelligence is the ability to perceive the visual world accurately. But spatial intelligence and visual perception are different. One may be able to visually remember what exists in a room but be unable to mentally rotate shapes. Even further removed is the ability to visualize and manipulate imaginary objects.[23]

Birds such as ravens have shown a fair amount of spatial intelligence, being able to distinguish between crossed ropes leading to food. It is difficult for me to believe that dolphins who constantly live and play in the three-dimensional world of the sea—and whose brains are larger than ours—don't have a highly developed spatial intelligence. They have been shown to closely mimic human behavior using their flippers to represent our hands. That at the very least is strongly sugges-

[21] Gardner, page 187.

[22] Ibid., page 188.

[23] Ibid., page 173.

tive of the ability to visualize their bodies and make direct spatial correspondence with ours.

On the other hand, linguistic and mathematical sophistication have not yet been found among other species to the same extent that we have developed them. I would caution that future research might cast this into doubt, with dolphins being one candidate worth further investigation.

This may explain the importance we attach to words. Many people are only able to think through words.[24] How one speaks not only determines where one originated but also one's class and one's educational background. Words play such an important part of our thinking that at one point some philosophers believed almost everything could be explained through a philosophy of language.

Clearly words and mathematical symbols have a special significance to our species. Most of what we recognize as communication is through words either spoken or written. Our books, poems, stories, and explanations all involve words. If we broaden the definition of words to include mathematical symbols then most of what we use to consciously explain the world around us involves words. Yet we have much commonality with other animals who don't use words. Their communication is entirely nonverbal. We should therefore expect to find that an element of our own communication is nonverbal. And indeed it is.

Some communication specialists claim that the bulk of our communication is nonverbal, with only 5% relying on the meaning of the words themselves. Changing the inflection of a sentence, raising or lowering the pitch at the end, or changing tempo can totally alter its meaning. A sentence such as, "I really like him," can be turned into a statement, a question, a sarcastic remark, an implication that I really dislike or hate him, a noncommittal statement, or one that says I adore him, all on the basis of sounds. In addition we have gestures, posture, facial expressions, hands, body activity, and skin color and other subtle body changes, all of which can transmit meaning without the use of words.

So much of our face-to-face communication is nonverbal that a person attuned to the nonverbal is a significantly better communicator than one who is not. In fact her skill can be so good that she can effec-

[24] I am referring here to conscious thinking, in which many people favor words. Unconscious thinking is mostly via images or other modes. Most dreams involve images and even in conversations in dreams the words are not heard so much as they are sensed.

tively get her way with people who are unaware of nonverbal cues. Those who are unaware of the great nonverbal language we all speak may deny its existence. They are "unconscious" of its effect and fail to see, hear, or feel it—at least consciously. But they notice it unconsciously. Denying its existence does not hamper its effectiveness; in fact, it only makes it more potent. Those things of which we are unconscious have the greatest effect on us. Since we are unaware of them we are unable to alter, filter, or change them. And therefore, they have full reign over us.

Our minds constantly induce us to believe that we have a full and complete picture of the world even when the contrary is staring us right in the face. And I mean this literally. Let me give one example. Each of us has a blind spot in our eye. We can be made conscious of this. Hold a full-size book so as to be able to read it. Close your left eye and with your right eye focus at the top right section of the page. Point your index finger and run it across the left page toward the bottom. Keep looking at the top of the right page while moving your finger along the bottom part of the left page. At one point the tip of your finger will disappear. As you move your finger out of that spot it will reappear. Move it back in and it will disappear. This occurs because the nerves that transmit the signals to the brain at the back of the eye bunch together in the spot corresponding to this part of your vision. As a result there is no place to record the light actually striking the eye at that point. Each eye has a blind spot. When you use both eyes the blind spot of one eye is seen by the other, resulting in a full picture. But when you close one eye, the mind, rather than present a gap in your vision, maps the ends of what it does perceive and seamlessly stitches them to present a picture of the world with no gaps.

Just as nature abhors a vacuum our minds seem to automatically avoid presenting us with blind spots. I postulate this is a more general rule. Our minds will not present us with an incomplete picture. It represents our model of the world as being complete and continuous. And further, we have an ingrained distrust of anything foreign to that view. That distrust may be related to our survival skill and our need to bond into a tribe.

We seem to have a built-in mechanism that leads us to believe that our model of the world is *the* world and that our model is complete, total, and continuous. This makes it difficult to appreciate when we are being influenced by anything other than what we can see, feel, or hear. Many psychologists of the nineteenth century and early twentieth century denied the existence of the unconscious mind. William James, the noted American psychologist, doctor, and philosopher, gives a list of reasons in his major work on psychology explaining why the unconscious or subliminal mind, as he calls it, need not exist.

For optimal effectiveness in the twenty-first century, managers need a model of people and reality that is current. The nineteenth- and twentieth-century model of a single intelligence, a belief that communication only occurs through words and that we can control everything including ourselves through just the conscious mind, is obsolete. Even some of the models that were developed by observing machines are limiting our understanding of economics and organizations. The metaphor of an organization as a machine needs serious modifications.

CHAPTER 13

TOWARD   AN   ECOLOGY
OF   COMMERCE

We used to think of humans as being distinct and apart from the rest of the planet because of several widely accepted beliefs. Among these was a belief that humans were the only intelligent or conscious beings on the planet. This placed animals and the rest of the natural world on a level with inanimate objects.

Another key belief was that the rational, conscious function was the only function of the mind. When other functions, such as feelings and intuition, were recognized, they were downgraded in importance. Rational thinking represented cognition and sentience; I think, therefore I am. And since we could see no evidence that other species thought, since none could communicate to us in the way we most cherished, with words, we alone were sentient. We alone were special and distinct from the rest of creation. Only the species that could think as evidenced by speech could be conscious.

Yet evolutionary theory claims we are of the same stuff as the rest of life on earth. We are mammals just like cows, just like whales, just like dolphins. We are primates, just like gorillas, orangutans, and chimpanzees. We are a distinct species, just like each of the other species, and have differentiated through the same process. We have some unique qualities, such as a highly developed larynx that allows speech and a gift for tool making that extends to tools that make tools. But we are not the only ones living in a society. There are tribes of chimpanzees, extended families of gorillas, pods of whales and dolphins.

Our modern investigations into the societies of other species is teaching us that these higher animals have more in common with us in terms of reactions, emotions, and processing than anyone but the most extreme animal lover would have claimed even as recently as thirty years ago. But there is one major difference. When a whale needs to feed it searches through the ocean and interacts with the rest of nature. When a chimp needs to feed it swings through the trees looking for fruit, climbs down to scavenge, or goes on a hunt. It too has direct interaction with the rest of nature. When we need to eat we go to a store and interact with other humans but not with nature. People who operate the store do not interact with nature either. Each interacts with other humans. Farmers have some interaction with the soil but it is controlled, especially if they are in air-conditioned combines working the controls.

We have created a new kind of ecology that, while having some interaction with the rest of the earth (in the air we breathe, the minerals we take in, weather, floods, and so on), is to some degree self-contained, semi-encapsulated. This ecology does not just include humans; our domesticated cats and dogs are a part of it. They too no longer hunt or scavenge for food. They get served out of a can as well. This ecology that provides for the needs of the human race is called an economy. While it may be different than other ecologies, if we are to believe evolutionary theory, biology, and psychology, it is an ecology nevertheless subject to the same general laws as other ecologies.

Economists should be able to learn from ecologists, and vice versa. One difference is that our human ecology, the economy, has the ability to change more rapidly than other ecologies. This should give those ecologists who study economics a leg up, helping them discern the universal rules that apply to both more quickly.

We have placed too much reliance on mathematical and scientific theories based on the physical sciences. Linear equations, normal distributions, and computer modeling are all useful, but they have their limitations in describing life, and that is what we do when we attempt to understand business. Business is a branch of life and therefore life sciences are as applicable in understanding it as the mathematical sciences.

Assumptions of Rationality

Some of our best minds consider rationality, the ability to speak coherently and use mathematical symbols, the pinnacle of development. It was assumed that speaking was significantly more complex and required much more memory and processing power than some of our other basic functions. Isaac Asimov, the prolific science fiction writer and scientist, made those assumptions explicit in one of his best-known works, the novel *I, Robot*. Published in 1950, it is about a basic robot manufactured in 1996. Robbie the robot is capable of taking complex commands, such as running, bending, and playing with children, and making judgments. In one spirited passage Robbie, who was separated from his original owner years earlier, is now working in a factory. He recognizes the young girl, his former owner, running toward him with joy. He sees that she is in danger of being crushed by an oncoming vehicle and makes a decision to abandon his assigned work, run toward the girl, and save her. Not only does he make a complex split-second decision, he makes an ethical judgment that saving her is more important than his assigned work. But Robbie couldn't speak. A few years later a talking robot prototype is developed. This robot is housed in a large room with immense circuitry and he can just utter the answers to a few basic questions before blowing his circuits.

The actual development of modern computers is precisely opposite of that predicted in the Asimov novel. We now have machines that play a decent game of chess and answer questions in a particular field. But we are not even close to having a machine that can understand human emotions and react to them or make complex judgment calls to abandon work and run at a speed calculated to save a little girl from being run over.

The development of computer software, especially since the advent of the PC, has brought into question some of the unstated presuppositions of previous generations. While we have been able to create programs that handle complex mathematical formulas and perform spelling and grammar checks, we are still developing peripherals and software that can instantly recognize people, a task humans and other animals do automatically. Handwriting recognition and voice recognition are still in developmental stages and what is available can only run on the newest machines with lots of memory and extreme processor speeds.

At the very least we should recognize that the basic biological functions we take for granted are extremely complex phenomena, requiring immense memory and processing capability. They require immense intelligence. This should leave us in awe of the complexity of life. Emotional decisions can in fact be quite intelligent based on the survival needs of life on Earth. This is counter to the earlier assumption, based on the supremacy and singularity of thinking, that emotions only cloud our judgment. The dream of creating new life forms just from silicon will probably remain a dream for quite a while. It seems much more likely instead that silicon processors will be grafted in some way onto biological life.

Psychological Type and Multiple Intelligences

We have introduced two distinct notions of human differences: psychological type and multiple intelligences. Each theory deals with categories that are to some extent independent. It is possible, for example, for a person to be intelligent both mathematically and musically. It is also possible for another person to be very intelligent in one and have little talent in the other. Likewise with psychological functions, it is possible for someone to be able to access feeling and thinking but it is more common for a person to be able to access one but not the other in a given situation.

How do these two theories relate? Jonathan P. Niednagel, an expert in the Myers-Briggs System of psychological types mentioned in Chapter 11, believes our psychological type has such a profound impact that it even affects the way we move. He prefers to use the term Brain Types. He has used it in athletics to evaluate who will make the better athlete under different conditions. Some types work best when the pressure is on. These are the ones you send in during a do-or-die situation. He has also used it to evaluate which college players will eventually make it in the pros. In his book *Your Key to Sports Success* he covers each of the types, their athletic skills, and the optimal coaching method for each type as suggested by the theory.

In Chapter 11 I used one type, INTP, to make a statistical point concerning the distribution of types in an organization. For a moment let's focus on that one type again. INTP stands for *I*ntrovert, i*N*tuitive, *T*hinking, and *P*erceiving. Niednagel says the nickname for this relatively rare type is "Logician," but I think "Theoretician" is more accurate.

Niednagel has identified several well-known people as INTPs. Among these are Albert Einstein, the great physicist; Mikhail Baryshnikov, the great dancer; Arthur Ashe, the tennis champion; Steven Spielberg, the renowned movie director; Jane Goodall, the eminent naturalist and leading expert on chimpanzees; John Lennon, of the Beatles; Nelson Mandela; and Leonardo da Vinci. It's pretty clear that Carl Jung, the eminent psychiatrist, and Charles Darwin, the naturalist, also belong here. I chose these out of a more extensive list to highlight the differences in intelligences within the same type.

Is one more intelligent than the other? Is Einstein more intelligent than Jung? They were both Swiss citizens and had some contact. In one of his writings Jung said that Einstein talked to him about physics and he was quickly lost. But then Jung started talking about the psyche and it was Einstein's turn to be totally befuddled. Is Mikhail Baryshnikov more or less intelligent than John Lennon? For me, at least, when the question is posed in this way and with the benefit of the knowledge of multiple intelligences, these questions become nonsense and certainly not worth answering or pursuing.

Rather, much more interesting and important questions come up. Why have some people reached such heights in their chosen fields? What must we do in organizations and societies to make it possible for the optimal number of people who wish to achieve to be able to achieve?

For additional insight we need to turn to another distinguished psychologist, Dr. Abraham Maslow. Maslow was a professor of psychology at Brooklyn College and chairman of the Department of Psychology at Brandeis University. He was an active clinician and researcher from the late 1930s until his death in 1970. Much of early clinical psychology focused on people who were experiencing severe problems. They were sick or, in clinical terms, experiencing psychopathology. Models developed based on studying these people were naturally skewed toward sickness. They did not show a healthy human being. Dr. Maslow, on the other hand, spent much of his time studying psychologically healthy people.

Maslow's observations led him to postulate the existence of a hierarchy of needs in people. The most basic of these needs are physiological: food, clothing, and shelter. As long as these are unfulfilled they are the prime motivators in a person's life. Once these are satisfied, however, a new need becomes prevalent: the need for safety and security. While unfulfilled, safety and security are of prime importance. But once fulfilled they fade in importance while a new need emerges, a social need. This is the need for love, affection, and affiliation. And once these are met the need for esteem becomes paramount. After all these basic needs are met, however, some people seem to move toward self-actualization.

Perhaps self-actualization is better thought of not as a need per se, but more of a desire. For only when all the needs of a person are met can he become self-actualizing. Maslow initially called what emerges a metaneed to fully become oneself. Self-actualizing people naturally achieve and are more creative than others. Creativity here is not limited to the more conventional forms of creativity such as art, music, drama, or creating new theories. Creativity here refers to the creativity of everyday life. Instead of being driven by needs and living to fulfill these needs, life itself becomes the quest. Creativity comes through in everyday occurrences. These might include the way a house is kept and organized, the way a garden is tended, the way words are used.

In Maslow's research self-actualizing people represented a very small percentage of the population, about 1%. All were in their late fifties or older. Having all the basic needs met does not necessarily result in self-actualization. We all know people who have plenty of money but still yearn for more. According to psychological theory, some of these people may have an unfulfilled early-childhood need. Regardless of how much they get now it cannot fill the unmet need of childhood. We do not know if or how someone who is basically healthy and has all his or her needs met will become self-actualizing.

Self-actualization is related to another phenomenon that Dr. Maslow investigated and named peak experiences. A peak experience is a wonderful life changing moment when an insight, a picture, or an idea seems to lead to whole new ways of experiencing life. Athletes have described being so "in the moment" that they meld in some way. They and their teammates become one; an event can take on a slow-motion effect where the athlete becomes the jump, the run, or the movement. Virtually everyone who has experienced it wants to re-create that feeling. Today people talk about being in the zone and use Zen language to refer to this desired state.

People who had peak experiences, whether they were athletic, artistic, scientific, or spiritual in nature, described what they felt in very similar terms. They described a unity with others while at the same time feeling more aware of their existence and more alive. "The emotional reaction in the peak experience has a special flavor of wonder, of awe, of reverence, of humility and surrender before the experience as before something great."[25] "The peak-experience is only good and desirable, and is never experienced as evil or undesirable. The experience is intrinsically valid . . . complete and needs nothing else."[26]

Peak experiences also have some aftereffects. According to Maslow they can have therapeutic effects removing certain neurotic symptoms. They can change a person's view of himself in a healthy direction. They can change his view of the world or aspects of it. "They can release him for greater creativity, spontaneity, expressiveness, idiosyncrasy."[27] "The person is more apt to feel that life in general is worthwhile even if it is drab, pedestrian, painful or ungratifying, since beauty, excitement, honesty, play, goodness, truth and meaningfulness have been demonstrated to him to exist."[28] In a peak experience many dichotomies are resolved. Self and others—selfishness and selflessness—lose their distinction. One feels more alive and aware while also feeling more connected.

A person in a peak experience takes on many of the characteristics that Maslow found in self-actualizing individuals.[29] When he first ran across self-actualizing people he was struck by the vague perception that their motivational life was in some important respects different from all he had learned. He first described it as expressive rather than coping. Then he pointed out that it was unmotivated or metamotivated (beyond striving), rather than motivated. But this statement rested so heavily on which theory of motivation one accepted that it created more problems than it solved. But with the added insight of his study of peak experiences, he could define self-actualization as "an episode, or spurt in which the powers of the person come together in a particularly efficient and intensely enjoyable way, and in which he is more integrated and less split, more open for experience, more idiosyncratic, more perfectly expressive or spontaneous, or fully functioning, more creative, more humorous, more ego-transcending, more independent of

[25] *Toward a Psychology of Being*, by Abraham Maslow, second edition, page 88.

[26] Ibid., 81.

[27] Ibid., 101.

[28] Ibid., 101.

[29] Ibid., 97.

his lower needs, etc. He becomes in these episodes more truly himself, more perfectly actualizing his potentialities closer to the core of his being, more fully human."[30]

In this definition self-actualization can come to anyone at any age. Those people who he first identified as self-actualizing experienced this more often, more intensely, and more perfectly than the average person. Self-actualizing people come to such a high level of health, maturation, and self-fulfillment that they seem almost like a different breed of human and have so much to teach us, according to Maslow.

In the spectrum of human development there are people who suffer from some kind of psychopathology or sickness of the psyche; there are people who are strongly motivated by some unmet needs; there are people who have all their needs met but are still seeking more; and then there are self-actualizing people.

Clearly, what may be effective to people with strong unmet needs might be ineffective with self-actualizing people. Addressing just one basic human need such as money would not be a powerful force to someone who needs a strong sense of affiliation. In addition, people have different psychological types and intelligences.

For an organization to be really effective it must allow for growth for its people who will be at different stages of development. What is appropriate for one person may backfire or be inappropriate for another. One way to lose good people is to have a manager who wants everyone to be just like him. Another way is to have a manager who treats everyone the same. He may treat everyone as if their primary or only motivation were money. Those who value ethics or creativity will be turned off. They will be less productive and will eventually leave, denying the company the benefit of their talents. But the manager could also treat everyone as if they were self-actualizing when in fact they need much more guidance or motivation at this point in their development. And this would also lead to loss.

A corporation has two main products. First it has the economic product that it creates for payment. Remember that all the innovation a company creates eventually gets passed on to society. In order to create additional profit it needs internal creativity of some kind. The three main principles of The New Management—External Quality, Internal

---

[30] Ibid., 97.

Quality, and Continual Improvement—all require a constant infusion of intelligence and creativity. This means people. The second product of any corporation is its people. But the people who are most critical are the managers. One worker who makes a mistake may have a deleterious effect on the company, but nothing compared to the ill effects of one poor manager. The higher up the corporate ladder, the more leverage the ineffective manager has and the more harm he can do not just to the company but to all of society.

In order to be successful long-term, a company must give great attention to the training and development of its managers. This doesn't mean just technical training in the trade of the organization nor is it limited to knowledge of psychology. It means that a corporation must pay attention to the development of its people, especially its managers, as fully functioning humans.

The Eighth Intelligence

Of the several eminent people on the short list of well-known INTPs listed above, the one I respect most is Nelson Mandela. He was persistently denied his rights by the former government of South Africa and was imprisoned not for any crime but because of his beliefs and his refusal to accept or legitimize racism and injustice. Yet when he came to power and became the new president of South Africa, he did not act out of malice. He did not seek revenge. There were no mass accusations or punishments. Rather there was a call for justice and to find the truth in a most noble display of equanimity and balance.

But which intelligence does this represent? Howard Gardner has stated that he is inclined to add an eighth intelligence, perhaps called spiritual intelligence. Mandela's actions, however, I would prefer to call ethical. Not in the sense of following a set of written rules, but ethical in a much higher sense of ethics. This is the ethics that emanates naturally from one who develops himself as a person. It may reflect the development of all or several of our intelligences. It seems to me to represent a high point of self-actualization. Mandela is a model for all of us. He epitomizes what humans can become, a potential for action that is just and healing, action that while being selfless is also in the very best interest of the person. Nelson Mandela is a model for great management.

CHAPTER 14

LIFE AND CHANCE

In the early days of the American space program the scientist James Lovelock was concerned with the question of how best to test for life on Mars. The conventional approach in the late 1970s was to sample the Martian soil to determine its suitability for microorganisms. Lovelock's thinking began to change when he started to consider the highly unlikely composition and movement of the chemicals and energy observable on the Earth's surface. In order to support life, Earth needs to maintain key elements in ways that are not just highly unlikely but virtually impossible in an inorganic environment. Further, these key variables are maintained on the Earth within very tight limits. In his words, "The composition of the Earth's atmospheres was so curious and incompatible a mixture that it could not possibly have arisen or persisted by chance. Almost everything about it seemed to violate the rules of equilibrium chemistry, yet amidst apparent disorder relatively constant and favourable conditions for life were somehow maintained."[31]

One example is the level of oxygen in the air, which at 21% represents the "safe upper limit for life."[32] For each 1% increase in the oxygen level above this, the probability of forest fires being started by lightning flashes increases by 70%. At 25%, very little land vegetation would go unscathed. Perhaps even more startling is the temperature of the planet, which has remained quite stable over long periods of time

[31] *Gaia: A New Look at Life on Earth,* by James Lovelock, page 62.

[32] Ibid., 65.

despite the Sun's temperature, the surface properties of the Earth, and the composition of the atmosphere having varied greatly.[33]

On the other hand, even from a distance Mars displays all that would be expected from a chemical reaction. Its chemical composition is predicted by thermodynamics with the simplest products being most abundant. The temperature at the surface varies greatly depending on the amount of sunlight reaching the planet's surface. A Martian day experiences temperatures hundreds of degrees warmer than anything on Earth. Temperatures during a Martian night are several hundred degrees colder than anything on Earth. There is nothing chemically or physically improbable about Mars. Even from a distance it appears lifeless.

The planet Earth has an extremely sensitive, sophisticated, and effective self-regulating system. The self-regulation serves to make the planet habitable for life. The inference is that in some sense Earth is alive, while Mars is not. This highlights the gaping difference between life and nonlife. While life seems to obey many of the same physical and chemical laws of inert matter, in very real and fundamental ways it behaves quite differently. It seems to defy the second law of thermodynamics. The second law is often stated as a system left on its own will experience an increase in entropy, meaning it will wind down and decompose to simpler states requiring less energy. But not only does life not wind down, it is self-regulating and maintains key parameters such as temperature and oxygen levels inside its borders. Entropy not only doesn't increase but through growth, reproduction, and evolution actually decreases. Physicists might argue that the second law of thermodynamics is not truly violated since energy is taken from outside to decrease entropy. But if life doesn't technically violate the second law, it fails to go along the route predicted by thermodynamics. The laws describing the physical world are inadequate to describe life.

Systems Thinking

And that brings up a key question: "Is a corporation a living entity?" If the planet is in some sense alive, if the biosphere and the ecology are only explicable with laws of life, where does that leave human organizational forms? After all, the components that make up a corporation

---

[33] Ibid., 9.

are for the most part people. True, there are capital assets such as plants, equipment, and real estate, but these are all inert and will not produce an ounce of good or a penny of profit unless there is life to drive it. Most great managers recognize it is people—the other managers and the associates—that make a company great. Yet our very way of measuring the value of a corporation relies on our measurement of the inert, nonlife-like products. It is as if we measured the success of a species by the amount of manure it produced. Shouldn't there also be some measure of the creativity or life force of the organization?

If a corporation is a living entity, then we need laws that more closely describe its life-like characteristics. The best we have in this regard, at present, is systems thinking. Systems thinking is one of the necessary legs of MetaKnowledge. One cannot optimally manage an organization without it. One way in which systems thinking is different than other conceptions of the organization is its emphasis on the whole and not the parts. A traditional approach would look to maximize the performance of the organization by seeking to have each part maximize its performance. As a result, every part of the company is trying to increase its profitability or lower its costs. But this leads to sub-optimization and waste.

Suppose for an instant an item was heated in an oven to give it certain properties. It might be tempting to find ways to lower the time spent in the oven. But doing so may create significant problems for succeeding steps of the process. By trying to lower the cost associated with the curing process, the total cost of the product can increase. Lowering the cost of key processes often times raises the overall cost. Trying to save time in one step can backfire when the whole system is considered. If you understand this you realize that many times some part of the process needs to be sacrificed for the good of the whole. You might need to spend extra time or extra money in a critical part of the process. This might seem like a luxury until it is examined from the point of view of what is best for the whole company.

In a creative process often the up-front work needs to get extra time and care. If a new product is well conceived and designed much can be saved in later stages. In fact, one might even think in terms of "wasting" additional time at the beginning to get it right.

If systems thinking leads to enhanced performance for a company, there is reason to believe that it may also be applied to the whole economy. This may create a paradox. A healthy capitalistic society, where profit is a suitable objective, does best and creates the most wealth when certain sectors of the economy are sacrificed and neither profits nor wealth are maximized in those sectors.

Some obvious examples of this are government regulations such as safety and health. In order to ensure that these regulations are complied with, we establish agencies that do not receive any revenue as a direct result of their work. A bridge could make a great deal of money by charging a toll but doing so would slow down traffic and discourage business, creating a loss for the economy many times greater than the tolls collected. A less obvious example might be banking. To have currency flow freely in the economy, banks do not charge for changing currency from paper money to coins. Perhaps that should be extended and banks should be mandated to keep certain fees to a minimum to ensure an active circulation of money. Why should it take seven days to clear a check? Certainly there is no technological reason for that. But if the banking system is motivated by profit it has no incentive to bring down the time it takes to clear checks. A strong argument could be made that a bias toward lower interest rates and lower spreads between lending and borrowing rates would be better for the overall economy although less profitable for the banks.

The notion of a self-regulating economic and social system that regulates for the good of the whole was an important part of Adam Smith's *The Wealth of Nations*. Individuals acting in their own selfish interests were somehow kept in check by the invisible hand of the system. While each person was looking after herself and maximizing her own profitability the invisible hand kept things in check. Smith was aware that all too often, however, regulations favored the wealthy and powerful. He also observed that many regulations that were supposed to help the poor or provide support often had the exact opposite effect. But in order to understand how some regulations were counterproductive one had to look at a much larger chunk of the system. Just analyzing from the local perspective led to dysfunctional regulations.

Specialization, Diversity, and Optimization

Lovelock built a computer model with two different kinds of daisies called Daisyworld. One was brown while the other was light colored.

He ran some computer simulations changing the luminosity of the sun of his Daisyworld over a wide range. When the temperature on the planet was cold and sunlight was weak, the darker daisy could absorb more light and heat and grow and prosper. But as they prospered the color of the planet became darker so it absorbed more light and the mean temperature on the planet increased. This made it possible for the lighter shade of daisy to grow as well. On the other hand when the sun became warmer the dark daisies absorbed too much light and could not prosper. These were ideal conditions for the lighter daisies that would then prosper and take over most of the planet. But in so doing they would change the color of the planet, making it lighter and therefore reflecting more of the sun's light off the planet. This moderated the temperature of Daisyworld.

This simple two-daisy model was able to regulate the temperature of the planet, keeping it fairly constant even with fluctuations in the luminosity of its sun from 60–120% of the luminosity of our Sun. Even more interesting, when the number of different kinds of daisies was increased the temperature became more stable and the system became more robust. In his model, diversity created a more robust ecosystem that was better able to tolerate disturbances and perturbations from outside the system.

This relates to organizations in several ways. It is more fruitful to consider an organization as a living entity. If you push it, it will push back. The obvious, straightforward solution can backfire. An astute manager understands this and manages accordingly. She is respectful of the people, the systems, and the beliefs. A manager who treats the organization as an inanimate object that can be cut and sliced like a dead fish is sorely disappointed.

Both a company and an economy are most robust when there is diversity. The presence of diverse specialized skills and specialized processes allows a company to be more effective and weather external changes better. Diversity is most important when there are great changes in the external environment. When a company finds a niche it needs to simplify and streamline its approach. Long periods of stability lead to companies specializing in a particular niche. This is fine as long as the niche is permanent. However, during periods of rapid change and turbulence, when the niche shrinks and new ones arise, the organization or the economy that has the greatest diversity does better.

Systems and Subsystems

Every organization is a system comprised of several interacting subsystems: a system of beliefs; a system of people; and hard and soft systems for the creation and delivery of the economic product.

A SYSTEM OF PEOPLE. People with very different talents and personalities are required for a successful organization. Their differences add strength and agility. With great diversity it is important for people in an organization to share values and agree on the mission. The right people need to be in the right positions. No one can do every task or every assignment. Some will never make good accountants and should not be asked to take on that responsibility; some will never be effective at sales; others will not make very good managers. Management needs to be cognizant of individual strengths and differences and guide people toward appropriate positions.

Some key personnel may appear to be irreplaceable. Yet keep in mind that in a successful self-perpetuating organization all the people are eventually replaced. This mimics the human body. Every molecule and every cell in the body is replaced with regularity. The form and the structure allow for the existence of the person over time despite every cell and all physical material being replaced.

HARD AND SOFT SYSTEMS. Hard systems are relatively easy to map. The basic system that creates and delivers your economic product is easily flowcharted. These include business functions such as billing, collections, and sales. The hiring, firing, and promoting process can also be mapped. But other processes are not easily mapped. How does the company treat people, handle disagreements, "unsatisfactory results," conflicts, exceptions? These are part of the soft systems. Soft systems are characterized by processes that are subtly linked and by networks or associations. In addition to the more obvious processes there are networks or associations that are not on the organizational chart or any flowchart. Two individuals in different departments may be friends and work together to enhance operations. They may be the people others go to when there is a crisis or a difficult situation, yet their association receives no recognition on the organizational chart. These networks are a vital part of the organization and often exert a strong influence on key decisions.

These soft systems often determine the character and flavor of the organization. They are magnified by the leverage inherent in the hard systems. An outsider's perception of the character of the organization is very much influenced by soft systems.

BELIEF SYSTEM. Underlying hard and soft systems and people systems are beliefs. This has already been covered in an earlier chapter but I just wish to remind the reader that beliefs as used here include values and beliefs about the universe or what we often refer to as knowledge. These are the key beliefs that serve as a foundation for how we live our lives and how we conduct business. In my opinion this is the most fundamental system in an organization.

BELIEFS ABOUT PEOPLE. One very well-known dichotomy of beliefs was laid out by Douglas McGregor who coined the terms Theory X and Theory Y. A person with Theory X beliefs assumes people do not wish to work and must be forced, coerced, and motivated. Sticks and carrots must be used to assure constant work. It is assumed the average person prefers direction and seeks security. She holds no internal ambition or need for greatness.

Theory Y followers believe that for the average person, work is as natural and desired as rest or play. Most people have a desire not just to earn a living but to perform a full day's work and be part of a team. They display self-initiative, seek responsibility, and desire to create and complete projects. Motivation comes from positive rewards such as pay, good work conditions, and being respected, but it also comes from personal satisfaction and joy of work and joy of creation.

The better organizations of course subscribe to Theory Y. But a great manager knows that some people will be better characterized by Theory X. He may have or need some of these people in his organization, perhaps because of their skill or the need to do a repetitive task others find boring. But by creating the right environment a Theory X person can develop into a Theory Y person.

BELIEFS ABOUT ORGANIZATIONAL PURPOSE. There are beliefs about the nature of business. For some the purpose of a company is to make as much money as possible. For others it is to maximize wealth, which can translate into keeping the share price as high as possible. But a very different belief is that the organization exists to provide a function and service to society. In this view a healthy profit is the result of properly fulfilling the social and economic role of the organization. Different beliefs lead to managing in different ways, to looking for validation in different ways, and to very different actions, especially under stress.

Systems and Metasystems

The basic system in an organization is the interaction of those processes that create and deliver the economic product. This system turns the inputs of the organization into its output. It creates profits or losses resulting in growth or decline. The person at the center is the chief executive officer who has at his disposal significant leverage. He has organizational, financial, operating, and knowledge leverage. The company may also employ knowledge tools and/or physical tools. A CEO who effectively leads the organization and effectively makes use of the people and leverage of an organization can have a dramatic effect on performance and results. A good CEO can take a poor or mediocre company and make it successful.

But there is a lot more involved. In addition to the systems that create the deliverable there are systems to perpetuate and improve the organization. Among these are human development, training, management development, succession planning, long-term planning, process improvement, and research and development. These can be called metasystems because they operate on the basic system and are one level removed from the actual delivery of the economic product. The improvement process can work on the basic system or the metasystems (i.e., improvement of the decision-making process, training or hiring). So it can be considered both a metasystem and a second-order metasystem (improvement of a metasystem).

While good metasystems may not lead to immediate results or immediate profitability, they lead to the perpetuation and renewal of the organization. A manager might be an outstanding leader, from the point of view of producing excellent results today, yet by neglecting the metasystems he could lead the company to ruin. One example is Stanley Gault, a GE executive who became CEO of Rubbermaid Corporation. With his appointment, Rubbermaid went from a mediocre to an outstanding performer. The financial performance was extraordinary, the stock soared, and the company grew. It generated a great deal of attention from the financial press. In the late 1980s it was consistently named one of *Fortune* magazine's most respected companies in America. But as soon as Gault retired and left the company, it drifted, faded, and returned to mediocrity or worse. It was soon acquired and became a division of Newell Corporation.

Executives who focus not just on the system but also on the meta-systems and build an organization that is self-regulating and self-perpetuating, do not garner as much press. In *Good to Great: Why Some Companies Make the Leap . . . and Others Don't*, Jim Collins documents eleven companies that not only went from mediocre to excellent, but continued to excel once the architect of the change retired. In each case the CEO was a quiet, self-effacing individual. But what comes through is that each was an extremely intelligent, resolute, and secure individual who did not need personal glory. They have the attributes characteristic of self-actualizing individuals.

Chance and Creation

A popular science book of the 1950s set up a hypothetical experiment of monkeys who, without any knowledge of the alphabet, were taught to pound the keys of typewriters. Suppose thousands of monkeys were so equipped and kept pounding away indefinitely. While this seems pretty far-fetched, the point is that if enough time passed enough combinations of letters would be hit that a monkey could accidentally write a Shakespearean play. After all, infinity is a very large number. Given enough time almost any combination of events is possible if any single event, such as the striking of any possible letter or punctuation mark, is possible.

This example was very influential and reflects a view of probability theory. With enough time any event is possible. After reflecting on this example for years I concluded that it is deeply flawed. For starters, no one, and I infer no monkey, *ever* hits the keys randomly. Instead we tend to hit the same keys repeatedly, resulting in repetition of similar non-sensical words.

But let's not throw the baby out with the bathwater. To correct this we could have the keystrokes generated by some mechanical or electronic means to produce something more "random." Perhaps a computer with a random letter generator would do. Once again we could get some repetition if each keystroke were equally likely each time, or what is called choosing with replacement. We could instead have our computer choose without replacement so the same combination never occurred twice. This would require some very sophisticated programming—we are already quite far from a natural occurrence of chance. But let's pursue this thinking further and reframe the issue. Is it possible to create a Shakespearean work with a computer operating randomly in a strict sense of the word "random"? Running it fast enough and with enough time, it does seem conceivable that some real gems might be generated this way. Especially when you consider the speed of modern computers. Eventually a Shakespearean play might be "created" this way.

But now we come to a fundamental problem. Suppose all these combinations of letters were printed out on paper. We would be creating huge amounts of written documents, huge amounts of waste. How would you recognize that a given sheet was intelligible? You would have a situation that dwarfed the proverbial needle in a haystack. This problem is much larger than the problem facing an author contemplating a new work. Each page would have to be read, deciphered, and judged. Each would have to be compared to something. This already assumes intelligence. And it assumes a phenomenal ability to process billions of tons of garbage and compare it to something or some standard to get an ounce of worthwhile prose. In order to determine something worthwhile, the ability to recognize coherence would be necessary. In other words, there would have to be some intelligence around to make that judgment. And the work that would be required to actually find the gems would be so onerous that it would be easier, by far, to just create the gems ourselves.

In physical terms all the waste created, whether on paper or in the memory of the computer, would be a huge increase in entropy. The gems in there would be so hard to find that essentially they would be useless—one might even say that for all intents and purposes they would be nonexistent.

While there is a mathematical possibility that chance can create a Shakespearean play, there is no physical possibility for that to occur. To me this also casts doubt on the idea that life developed by chance out of a primordial soup of chemicals that existed billions of years ago on the earth.

Proto-Life

But some fascinating discoveries made in some loosely related fields over the last thirty years or so present new possibilities. New mathematics and new science have developed around the idea of self-organization. Chaos Theory, complexity, nonlinear dynamics, systems dynamics, dynamical systems theory, cybernetics, and other terms are used to describe this new area. One startling realization is that under certain conditions, far from thermodynamic equilibrium, it is possible for self-regulating, self-perpetuating, nonliving phenomena to spontaneously appear. Under the proper temperature and pressure certain chemical processes jump into a dynamic state that, while constantly in flux, maintains key characteristics over time. These systems even grow and evolve. A funnel of water formed when a bathtub is draining is one example. On a larger scale a tornado exhibits many properties of self-regulation and growth while conditions are right. On an even larger scale the huge red spot on the planet Jupiter is a dynamic system constantly in flux, yet observable as an entity since it was first noticed decades ago.

The first description of self-organizing systems was the theory of "dissipative structures" by chemist and physicist Ilya Prigogine, Nobel laureate and professor of physical chemistry at the Free University of Brussels. Prigogine was interested in the questions of life that he thought were telling us something very important about nature. But he studied a much simpler phenomenon of heat convention known as the Bernard instability. When a thin layer of liquid is heated from below, the heat is transferred without any motion of the molecules themselves. At a certain critical point, however, a threshold—a striking pattern of hexagonal-shaped cells—suddenly appears. The molecules organize into six-sided cells that move and in so doing transfer heat.

Humberto Maturana, a neuroscientist with the University of Santiago in Chile, in collaboration with Francisco Varela studied living cells. Their work led them to coin a new term, autopoiesis, which means "self-making" or self-creating. With Richard Uribe, they developed a mathematical model for the simplest autopoietic system, the living cell.

Chemical autopoietic systems have been hypothesized and synthesized in the laboratory. A definition of autopoiesis is "a network pattern in which the function of each component is to participate in the production or transformation of other components."[34] Gail Fleischaker, a biologist and philosopher, has summarized three basic criteria of an autopoietic system: It must be bounded, self-generating, and self-perpetuating. Most successful corporations are bounded, where there is a distinction between inside and outside. That distinction is not made through any kind of physical barrier but rather through identification. Like the cell with its semipermeable wall, the identification barrier is semipermeable. People leave and enter the company, but the functions maintain stability.

Corporations are self-generating, as long as they are profitable. Profitability requires, however, that they serve a niche in their ecosystem, their economy. It also requires health. Corporations do get sick. They have internal and external diseases. They also show the ability to grow. But growth shouldn't be seen as necessarily getting bigger. Growth in people means they are getting smarter, developing more. Systems can also grow, improve, and become more refined.

The most difficult criterion to satisfy is self-perpetuation. Peter Senge claimed that the life expectancy of a Fortune 500 company was forty-two years, less than the life expectancy of one of its parts—humans. Some of the longest-lasting organizations are religious. The various churches of the world tend to all be long-lived. The Roman Catholic Church, for instance, has been around for close to 2,000 years.

Long-lived organizations seem to have at least two factors in common. They have a mission that involves something far greater than personal success or survival. In the case of churches there is a belief of a greater being and in many cases eternal life. Their mission can be expressed as "saving souls," or "putting people in touch with a greater consciousness," "salvation," "enlightenment," or some other "higher goal." Secondly there seems to be respect for the organization in and of itself as something worth perpetuating. The church or the company is respected as an entity. There is a desire for its self-perpetuation. Self-perpetuation requires a belief system that emphasizes the organization over the individuals. It requires strong metasystems. An organization is therefore not autopoietic unless it has developed metasystems.

[34] *The Web of Life*, by Fritjof Capra, page 208.

Implications

One implication of Chaos Theory, dynamical nonlinear system theory, and autopoiesis is that these phenomena are occurring on all levels of the universe, the very small to the very large. It is not something rare; on the contrary it is ubiquitous. We are just starting to notice them because the shift in our understanding allows us to recognize them. These insights have led to a new theory, a new map of reality very different from the mechanical, atomistic map that has been developed by Western science since the sixteenth century, which is heavily influenced by Newtonian mechanics.

The older map has been extremely successful in explaining phenomena from the very small to the very large, and it helped make possible the incredible increase in our material well-being. The older map won't be obliterated or replaced as some observers have suggested. It will always be an important intellectual tool. Newtonian ideas for the most part flow from the part to the whole. Systems theory to a large degree flows from the whole to the part. The two supplement and complement each other. We now have two very powerful maps to explain the world. Both are necessary to lead us to our next level of cultural evolution.

CHAPTER 15

LANGUAGE, DIMENSIONALITY, AND LOGICAL LEVELS

The White Knight

"You are sad," the Knight said in an anxious tone: "let me sing you a song to comfort you."

"Is it very long?" Alice asked, for she had heard a good deal of poetry that day.

"It's long," said the Knight, "but it's very, very beautiful. Everybody that hears me sing it—either it brings the tears into their eyes, or else—"

"Or else what?" said Alice, for the Knight had made a sudden pause.

"Or else it doesn't, you know. The name of the song is called 'Haddocks' Eyes.'"

"Oh, that's the name of the song, is it?" Alice said, trying to feel interested.

"No, you don't understand," the Knight said, looking a little vexed. "That's what the name is called. The name really is 'The Aged Aged Man.'"

"Then I ought to have said 'That's what the song is called'?" Alice corrected herself.

"No, you oughtn't: that's quite another thing! The song is called 'Ways and Means' but that's only what it is called, you know!"

"Well, what is the song, then?" said Alice, who was by this time completely bewildered.

"I was coming to that," the Knight said. "The song really is 'A-sitting on a Gate': and the tune's my own invention."[35]

While this may seem like nonsense to most of us, to students of logic and semantics this all makes perfect sense. Martin Gardner, an eminent

---

[35] *The Annotated Alice*, by Lewis Carroll, with notes by Martin Gardner, page 243.

student of logic himself, writes, "The song *is* "A-sitting on a Gate"; it is *called* "Ways and Means"; the *name* of the song is "The Aged Aged Man"; and the name is *called* "Haddocks' Eyes." Carroll is distinguishing here among things, the names of things, and the names of names of things. "Haddocks' Eyes," the name of a name, belongs to what logicians now call a "metalanguage." By adopting the convention of a hierarchy of metalanguages, logicians manage to sidestep certain paradoxes that have plagued them since the time of the Greeks."[36]

Definition of MetaKnowledge

"Meta" can be used to denote beyond the subject matter as Aristotle did when he coined the term metaphysics; it can be used to denote knowledge about the subject matter that is not the subject matter itself; and it can be used in a reflexive sense. A metalanguage can be a language of languages, or a language used to talk about language and syntax, or it could refer to communications beyond language.

All three meanings apply to MetaKnowledge. It is definitely about knowledge, one of its branches is knowledge about knowledge, and it is beyond the specific, substantive knowledge we use every day to accomplish tasks. It is at a different level, informing our actions with wisdom. We have already touched upon several parts of this system of knowledge including theory of knowledge; knowledge of variation and inference; knowledge of people, including psychological types, multiple intelligences, and development of healthy individuals; systems thinking; a theory of the economic impact of knowledge; leverage and compounding; principles of The New Management; knowledge of how we learn; a theory of organizational transformation; ecology; and chaos and self-organizing systems. I would like to briefly cover three other areas that we constantly touch upon but have not dealt with explicitly—a theory of language, dimensionality, and logical levels.

Theory of Language

Several decades ago a philosophical movement, the Philosophy of Language, tried to explain everything by analyzing language. Today that

[36] Ibid., 245.

seems a bit naïve given our new appreciation of nonverbal interactions, communications, and cognition. Still, language plays a dominating role in the conscious communication and thinking of many people.

One contribution of the theory of language was to distinguish two different kinds of language within our everyday usage. One they called Technical Language. In science, technology, music, art, or any discipline for that matter, a word needs to take on a specific and precise definition. This allows clarity and precision. It allows specialists to communicate with each other quickly, with less room for miscommunication. But it also closes the door to the nonspecialist who has not learned the precise meanings of the language of that trade.

The other language-within-a-language they called Ordinary Language. This is the everyday language most of us use daily. Typically we use words in a rather loose way. The meanings are approximate and we assume other people understand them in roughly the same way we do. Often disagreements turn on what we mean by a specific word. Ordinary Language has the drawback of lacking clear, well-defined meanings for each word. This lack of precision leads to words being applied in ways that are loosely related. While at times this can be a drawback, it can also be a great asset. It allows us to communicate with many more people. This very lack of an "exact" and therefore limited meaning allows for more analogies, metaphors, and connections between ideas. It leads to a richness of thought and imagery not possible with Technical Language. And it also happens to be the way we communicate and think much of the time.

In addition, every word has two meanings when used. One is the denoted, dictionary type of meaning, the other is the connoted, or flavoring of that word. Two words can have the same denoted meaning, yet have very different impact because of their connoted meaning. Cheap and frugal can both be applied to the same kind of behavior, but "cheap" is more likely to have a negative flavor or coloring. It implies that the person could afford more and should buy better, say because of long-term consequences, yet does not. "Frugal" has a mostly positive connotation implying that there is no excess spending or waste. The connoted meaning or flavor or coloration can be outside of conscious awareness, thus a person called cheap might not know why they are upset, yet respond positively to being called frugal.

Dimensionality

There is a kind of numerical illiteracy rampant in business literature. People look for the one number or indicator that will tell them how to act. But as we have pointed out, reality is multidimensional and that requires several numbers or indicators to describe and understand. One example discussed extensively is IQ, which we have argued is virtually meaningless as it stands. But there are two other areas of immediate relevance to commerce—profit and purchase price.

Profit

The unsophisticated investor, especially during bull markets, is drawn to that single number, profit, to tell him whether to buy, hold, or sell. A corporation is a complex phenomenon with many dimensions. Corporations have personalities made up of many factors. No single adjective or number is sufficient to describe a company. And no single number is an adequate predictor of success.

The Great Depression of the 1930s accompanied a rash of bankruptcies and banking failures. A study done afterward showed that five numbers were required to adequately predict financial strength. These included current ratio, working capital, and debt-to-equity ratios. To rely solely on profit as a measure of a company's prospects is not just madness, it is stupid. Of course during a stock market mania the whole market responds to earnings but at that point you are not trading companies as much as you are riding a wave, just like the Dutch tulip bulb mania of the seventeenth century that saw tulip bulbs fetch more than their weight in gold.

Purchase Price

Another example is purchase price. Purchasing, particularly in a business setting, just on the basis of price is counterproductive. Price without reference to quality is meaningless. An item can be the lowest price coming in the door, but because of poor quality can be the most expensive going out the door. You could buy the cheapest paint, but it might require two or three coats instead of one. So yes, the price of the paint is less but you incur additional labor costs and may have to purchase much more paint to get the job done. To complete the job can actually cost more even though the price of your input is less. And worse, the end product is never as good.

Descriptions of dimensions are not limited to numbers. Words in some cases are as good or better. But if there are six important factors, you need six qualities with either a numerical or verbal assessment to do it justice. The qualifications for a position might include good communication skills, the ability to speak in front of large groups, knowledge of certain areas, and so on. Here you implicitly recognize that a job is multidimensional, and just being strong in one dimension is not sufficient to do the job properly. To try and add up all these factors to come up with a single number borders on the insane. Of course, some of you are saying, "But that's the way we do it in our company." But that does not make it right.

And this brings up a related point. The old corporate map was an organizational chart. People hired were supposed to fit into boxes on the chart. If they didn't have the exact qualifications, they couldn't go into the box. If taken too literally, and they have been taken too literally, organizational charts lead to bureaucracy. If people are unique, then forcing them to fit into boxes can be dysfunctional. Of course a person must adapt to an organization, but the organization must adapt as well. If you are to get the most out of each person, his or her uniqueness has to be appreciated.

Logical Levels

Related to dimensions is the concept of logical levels. While logical levels and dimensionality have different origins, they both add depth to simple analysis. A logical level such as metalanguage allows us to extract the essence of language and avoid contradictions and paradoxes. An example is the maxim, "The more things change, the more they stay the same." This is clearly a paradox: in changing more something stays more the same. The paradox can be resolved by understanding that what changes and what stays the same are at different logical levels or of different logical types. Every year a squirrel circumvents my anti-squirrel mechanisms and manages to feed in my bird feeder. Yet squirrels only live a year or two. While the individual squirrels themselves are constantly changing, squirrels as a group occupy the same niche, go over the same territory, have the same fights year after year.

Similarly, a river constantly changes and the water in it is never the same. The exact choppiness of the river is never exactly the same but the general conditions of choppiness repeat time and again. With all this change the river remains the same. "The river" is a different logical type than the atoms of water and different from the variations of choppiness even though water and choppiness make up and characterize the river. The individual and the class to which it belongs are at different logical levels and to mix them up in the same sentence without distinction is a logical fallacy that leads to contradictions, paradoxes, and wrong conclusions.

Darwin's theory of evolution applies to species, not to individuals. It is a mistake to assume that one person having a lot of children guarantees the survival of his progeny and his genes. What do survive are whole sets of genes carried by multiple individuals. A species survives not because of one person's genes but because of a whole set of genes spread out over many individuals. A species survives over generations, individuals do not. It might be that in order for the species to survive during swings in climate, different sets of genes must flourish at different times. If one set were to overpower the other, the survival of both sets could be lessened.

Foreground

So far much of our discussion of MetaKnowledge has been against a backdrop of one very powerful, long-lived trend—a constant improvement of material well-being that has accelerated since the onset of the industrial revolution and especially over the last one hundred years. Two related trends are also driving businesses and the world.

One is a communication revolution with numerous tools and channels for expression. Among these are the telegraph, telephone, camera, movie camera, radio, television, fax, copy machine, camcorder, VCR, cellular phone, digital technology, and computer. And all of these appear to be converging into the Internet. This new communication trend is possible because of our improved ability to create physical goods, but it is also having an impact on our production and management capabilities. The communication trend also has its roots deep in the early years of the human race.

The other significant trend transforming the world is globalization.

CHAPTER 16

COMMUNICATION
REVOLUTIONS

Imagine walking into a cave and encountering wall paintings of exquisite craftsmanship and power. The paintings were drawn with such skill that the animals, people, and spirits they portray come to life. Colorful, with great detail, they evoke feelings of awe and beauty. The Lascaux Cave paintings discovered in southern France in 1940 do just that, displaying artistic skill and sensitivity similar to what we associate with great art of our time. The cave has inspired comparison to modern masterpieces and has been labeled the prehistoric Sistine Chapel. Yet the paintings are 17,000 years old. The recently discovered Cave of Chauvet is more than 30,000 years old. These caves present a strong case for the existence of human sensitivity, exquisite craftsmanship, culture, and a developing intellect tens of thousands of years ago.

What distinguishes us from our ancestors of 40-, 80-, and even 100,000 years ago are not biological differences in our body or minds. It is our cultural evolution and the development of our ability to manipulate the physical world. While our main interest from a commercial point of view are the implications of future communication innovations, a historical comparison of prior breakthroughs can give us some perspective. The past is prologue and contains clues to the future. We will trace the major developments of communication leading up to some of today's business practices and the advent of the modern corporation.

Our cultural evolution can be analyzed in four waves, each corresponding to a revolution in communication. But are we the only species to communicate among ourselves? The accepted answer to that has shifted radically over the last few decades. We now know we are not the only communicators. A massive amount of evidence has led to a revolution in our perception of other species. Whales sing intricate songs transmitted over thousands of miles. Bird's songs have meaning to other birds. Bees perform a complex dance to indicate to the hive the location of a source of food. Wolves hunt in a complex and coordinated manner with members of the pack taking on different roles. We may not be able to read their messages, but they certainly can.

Most relevant, and perhaps most startling, is the discovery that gorillas have their own language and can be taught to communicate with us. Two scientists, Penny Patterson and Ronald Cohen, from the University of California trained two African gorillas to communicate with words. Koko, the first of the gorillas to be trained, was a female orphan. As an experiment Penny began teaching Koko words while the gorilla was still a toddler, but Koko's ability to learn exceeded all expectations. She was learning at a rate one year behind a normal human child. An IQ of 100 is considered normal for humans. Since Koko was a year behind an average child, her IQ was assessed at 85. In time she developed a one-thousand-word vocabulary.

But the language she learned to express herself in does not make use of spoken words. She was taught American Sign Language, and all her "speaking" was done with hand signals. As she progressed she and her companion, Michael, combined words they knew to create new meanings. "Scratchcomb," for instance, was created to mean brush. As the proportion of a gorilla's thumb to fingers is different from ours, a gorilla cannot form some words in the same way we do. Their adaptations led to Gorilla Sign Language.

Afterward it was discovered that gorillas have their own gestural language used in the wild, indicating they have a natural predisposition to learn a language based on hand signals. They do not, however, have a highly developed larynx and cannot vocalize words. Interestingly enough, however, Koko developed the ability to comprehend spoken English. It is fascinating, observing the interspecies communication of the human Penny speaking to Koko the gorilla in English and Koko answering back in her Gorilla Sign Language. Koko and Michael displayed a wide range of emotions such as grief, shame, and guilt, which we used to think were unique to humans.

The First Communication Revolution—Spoken Language

Our ability to communicate through spoken words gave early man an advantage over other primates. While we like to view ourselves as categorically different and more intelligent than other species, the example of Koko and Michael suggests quite strongly that the difference between our two species is not as great as we had believed. Our intelligence is only incrementally greater. Of course, small incremental differences can make a huge difference in the race for survival and dominance.

Spoken language's importance is not just that it allowed us to communicate rapidly over distance. Words, once established, can live independent of the person who first speaks them. Thus a poem or a story becomes an entity outside of the individual. Words create an external medium that further stimulates our cognitive abilities. They become a recording vehicle, allowing us to set down our achievements. It is natural for us to use words to indicate physical objects such as tree, rock, sun, father, mother, and brother or sister. It is a natural extension to note the relationships and actions of these objects. But once language was established, new concepts could be developed. Show me a "subtle" or an "esteem" or any one of various concepts, adjectives, and verbs that we have developed to explain our world and our ideas. They don't exist as physical entities. It is hard to conceive of some of these concepts without language. It seems likely they are invented concepts that would not have developed in the absence of language. Indeed, could our more subtle concepts develop in the absence of language?

The Japanese snow monkey was extensively studied in Japan. In the early 1950s scientists were surprised when they witnessed the monkeys learning from one another. A new food, a sweet potato, was introduced to the tribe. When one individual, called Imo, figured out how to clean it by putting it in water, other monkeys observed and copied her. So the ability to learn from others precedes spoken language. But language increases the speed, specificity, and amount of learning passed on from one generation to the next. It accelerates the accumulation of knowledge over generations. The child can learn from the mistakes of the parent. The whole species can learn, not just the individual, from the lessons and mistakes of our ancestors. The epic poems passed orally from generation to generation show just how much we were able to accomplish with spoken language.

The four communication revolutions as I define them are (1) spoken language, (2) written language, (3) the high-speed printing press, and (4) the advent of mechanical and electrical means of communication. Each of these revolutions has had a profound and dramatic impact on the welfare of humanity and left its imprint on the ecology of the planet. Since we have such an emphasis on the new, it is easy to overlook the revolutionary changes that resulted from earlier revolutions. It is also easy to forget how many innovations, modern ideas, and tools were developed during one of the earlier communication and cognitive revolutions.

Literature, art, interchangeable parts, clothing, metal forging, and craftsmanship were all developed during the first revolution, without the aid of written language. Some items from earlier revolutions have survived and were adapted over time while others have disappeared. We still are enthralled by the oral epic poems such as "The Iliad." We still wear leather shoes and use ceramic cups. But few of us ride our horses to work.

Each revolution has had profound effects in three areas: organization, tools, and intellectual achievements.

ORGANIZATION IN THE SPOKEN LANGUAGE REVOLUTION. Once again, to gain some perspective it is helpful to look at our primate relatives. Jane Goodall is the world's leading scientific expert on chimpanzees. Her extensive observations of chimpanzees in the wild have changed our views of chimps, other animals, and ourselves. Where once we thought we were the only mammal to wage war, to hunt in groups, and to kill members of our own species, we have learned otherwise.

Goodall observed a group of chimps for many years. At one point the group broke up and a smaller tribe formed and occupied a different territory. For several years the two tribes existed peacefully, but at a later point the larger tribe attacked and massacred the newer, smaller tribe. Even though members of the smaller tribe had once been part of the larger tribe, they were decimated. The idea of tribal identification seems to go far back in our evolutionary history and its implications can be brutal.

The tribe is the basic form of organization among chimps. This is not true of all primates. Orangutans are basically loners who spend most of their time by themselves and just come together for mating purposes. Gorillas live in harems with one alpha male and several adult females.

The tribe is also a basic organizational form for humans. In some respects it is more basic than the family. It certainly vies with the family in importance. Tribes have a longer life span than families, which break up and reform when the children come of age. Tribes have been more important in the survival of the species. For our species to have survived we needed to band together against other animals that were faster, stronger, and naturally better equipped than us. Tribal behavior is still very much with us and helps explain a lot of what occurs among and between groups of people.

Tribes appear to have an optimal size. When one becomes too large it breaks up into smaller units. Historically there were reasons why a tribe could not grow beyond a certain size. Probably the amount of land necessary to support life was a factor. Too many people living together tend to stress the land and may also have stressed the people. But spoken language added another twist to human society. People could identify as being related, not just by being in the same tribe but by their language. If they could communicate there was a sense of familiarity. Spoken language helped expand the idea of a tribe into related tribes.

Spoken language has a tendency to change rapidly. Groups that had little or no contact quickly developed different languages. Language helped bind and divide people into related groups. It helped identify friends and potential enemies. There is even a word for this. "Shibboleth" refers to the customary use of language distinctive of a particular class, profession, or tribe.

I am sure we have all had the experience of being in a strange neighborhood and feeling vulnerable. Why is it that we were told to avoid certain areas or certain people? For most of us, once introductions are made we discover the people to be little different from our own kind. Yet that fear of strangers or people with strange customs persists in most children. In fact, the word for foreigner in many languages is "barbarian." People not of our tribe, not of our immediate neighborhood, invoke a primal caution, almost a primal fear that is deeply ingrained in our psyches.

TOOLS IN THE SPOKEN LANGUAGE REVOLUTION. It is said that the history of man's progress is the history and progress of his tools. We are not the only species to use tools, but we have developed them to an unprecedented degree. Chimps shape reeds to pick out termites from their nests to serve as tasty appetizers. Crows use slim sticks in a similar fashion to lure out nutritious beetles from rotting logs. Our first tools were probably rocks, sticks, and related objects. Chimps shape the reeds for their intended purpose, but early humans went much further with much more intricate shaping. Rocks were smashed against each other to create shapes and edges for cutting. Tools were used to create other tools. Tool making is at once one of the most powerful indicators of our physical progress, as well as one of its creators.

Knives, spears, and arrows are of course tools. They are also weapons that could be used on animals or other humans. Some of the most profoundly important tools, however, are less noted. The needle is one. It made it possible for our early ancestors to fashion garments conforming to their bodies. This allowed them to function in colder climates, and it helps account for our ability to thrive in all kinds of climates. Interchangeable tools, such as harpoon points, were another major development. All these were developed by our hunter-gatherer ancestors before the advent of written language.

ASSOCIATED INTELLECTUAL DEVELOPMENTS IN THE SPOKEN LANGUAGE REVOLUTION. It seems likely that in addition to using words to describe the environment, there was a need for counting and measuring. We have no way of assessing when, how, or to what extent mathematics developed, but it seems plausible there was a need to distinguish the number of animals, length of time, number of years, age, and other numerical attributes early on in our history. Our fingers provide the perfect medium to describe numbers. They are a kind of early abacus. Given the ability of gorillas to use hand signals to communicate, it seems plausible that fingers were used to count. Additional evidence is the ease by which children who are learning to count use their fingers. Is it just a coincidence that we write mathematics based on a decimal system, a system based on ten?

Linguistic memory became particularly important. How could a legend, an epic, be perpetuated unless it could be taught, word for word, in its entirety? History and mythology require a method of recording. Memory was the recording device of our ancient ancestors. It must have worked well. Today, among cultures where oral epics are still told and recited, incredible feats of memory are routinely accomplished.

AGRICULTURE: A REVOLUTION OF ITS OWN DURING THE SPOKEN LANGUAGE REVOLUTION. Observation of the Sun, Moon, and stars led to timekeeping and an early form of astronomy. Most hunter-gatherer tribes moved with the seasons and the moons. And sensitivity to nature's timing was critical for another great achievement—agriculture.

Agriculture as a way of life is believed to have begun in the Middle East and coincided with the mutation of wild wheat into a plant that had larger seeds that were easily harvested. But this is a strictly Western-centric view. Agriculture also developed in China and the Americas, with rice and corn respectively as the major grains. When the Europeans came upon the new continents now called North and South America, they came across some advanced civilizations with cities, art, astronomy, and writing. The swift conquest of the Americas by the Europeans is often interpreted as the superiority of one more highly developed civilization over another that was less highly developed. But, in fact, Cortez was on the verge of defeat when he was fighting the Aztec king Montezuma in Mexico. It was an outbreak of smallpox that affected all the Native Americans at once that led to their stunning defeat. The Americas, isolated from the Eurasian-African landmass by oceans, had never been exposed to this virus and therefore had no immunity to it. The Spaniards had all been exposed to smallpox and had developed immunity to the disease. They unwittingly brought over the virus with them. The swift conquest was due to an early form of biological warfare.

The development of agriculture independently in several places indicates it was not an unlikely accident but rather a natural development of the co-evolution of humans and their environment. At first agriculture supplemented the hunter-gatherer's food source. But agriculture allowed for more people to be supported by a relatively small amount of land. It created a large advantage over societies that held on to hunting and gathering for their sole source of food.

Agriculture in turn induced many other changes in society. It allowed for larger villages. It also stimulated the development of the next major communication revolution.

The Second Communication Revolution— Written Language

With towns came a need to record information. One hypothesis is that a communal grain storage 4,000 to 5,000 years ago needed to record what each farmer brought in and took out. These notations on clay tablets may have been the beginning of written language in the West.

TWO KINDS OF WRITTEN LANGUAGE. There are two kinds of written language. The kind we use in the West is phonetic with words represented by sound. As the spoken language changes, the written language changes as well. The other kind uses a pictograph to represent a word or concept. In this case the written language is independent of the spoken language. The pictograph is constant even if the pronunciation changes radically. This is how Chinese characters are written. Each method has its advantages and disadvantages, but whichever is used, written language confers vast advantages.

ORGANIZATION IN THE WRITTEN LANGUAGE REVOLUTION. Agriculture required new concepts and social structures. Private ownership of land, an idea useless to hunter-gatherers, took on great importance. If someone works a fertile parcel of land, who is entitled to it once he passes away? Who determines the inheritance? Is it the society, the family, or the individual? Agriculture led to private property and created the concept of ownership of land. It also required laws that could outlive a single leader and survive through generations.

With the advent of written language and numbers, larger, more sophisticated organizations and more complex cooperation could develop. Villages could grow into towns, city-states, and empires. Written language was the first broadcasting system. It allowed a writer to communicate over distance and time while maintaining the integrity of the original message. Laws could be written. A document written in one place could be transported a great distance and read or posted.

Of course, you needed to be able to read to make sense of a posted message. This gave an aura of authority to anyone who could read. An educated person first and foremost was able to read. This made kingdoms, nations, and empires governable. Democracy and republics could develop. One example of an early republic was that of Sparta of ancient Greece. Both Socrates and Plato admired the Spartan Republic. Machiavelli was a scholar of political systems, besides being known for a rather opportunistic political philosophy. He claimed that the Republic of Sparta had lasted 800 years. To put this in perspective, remember that our own republic, currently the longest surviving one in the world, is just more than 200 years old.

WRITTEN LANGUAGE AS A STORAGE MEDIUM. Written language is a powerful storage medium. If it is in writing, we can refer to the original document. Memory and people's recollection of events were superseded when a written record was kept. This meant greater reliability and cast an aura of authority over the written word. People who write well are admired in all literate cultures. For many people, the fact that something is in writing is enough to give it an air of authority.

TOOLS IN THE WRITTEN LANGUAGE REVOLUTION. Besides paper and ink, which by themselves are major inventions, the written language revolution saw the development of masonry, wheels, chariots, shipbuilding, sailboats, intricate metal work, wrought iron, and steel. We developed roads, concrete, multistory buildings, and simple machines. The pyramids and the Great Wall of China were built. Indeed much of what we now call civilization was developed during this second communication revolution.

ASSOCIATED INTELLECTUAL DEVELOPMENTS IN THE WRITTEN LANGUAGE REVOLUTION. Philosophy, astronomy, written history, the Bible, republics, democracy, written or formal law, formal medicine, formal schools, libraries, written music, algebra, geometry, mathematics, and science were all developed during this phase. Painting, sculpture, athletics, drama, and religion all existed prior to the written word, but they were formalized, expanded, and improved. Oral legends were written down and became literature.

THE ROOTS OF WESTERN CIVILIZATION. What we call "Western Civilization" has its roots in the Roman civilization. Rome adopted the philosophy, metaphysics, and religion of the Greeks. In the latter part of its existence Rome adopted Christianity, a Jewish sect, as the state religion. Western science, philosophy, and mathematics trace their roots to ancient Greece. Christianity came to us from Israel through Rome. Our notions of justice, law, and organization are distinctly Roman. Modern science, representative forms of government, Judeo-Christian religions, engineering, mathematics, and Roman law are the main pillars of Western civilization and they all came to us from Roman civilization, too.

There is a great debate in education today about including non-Western works of literature and science into the required reading of American students. It is natural that this multiculturalism would meet great resistance, since it conflicts with our long-standing traditions and history. What makes it possible today, perhaps necessary, is that many of our citizens are not of Western descent and identify with more than one culture. Western civilization is broadening and taking on influences and ideas from the rest of the world, but this is nothing new. Western ideas have come to us from many cultures. Any culture or organization that fails to take in new material is doomed to stagnation.

One example is China. Almost ninety years prior to Columbus's voyage of discovery, a Chinese expedition with a fleet of more than 300 ships and 27,000 men was sent to explore the Indian Ocean and the east coast of Africa. The deck of each ship was large enough to fit all three of Columbus's boats. But after several expeditions the Chinese emperor concluded that the rest of the world had nothing to offer China. Subsequently all travel and most contact with the outside world was summarily stopped. Even in his epic work *The Wealth of Nations*, published in 1776, Adam Smith cited China as the wealthiest of nations. But the small and underdeveloped continent of Europe was not only to catch up with China, but to leapfrog it in terms of physical and economic development. In the twentieth century, China was one of the poorest of nations.

KNOWLEDGE AND CLASS. In this second communication era, knowledge had an elite and sacred quality to it. Books were not easily reproduced and were expensive. Formal knowledge was not easily shared or disseminated. Few had access to books. Few could read. In the Roman Empire, there were two types of citizens: the patricians and the plebeians. And in addition, there were many slaves. The patricians had access to knowledge and wealth. The plebeians, for the most part, did not.

The Third Communication Revolution—
The Printing Press

Johannes Gutenberg's invention of moveable type around 1440 led to the development of the high-speed printing press and revolutionized access to knowledge. The first mass-produced items were printed products such as pamphlets and calendars. The Mazein Bible printed around 1452 seems to have been the breakthrough product, sending a clear signal that a revolution was underway. Before, duplicating a book required that a scribe, with meticulous penmanship, hand copy the original. This was laborious and time consuming and required the service of a highly skilled and expensive craftsman. Even with adequate funding the process was slow and books were prohibitively expensive for all but the wealthy elite. Further, copying errors—both voluntary and involuntary—were immense. A scribe who didn't like a particular passage could take liberties and rewrite it more to his liking. This was in addition to unintended errors and omissions. The printing press required a fair amount of work to set up. But once prepared, copies of a book could be produced at a fast clip, with great accuracy and at a fraction of the cost. The skill was now in the setup.

ADVANTAGES. When books were individually copied it was not physically possible to make large numbers of copies. Making one hundred copies would have been a laborious process requiring years, and the one hundredth copy was just as difficult as the first. With the invention of the press, 100,000 copies became a reality. In fact, the more copies produced at a time, the lower the average cost per copy. The printing press created knowledge leverage. The time and cost to replicate a document became a fraction of what it was. Scribes were made obsolete. No doubt scribes must have feared that the machine was replacing the skilled worker and the world would never be the same again. They were right on both counts. But the benefits for the rest of society were immense. Books became affordable. The printing press gave us mass-produced books and led to mass education, self-education, newspapers, and personal libraries.

Knowledge, heretofore the sole province of the nobility and the priesthood, became available to everyone. The monopoly of knowledge was shattered and individuals became free to think on their own. The mass printing of the Mazarin Bible set the groundwork for the Protestant Reformation. As a side note, however, Gutenberg's printing business failed. He wasn't able to pay back the loans he took out to start his business, which were collateralized by his printing equipment. The lender took over the equipment. Gutenberg, one of the inventors of knowledge leverage, became a victim of financial leverage.

Not only language was revolutionized by the press. Drawings and pictures were also mass produced. Drawings and paintings have an older heritage than written language. All the verbal descriptions in the world can't describe the Sistine Chapel, but a good etching gives a fair representation of it. Art too now became available to a mass audience.

ORGANIZATION IN THE PRINTING PRESS COMMUNICATION REVOLUTION. The press allowed for new forms of organization. Stock certificates could be issued. Paper money became practical, as did bearer securities such as bearer bonds. Security markets developed. The modern stock corporation was born. Strangers could combine for large ventures requiring more capital than any single person had on his own. This made possible the modern split between management and ownership. It allowed Europeans to raise large amounts of capital and form huge companies to explore other parts of the world.

While Columbus sailed for the Spanish crown, many of the British explorations in the Americas and Asia were private corporations that raised capital by selling shares. The British East India Company, incorporated in 1600, was given monopoly privileges on trade with the East Indies. It in time governed India. The printing press and the organizational developments of the time made possible colonialism, modern nations, and modern economics.

Another innovation was paper money, which allowed for the transfer of large amounts of capital without the bother and expense of transporting heavy loads of gold or silver. Paper money requires unique and expensive printing devices that can print in ways that are not easily replicated. If everyone could print money it would become worthless. Recent advances in small sophisticated printers are forcing governments to adopt even newer printing technologies, such as embedded laser sensitivity, that forgers cannot readily duplicate.

TOOLS IN THE PRINTING PRESS COMMUNICATION REVOLUTION.
Knowledge was no longer limited to religion or philosophy. Knowledge about the physical world, engineering, science, or just tinkering could be rapidly communicated to others. Around 1650 population pressures in Holland helped stimulate new agricultural methods that allowed more food to be grown with fewer people. These methods were copied in England within decades. The new methods created greater food abundance and wealth, but they also freed people from farming and helped create laborers who could be hired to work in nonagricultural sectors.

At about the same time an energy crisis was developing. Wood, the main energy source, was becoming scarce as the forests of Europe were being cut and England was quickly losing what was left of her forests. This led to a search for new energy sources, first water, then coal. A whole new set of tools, machines that could do the work of several people, were developed, mostly in England. Cottage industries began to develop with households turning out large numbers of goods, initially textiles.

Abundant food, willing and sufficient labor, new sources of energy, a free trade area in England, and an experienced merchant and business class with an established and proven structure of doing business were all precursors to the Industrial Revolution. In 1698 Thomas Savery patented a steam pump used to clear mines of water. This was much improved by the inventions of Thomas Newcomen. In 1776 James Watt put into use a much improved steam engine that used a separate condenser. The coal-powered steam engine from then on was used extensively in industry throughout Western Europe, but especially in England. The steam engine powered trains, ships, and factories. Physical leverage began to take its present form.

Not just industry and commerce were transformed. Louis Pasteur hypothesized the existence of germs that led to vaccination and pasteurization. Advances were made in chemistry, biology, mathematics—in fact, in every field of knowledge. Inventions proceeded at a rate never seen before. The scientific and technological revolution that was stimulated when Europe made contact with other cultures was fed by the mass distribution of data, information, and knowledge, made possible by the proliferation of fast presses that were in turn made possible by Gutenberg's breakthrough.

ASSOCIATED INTELLECTUAL DEVELOPMENTS IN THE PRINTING PRESS COMMUNICATION REVOLUTION. The printing press was a catalyst for the Protestant Reformation, the Renaissance, and the Industrial Revolution. When Gutenberg invented moveable type the Earth moved—literally. With the Church losing its monopoly on knowledge, other points of view—both religious and temporal—could develop. A new secular science took hold that accepted ideas previously considered heresy. Among these was the heliocentric view of the solar system. Yes, the world began to move around the Sun and it began to rotate as well.

How significant was moveable type? Well, just consider that in the Middle Ages, Europe consisted of small villages, in many ways a throwback to much earlier or Paleolithic times prior to the development of Greek and Roman civilizations. In conflicts with the Arab world, it kept finding itself on the losing end. China was a major civilization with seagoing vessels large enough to hold several European sailing ships on the deck of a single ship. And then within a few centuries Europe became the dominant force in the world, humbling the former great powers in battle, developing new bodies of knowledge and a standard of living that became the envy of the rest of the world.

The printing press was a catalyst for the modern corporation, modern science, and the modern nation-state. It was one of the tools that led to Europe's preeminence as a cultural, financial, military, and political power.

The Fourth Major Communication Revolution— Mechanical-Electrical Communication

But this was to change and Europe would be displaced by North America. A new invention, the telegraph, was to quietly mark the beginning of a new era. Its inventor, Samuel F. B. Morse, was prescient in his first transmitted message on May 24, 1844: "What hath God wrought." By itself it was a major invention, but few could imagine the new invention to come on its heels, which would totally transform our world—the telephone.

That was followed decades later by radio and then cameras, moving pictures, television, tape recorders, copy machines, fax machines, camcorders, wireless phones, and computers.

Whereas the printing press had been a revolution that mostly impacted the written word, telephone, radio, and television were revolutions in the spoken word. Several of the new inventions of this era, including the camera, film, and television, created a revolution in images.

These inventions increased the speed, reach, and immediacy of communication. Language, images, and music became forms of mass communication. Films, videos, sound recorders, and cameras have created new art forms and allowed for the storage of visual images and sounds. They have done to the spoken word and acting what books did to the written word. In the past a book had longevity beyond its author, but a performance of music or theater was like pastry—finished after the first viewing. Camera and voice recordings changed all that. Now a singer could be listened to well after his death. A particular performance could be viewed and listened to again and again. Music and art were democratized and made accessible to great numbers of people.

TOOLS IN THE ELECTRO-MECHANICAL COMMUNICATION REVOLUTION. From the point of view of sheer numbers the current period has dwarfed all others in terms of inventions and the advancement of knowledge. A brief list of inventions would include the internal combustion engine, automobiles, airplanes, jets, tractors, power tools, lasers, radar, submarines, methods to control electricity, satellites, computers, software, television, the paper clip, antibiotics, penicillin, genetic coding, and on and on.

ORGANIZATION IN THE ELECTRO-MECHANICAL COMMUNICATION REVOLUTION. In terms of size, the modern corporation dwarfs all prior organizations. Wal-Mart employs more than 1.3 million people. The twentieth century saw the development of a professional managerial class, management theory, and the study of organizations as a discipline. But interestingly most modern corporations have a limited lifetime. In *The Fifth Discipline*, Peter Senge claimed that the average life of a Fortune 500 corporation was forty-five years, less than the life expectancy of a person. On the other hand, some religious organizations have survived for hundreds and even thousands of years—the Catholic Church is close to 2,000 years old.

Organizations—like people—have life cycles and personalities. Some are young and energetic, some are old. Some are flexible, some are rigid. It is a mistake to categorize all organizations as being the same just as it is a mistake to lump all people together. While a complete treatment of this subject is a work unto itself, one important distinction can be made between organizations that are essentially institutions and those that are primarily vehicles. An organization can be a vehicle to make money, develop a technology, or get its founders rich. You would not expect one of these to have a long life. Once their mission is accomplished they can be sold, liquidated, or merged. But an organization that is an institution has a purpose in and of itself. Its purpose requires, or at least includes, its perpetuation. An institution has built-in safeguards that limit what the chief executive officer can do. In most companies the CEO can sell the company if he deems it necessary or profitable. But in an institution such an action must meet with the approval of other seats of power. One example of an institution is the U.S. government. The president cannot sell or merge the United States. He cannot lead it to war for very long without congressional approval. And as was demonstrated during the Vietnam War, even a small but energized minority can thwart his desires.

ASSOCIATED INTELLECTUAL DEVELOPMENTS IN THE ELECTRO-MECHANICAL COMMUNICATION REVOLUTION. Psychology, quantum mechanics, astrophysics, molecular biology, Chaos Theory, computer simulations, and computer graphics are just a few of the fields that did not exist when the telegraph was invented. Our knowledge base is now so immense that no single person—or even a group of people—can grasp anything but a small part of it.

Each of the four communication revolutions has been associated with an acceleration of human development. Each has initially favored societies who adapted and adopted over those who lagged. Literate societies ran over hunter-gatherers. The printing press helped Europe achieve economic and industrial preeminence. The electro-mechanical era favored North America. Now the more interesting question is, what lies ahead? In order to answer that, we need to look at some characteristics of trends. We can start by examining financial trends, in which people have invested a lot of effort to understand.

CHAPTER 17

THE POWER OF TRENDS

Several years ago I learned firsthand the power of long-term trends. I was active in New York City real estate and had been through some of its ups and downs. I felt strongly that the market had reached a peak and so I sold everything. Sure enough I was right. The market declined and a liquidity crisis ensued. Successful, multimillionaire real-estate entrepreneurs lost their capital almost overnight. Major developers including Olympia & York, the largest at the time, failed.

I looked good. While the rest of the real-estate community was reeling I was flush with cash. But in retrospect, although the timing of my move looked brilliant, I would have been better off financially if I had just held on to my properties because a few years later the market came roaring back. Had I not been so smart and done nothing, instead of selling at the top I would have been much better off down the road.

This experience vividly demonstrated to me not only that long-term trends exist but also that identifying and riding them can be very lucrative. Even if a person is wrong short-term, a powerful long-term trend can eventually bail him out as long as he manages to stay solvent. I had initially purchased my property during the 1970s, a time when New York City was still recovering from the effects of a mass exodus of people to the suburbs. It was evident to me at the time that, long-term, New York had a bright future as one of the major cities of the international economy. Gentrification had also begun, and this turned out to be another long-term trend. I had failed to grasp just how long-term these trends were.

Trends vs. Cycles

But how can you tell a trend from a cycle? A *trend* is a powerful movement that proceeds in a given direction for a term longer than our investment horizon. For investment purposes the best trends are those that stay intact for the remainder of the investor's life. A *cycle* reverses itself regularly and therefore requires constant surveillance. A cycle can also have very long swings, going up in one phase for many years and then down in another phase for years. How do we know that a trend won't reverse course and head the other way? We don't, not with the same degree of belief as we know a physical law that has been subjected to experimentation. Our degree of belief in the existence of an economic trend must necessarily be weaker and more tentative. But we can look back at past data and make an informed decision as to the longevity and strength of a long-term trend.

Trends and cycles do have similarities. No trend continues unabated. There are periods when the trend seems to die or other factors overwhelm it. But with a trend each succeeding high is higher than the prior one. Each succeeding low is also higher than the preceding low. There is no discernible direction among the lows and the highs of a cycle. Therefore if you happen to miss a low entry point and fail to purchase at an attractive level, it's not a major problem for that level will come back in time.

But even the largest and most powerful of trends may stop or reverse. One of the differences between a cycle and a trend is the time scale. A one-hundred-year cycle, with a fifty-year upswing followed by a fifty-year downswing, is effectively, for business and investment purposes, two trends. One generation that comes of age around the beginning of the upswing will see a trend throughout its business life. Another generation that comes of age around the beginning of the downswing will see the reverse trend. An important business and investment decision is determining which economic movements are cyclical and which are likely to be long-term trends.

The Trend as a Friend

Consider the implications of a trend as defined above. Each peak is higher than the preceding one. Each low is higher than the prior low.

Suppose you buy at the high. The market corrects and you feel foolish, but you are too proud to sell. Eventually the market recovers and the trend bails you out. On the other hand, suppose you sell at the high. You look good for a while. But when the trend recovers and restarts its upward move, you may not look so good. Thus the expression heard in commodity pits: "The trend is your friend."

Of course if you happen to sell at the high and buy back at a lower price you get the best of both worlds. But this requires an even higher level of skill and in most cases some luck. We need to distinguish between trading and investing. A trader will be moving in and out of the market and for him it might make a great deal of sense to sell in a trend if he purchased at a lower price. Trading is a different discipline than investing. Some good investors are good traders, but many are not. My comments here are really directed at business people and investors.

The Major Trends

The major trends we are dealing with are of extremely long duration. It is their duration that gives us confidence of their continuance. The first trend that we have been dealing with is man's conquest of material needs and the emergence of knowledge as the primary economic advantage. This trend started at least as early as when humans began making tools. The second trend, the Internet, is part of a communication trend that goes back to at least when humans first started speaking.

But is the Internet a powerful trend or is it just a fad? I argue that the Internet is a powerful trend with significant implications, not just for the human race but for the planet. First, the Internet is international in scope. It already spans the globe. It has several advantages over some of the other international communication media, such as television and telephone. It is more flexible: It can be a broadcast medium allowing you to broadcast to many like television and radio, or it can be a one-to-one communication vehicle like the telephone. It allows you to communicate in real time with a live person on the other end, but it also allows you to communicate off-line. One can leave an e-mail message or set up a website that others can access at will. And the cost of broadcasting is but a fraction of the cost of other media.

The Internet is less expensive than other media, but as interesting is the costing model. Once you pay to be on-line, most service providers allow you to spend as much time as you like on-line.

The Internet is global, ubiquitous, constantly gaining users, flexible, and inexpensive. But it has two other fascinating features. One, it is connected to a computer. This allows the integration of all the other communication tools such as radio, videos, movies, and voice and video recordings. It is the perfect tool for knowledge transference. It allows you to communicate in several different ways such as video, voice, or text. And two, it has unlimited development possibilities. It also feeds in beautifully with the other two trends—our move toward a knowledge economy and globalization.

There are alternatives to the Internet. Interactive satellite television is one. This is a medium broadcast through a television by satellite directly into homes and offices. In addition to allowing you to get programs from the service provider it allows you to access the Internet. And this is the key. It has access to unlimited connections with others and vast amounts of information that is different from all other media forms. How the universal forum is accessed will not make a difference to the big picture, but it may make a difference in terms of the financial return of one company over another.

Andy Grove, former CEO of Intel, wrote a book in the mid-1990s called *Only the Paranoid Survive*. In it he identifies Strategic Inflection Points, which are times in the life of a corporation when a change is occurring of such a magnitude that it threatens the life of the company unless the company quickly and forcefully changes behavior and strategy. He calls these 10X changes, to represent the fact that they are much more significant and more powerful than ordinary events affecting a business. They start out slowly but just seem to overwhelm companies that cannot respond. A Strategic Inflection Point sounds very much like a threshold as I defined them in Chapter 7. Recall that a threshold is a point where a linear change in one variable leads to a change in state, a discontinuous jump to a different level where the same behavior no longer has the same effect. Different rules apply when there is a change of state.

Grove mentions the Japanese invasion of the semiconductor memory business as a key Strategic Inflection Point for Intel and for him as the CEO. The Japanese were able to get higher yields and lower prices in memory chips, and Intel could only lose money in that business. As a result, as he states, Intel shifted strategy, left the memory business, and refocused on microprocessors, the brains of the personal computer. But what he does not mention is that Intel was also forced to radically improve the quality of its manufacturing techniques. They were forced to adopt process improvement tools and thinking that are essential for what I call internal quality in Chapter 4. Internal quality is one of the key components of The New Management. Like it or not, in order to survive Intel had to adopt Japanese methods and the quality ideas of Shewhart and Deming. This is a stark example of a powerful trend at work.

In his book, Grove concluded that for Intel, at least, the Internet was not at that time a 10X change. Intel's present strategy didn't need to be adjusted. In my opinion, the Internet shouldn't be looked upon as a 10X change—that is missing the point. It is more like a 100X change. It is of a different logical level. It will not work over ten years—but over one hundred years or more. It is creating a whole new medium. But one or several new innovations can very quickly turn the Internet into a threat to any established business or industry. Those inventions—whether hardware or software—that make use of the Internet can become the 10X factors that threaten individual businesses. And the Internet promises to spawn many of these inventions, which by definition none of us can see on the horizon right now.

One example is the ability to download music from the hard disks of other on-line computers. Napster, Gnutella, and other programs, mostly designed by very young people, have opened this Pandora's box. The record companies are protesting and using whatever legal means are at their disposal to try to stop it, but so far, though they have experienced some legal triumphs, their efforts have been futile.

Will the Internet lead to a new country or a new continent becoming preeminent? That is certainly a possibility but so far the trend appears to signal the emergence of a wealthy and upper middle class that spans the globe. An income disparity seems to be emerging with a well-educated, technologically savvy class earning much more and having ample opportunity while many others are stagnant in their earning power. And both groups are represented on every continent. You need not be in technology to prosper. Those who service the well-to-do, such as bankers, stockbrokers, and real-estate brokers, are also becoming part of the new elite.

The Effect of a Trend on Past Trends

We have very persuasive examples of newer technology completely replacing older technology, leading to the demise of established companies. The car, for instance, completely replaced the horse and buggy and destroyed the carriage-making industry, along with manufacturers of whips, boots, and other related accessories. The development of the integrated circuit made the inexpensive calculator and programmable calculators a reality. This eliminated the slide rule and all of its manufacturers.

But we also have some powerful counterexamples. Despite a slew of new materials, most of us still wear shoes made of leather, a material that dates back hundreds of thousands of years. Wool and cotton, two more very ancient materials, are also very much in use today.

The invention of moving pictures was seen by some as the death knell for reading and books. Television was to have destroyed movies and book publishing. The video game and the computer were signaling an end to books and writing. But book sales throughout these revolutions and technological developments only continued to grow. Writing as a vehicle of expression and communication has only found more uses and a larger audience. In fact, if you look back over the four communication revolutions as we defined them, each of them continues actively. The typewriter and the word processor did not put an end to handwritten notes. Virtually everyone I know, including those who grew up with computers, still writes some things by hand. No one, as far as I can make out, has given up speaking despite the development of writing. Computers, televisions, typewriters, radios, and movies have not put a dent in books, magazines, or the printing industry.

In fact, just the opposite has occurred. If anything the newer media have stimulated further growth and development of the earlier ones. Some people spend their whole days communicating with one or more of the available media. What has suffered is physical labor. Fewer of us are doing physical labor. As the need for pure human physical labor has declined, knowledge products—whether they be books, magazines, computer programs, movies, or television—have increased. The first trend, our conquest of the material, has enhanced and fed into the explosion of knowledge and communication products.

This has implications not just for work but for leisure as well. The person who does strenuous physical labor each day is not likely to go jogging early in the morning or upon her arrival at home after work. Instead her idea of leisure may be to sit around and be served.

But people who work sedentary or high-powered jobs with little physical activity need some kind of physical balance. This has helped feed the phenomenal growth in such unlikely activities as jogging, weight lifting, long-distance biking, and triathlons. Each year many more people than can possibly be accommodated apply to run the New York City marathon. Thousands of people are turned away.

Even here, however, in these very physical activities the need for knowledge goes unabated. Any of these activities is as much a mental game as it is physical. Knowing about your body, training, and eating requirements are essential not just for success but to prevent injury. And many people find music or tapes an essential part of their workout regime.

The Difference that Makes the Difference

Why have some technologies died with the development of new ones while others have survived? I believe there are several reasons. The car replaced the exact function of the horse and buggy. The calculator replaced all the functions of the slide rule and then added some more—it was just superior in every way. Most synthetic materials, on the other hand, fail to do one or more things as well as either leather, cotton, or wool.

In the case of communication media, however, there is one additional factor. I believe each major way of communicating, such as speech, writing, and singing and acting, involves a different part of the mind. As a result all the videos in the world will not satisfy the need for a book. Some people will have a preference for a book almost all the time while others will prefer a video format. Some people need both videos and books. And there are enough of each type of person to support many different media.

Printing technology has developed steadily for 560 years. Costs have declined, uses increased, and it has become entrenched in many industries. Printed products surround us in ways we take for granted. Virtually every mass-produced product has some printing on it. The press is used to make the images and words not just for our books, magazines, and newsletters, but also for all the canned and bottled goods we consume, for the wallpaper in our houses, and for the designs on our tissue papers and toilet papers. Indeed we are surrounded by images and lettering printed by presses that are the direct descendants of Gutenberg's press.

Effects of Newer Media on the Old

The newer media are impacting the older ones. One notable example is the way speech is being affected by television, radio, films, and videos. In the 1950s I traveled with my family to the southern states of Georgia, North Carolina, and South Carolina. We found it extremely difficult to understand many of the residents of those states. Yes, they all spoke English but it was very different from the mid-Atlantic American English I had grown up with. I had a similar experience in the 1970s when I traveled through Europe and happened to meet up with one English fellow from Liverpool. It took me several days to acclimate my ear to his speaking patterns and pronunciation. Even after several days I often had to ask him to repeat himself so I could understand him.

In more recent trips throughout the States, however, I have had a very different experience. On a trip to Texas I found many of the residents had relocated from the Northeast and the Midwest. While the long-time residents had a different inflection, the difference was minor and I had no problems comprehending them. Languages left in isolation change rapidly and different regions quickly develop not just different pronunciations for the same word but different words as well. The universal nature of television and films has ended the isolation of speech in every region in the United States. The average household has a television on for seven hours a day. We all grow up surrounded by television, radio, and film, and we can't help but be influenced by the language spoken in them.

Whereas British English used to sound quite exotic to the American ear, listening to BBC news on PBS I am surprised by how little their speech differs from ours. I have no difficulty at all understanding my friends from New Zealand or Australia. In fact, when my pen pal from Auckland in New Zealand sent me an e-mail joke describing ten ways that you could tell someone was from her city, I had to laugh. I laughed not because these traits were so different or unusual but because they would describe people on Long Island, where I live, just as well. One item on the list was "You spend more money on your coffee maker than on your washing machine." Another item was "You order organic fruits and veggies on-line, but eat out every night anyway."

Gourmet coffees, organic fruits and veggies, and really great parking spots are as American as apple pie. I was surprised to find that they are also as New Zealand as kiwi. It struck me that not only is globalization a reality but that we have already created, at least culturally, one large super-state. That super-state includes the United States, Canada, Australia, New Zealand, Great Britain, Ireland, and most of continental Europe. We buy the same items, the same brands, and watch much of the same movies. We get our news from the same sources and speak a common language. The fourth communication revolution has helped produce a common culture, part of what is being called globalization. Japan and parts of Asia are a part of the super-state as well, although because of language differences they are not as fully integrated—yet.

Earlier Globalization

Globalization refers to international investments, mobility of labor and capital across borders, transnational organizations, and development of a common culture. There was an earlier period of globalization that by these measures was comparable to the current era. The earlier period ranged from the latter part of the nineteenth century to the beginning of the twentieth century and ended, some would say culminated, with World War I.

Foreign assets accounted for 20% of the collective gross domestic product of the world before 1914. That declined to 5% in 1945. It took sixty years for that number to recover to its pre–World War I level. Today it stands at 57%. Half of British savings were invested abroad. Levels in Germany, France, Belgium, and the Netherlands were comparable. These are far higher levels than anything we see today in the United States and Europe.

There were no passports and minimal restriction on immigration allowed for what may have been the largest mass migration in human history. One-seventh of the world's working-age population emigrated to a different nation between 1870 and 1925. The development of the telephone made foreign investments more practical. In addition technological breakthroughs in transportation made it less expensive for Europeans to bring in grain from the Americas than to grow it in their own back-yard. At the same time, workers attracted by the cheap land and high wages of the Americas and Australia left densely populated Europe.[37]

Many benefited from that earlier period of globalization. The major economies of Australia and the Americas grew enormously, the standard of living of poorer nations improved, and wages in Europe improved. But at the same time there were some losers and people who wanted to protect their new prosperity. Native laborers resented the new immigrants who were willing to work for less. Landowners and farmers in Europe resented the foreign competition. Tribalism reared its ugly side and a world war sparked a rapid decline in international trade and globalization.

A Model for Transformation

In the late 1980s companies instituting some aspect of Quality Man-agement were experiencing dramatic improvements. I was anxious to bring these ideas to other companies, especially smaller and mid-size companies. Much of the improvement results from a focus on process over results. But I noticed that even companies that had experienced significant improvements often reverted to their old ways of doing things just a few years later.

As I became more involved with the actual change process, I devel-oped a model to map and effect successful change. For change to be effective and to last, especially radical changes or transformations, three levels of a corporation must be addressed. These are Beliefs, People, and Systems. Any organization you can think of has these three levels or dimensions. These are more basic and fundamental than are many other aspects of an organization. Not every organization has customers. A cus-tomer is someone who pays for the services he receives. If he is unhappy with the product or service, he can take his money elsewhere. Nonprof-its don't have customers. The people who pay for the services, the donors, are not the ones who receive the service. The actual service may be given away free or it may be subsidized by the donors. Government agencies don't have customers. The users have no alternative. They must

[37] *The New York Times*, August 11, 2001.

deal with the government agency to get their license, keep their property, or whatever other service is involved. Clubs don't have customers. But clubs, government agencies, and nonprofits all have beliefs by which they operate and people that provide their services and systems.

Most managers will fall into one of two categories. When asked what management is about some will answer it is about people. Others will answer it's about good systems. It is natural for a manager wishing to effect change to work on the one area where she feels most comfortable. Some managers will immediately examine the systems and then suggest changes. Others will look at the people and make changes there. Few will look at the overall beliefs and culture of a company.

Yet to be effective, change must operate in all three dimensions of a company. Of course if a company already has a good culture and beliefs, less work has to be done in that area. A company with good people but lousy systems needs much less work on people and more emphasis on process.

Rarely do managers appreciate the extent to which beliefs and culture must be impacted to have lasting change. Some politicians, especially revolutionary ones, have a strong appreciation of the power of beliefs in organizations and nations. Lenin was an example of someone who knew that he had to change the thinking of Russians in order to make his dream of a socialist state possible. The founding fathers of the United States understood the power of beliefs, as evidenced by the documents they created, the Declaration of Independence and the Constitution.

Change can get way ahead of the underlying belief system. When this happens expect a reversion. If the change has also left some people behind and hurt them in some way, violence and anger may accompany the reversion. A company that is not failing but realizes it needs to change may ask some outsiders to come in and give it new direction. Consultants will prepare studies if requested but these studies will have no effect. Most of the time they are requested to back up a manager's pet project. If they fail to do so the studies are ignored. But when someone comes in and starts to make dramatic changes, whether that person is an outsider or a new executive, she needs to convince the rest of the organization to go along. To force the change, the new executive might rearrange furniture, transfer people between departments, eliminate coffee makers or a lunch room, or do something else dramatic.

And the people in the organization, often referred to as the old-timers, will move to undo as much as they can. They will sabotage the new management, complain to higher executives if they exist, and/or bring in their own coffee makers—unless there is an acceptance of the idea that the old ways are failing and new beliefs must be adopted.

The same is true of change on a national or international level. Change must occur in beliefs, especially at the metaknowledge level, in order for it to be effective and take root. Let me give one example. During the Middle Ages, most of the philosophical tracts of the ancient world disappeared. With the burning of the library at Alexandria around the fourth century A.D., the West entered a period of intellectual intolerance. The writings of Aristotle, however, survived better than others. Aristotle and other Greek philosophers became the metaphysicians of the Church. Since the Church dominated Western thinking, Aristotle became the one writer that an educated man had to read, comprehend, and agree with. His thinking dominated Western thought. In fact, because of this, much of the progress of the West in science and philosophy has been the result of refuting Aristotle.[38] But in the beginning, to question Aristotle was to invite excommunication.

In Aristotle's thinking people could be property. This was nothing unusual or innovative. He grew up in a world where slavery was commonplace. The victors in war took the losers as slaves. Aristotle and the other thinkers of antiquity defended the practice of slavery as passionately as the practice of private property; slaves were property.

Subsequently the Western world had no difficulty accepting the institution of slavery when it was economically convenient to do so. The Church was powerless to do anything about it since Aristotle was so central to Church dogma.

This confusion of people with property has led to much misery and muddled thinking. It is relatively recent that this proposition has been overthrown. For most civilized people today the notion that people can be property is repulsive. We find the idea of having physical slaves unworthy of a civilized person who has received the benefit of an advanced society.

The question of whether people could be property was heatedly debated. In the United States, its resolution was decided by war. This is

---

[38] *A History of Western Philosophy,* by Bertrand Russell.

an idea at a metaknowledge level. Where slavery was commonplace, it was taken for granted. For many people its justification was probably unconscious. It was made conscious and debated in a political arena. But no amount of argument or empirical research could prove the question one way or another. This was part of our ethical development, which happens in the framework of larger beliefs that must necessarily change as we and our society grow, develop, and change.

We operate with assumptions about property. Property used to include people, land, mineral rights, animals, wives, and children. People who were adamant that all these things were property were willing to defend those assumptions to the death. Yet we have changed and have made different distinctions. Most people in modern society believe that people, wives, and children cannot be property. In order for us to have strong property rights, we must be clear as to what constitutes property and what does not.

When our assumptions—our metaknowledge—change, the world shifts. The changes occurring now are no less profound than the changes that occurred when our scientific belief changed from a static Earth at the center of the universe to the Earth being one of several planets revolving around an average size star, of which there were countless more in existence.

Our central location on the Earth as the only sentient beings is challenged by Koko the gorilla. The sperm whale has a massive brain many times larger than ours. It is an accepted idea of evolutionary theory that organs with little use reduce in size over time. It is possible that the whale's brain creates a "multi-dimensional living map of the oceans."[39] Such mapping would require great memory and processing ability. But such a large brain is almost certainly versatile. Is it possible that a whale thinks and feels on a thought level beyond our current understanding? Just the possibility of sentience and intelligence is enough to change our beliefs and eventually our laws concerning other animals.

Trends in Beliefs

Just for a moment suspend judgment and look at the trends in beliefs over the last century or two. In the sixteenth century just saying the

---

[39] *Gaia: A New Look at Life on Earth*, by James Lovelock, page 140.

Earth was not the center of the solar system was enough to lead to excommunication, torture, and death. In the last 150 years, our place as central and unique creatures of the earth has been increasingly challenged. The evidence continues to mount that while we have some special skills, we are a part of nature and not above or beyond her. There is the emergence of the theory of evolution through natural selection and genetics in science. The birth of the American Society for the Prevention of Cruelty to Animals is another. Rachel Carson's book *Silent Spring* was yet another powerful force leading to what has become a worldwide ecological movement.

Today in developed countries, many kinds of development need to be accompanied by environmental impact studies. Should an endangered species be threatened by that development, the project is almost sure to get scuttled. By international agreement, the hunting of whales, formerly of some economic importance to some countries, has been outlawed. In 2001 the killing of a pet dog by an enraged motorist drew national attention, and the man responsible was sentenced to three years in prison. Increasingly animals are being treated by society and the law not as property but as sentient beings.

Justice has become transnational. Generals acting on command from the state—even heads of state—are being tracked down and tried for actions they performed in the service of their country *but that violated human rights.* Our sense of justice is shifting. The nation-state is being relegated to a secondary position subject to a transnational sense of justice, a universal recognition of human rights, a respect for nature, and an enlargement of the community of sentient beings.

Just fifty years ago these developments would have been unthinkable. But there is a clear trend indicating that the accepted beliefs of the developed world are changing. Indeed there is a co-evolution between our beliefs, especially at a metaknowledge level, and the laws and accepted mores of the world. As our perception of animal sentience, our roles in nature, and the validity of nation-states change, so will our laws, our politics, and acceptable business practices.

One aspect of MetaKnowledge strongly influencing our behavior is the increasing acceptance that the systems view of ourselves, nature, and business must play at least an equal role to the more individualistic role. The systems view looks at explanations of behavior from the whole to the individual. It assumes we are all interconnected, and seemingly isolated actions in one part of a system can have unpredictable consequences in what may appear to be an unconnected part of the system. It is clear to me that the emerging global culture is embracing the systemic view of life and the economy. Other parts of MetaKnowledge will over time gain greater general acceptance as well.

CHAPTER 18

GLOBALIZATION
AND ECONOMIC
UNCERTAINTY

Two aspects of globalization are economic and cultural. Economic globalization in turn has two facets, financial and trade.

1. Financial Globalization. Financial markets are being integrated worldwide. Currencies, debt instruments, and equities of major firms are traded in major capital markets around the world. One can buy IBM stock in Singapore or Dallas. While New York and Chicago sleep, Tokyo, Hong Kong, and Singapore are busy trading. This is made possible by the communication links and computers of the modern world. Capital can and does move quickly from one market to another.

The amount of capital and liquidity available in the international markets dwarfs the liquidity available to any single major player, including governments. As a result governments are forced by the international financial markets to play by rules of openness and disclosure. To a large extent they are treated like any other borrower and forced to behave in a prudent financial manner. While governments still play a special role, their roles have been diminished and conscripted by their need to tap the financial markets for funds. This is true of Malaysia and the United States, although to different degrees. Developed countries like the United States have a capital base—this is part of what makes a developed nation. Developed countries can therefore attract a fair amount of capital from domestic sources, while a developing country like Malaysia needs capital from foreign sources.

But the United States enjoys a great advantage in that its currency is one of the hard currencies readily accepted as being a safe haven politically and economically. Because of this it can run large balance-of-payments deficits as foreigners feel safe holding dollars and reinvesting them in dollar-denominated assets. The fact that the U.S. government can print or create dollars in other ways and has taxing authority to raise dollars gives it extra credibility and strength as long as the dollar is considered safe by investors.

But even here there are limitations on what the U.S. government can do. Should it decide at some point to create more money to deal with its obligations, it might very well create a movement out of the dollar. The three main hard currencies of the latter part of the twentieth century were the U.S. dollar, the Japanese yen, and the German deutsche mark. The strength of the U.S. economy in the 1990s gave the dollar more strength and credibility than the other major currencies. But Europe's launching of the Euro, a currency issued to replace the deutsche mark, the French frank, the Dutch guilder, and the other currencies of the nations of the European Union, has created a currency that can challenge the dollar as the standard international currency.

There is one other way that the U.S. government has greater strength in international financial markets than less developed nations such as Malaysia and Argentina. Should there be a flight of capital out of the dollar into the Euro or some other currency it would not draw down the foreign currency reserves of the U.S. government. The United States is not obligated to defend the price of the dollar. The dollar is a floating exchange rate and its value relative to other major currencies is determined by the market. Second- and third-world currencies, often on the advice of the International Monetary Fund, are pegged to the dollar. These countries are obligated to defend the price of their currency. Should the market value their currency at less than the official rate they are forced to sell their foreign currency reserves to buy their own currency, raise domestic interest rates, or take some other strong measure. This can be disastrous for a country. One recent example was Argentina, which pegged its peso to the dollar in 1991. When the dollar kept rising in the 1990s, the Argentine government had to respond. The last years of the twentieth century left Argentina in a prolonged recession with unemployment rates reaching 20%. By the end of 2001, Argentina defaulted on $141 billion in foreign debt and in February 2002 the peso was floated and all dollar debts were converted into pesos by declaration of the Argentine government. Much of the savings of the Argentine middle class evaporated. It is ironic that the less developed nations were heavily pressured to peg their currencies while the strongest nations with the most capital had let their currencies float.

2. Trade Globalization. Multinational corporations with international brands such as Coke, Gucci, Chanel, Ford, Toyota, IBM, and Microsoft are recognized worldwide. Increasingly, the people of the world are buying in a common market. Lesser-known brands, nonbranded items, commodities, and services are also part of global trade. Although there are still many barriers to trade such as quotas and tariffs, goods trade more freely now than at any time in recent history. Government attempts to restrict trade lead to black or gray markets. The integration is more complete than the word "trade" would suggest. A French name brand product might be designed in Italy, manufactured in Malaysia in a plant owned by Ethnic Chinese, with Australian leather, financed by a British bank, and sold in New Jersey.

Labor has also taken on a global characteristic, but with a twist. While there is some emigration of labor and managerial personnel, the more interesting aspect today is the farming out of work, often highly technical and skilled work, from the developed world to other parts of the globe. Software programming, for instance, is being farmed out by North American companies to computer scientists in Pakistan and India. Advanced communication links make this feasible.

3. Cultural Globalization. Films, videos, music, and books have international audiences. American audiences enjoy the films of Japanese director Akira Kurosawa and Japanese audiences appreciate Steven Spielberg films. The National Basketball Association is viewed with the same enthusiasm in Hong Kong as in Chicago. The Olympics has helped make sports an international obsession. Opera, rock, and African music have audiences throughout the world. The three tenors, one Italian, one Spanish, one Mexican, had their concerts broadcast around the world. Art, science, and mathematics are already global.

Large gaps in this integration are begging to be filled. While I have a choice of Argentine or Italian parmesan to eat with my California figs and local cherries, for four years in a row, I could not watch Lance Armstrong win the Tour de France. I am a cycling fan but cycling is a minor sport in the United States, virtually ignored by the networks and cable stations. Instead I am treated to endless rounds of football and golf. But cycling is a major sport in Europe. I was able to view the Tour through videos obtained by someone in my cycling club from a European source. In my case, cultural globalization has not gone far enough.

This chasm in the global cultural network could be filled by the Internet. A glimpse at the future is provided by the now defunct service Napster. Napster allowed the direct exchange of any music file among users as long as it was on the hard drive of just one of its users. Napster used a central server to search each user's hard drive. A person could search for an artist and find hundreds of recordings by that artist in the hard drives of other users. It was then a simple matter to download one or more musical recordings. This attracted the attention of the record companies, since a copyrighted song could be transferred just as easily as any other. In less than two years, Napster attracted more than sixty million users. To put this in perspective, it took America Online more than fifteen years to gain twenty million users. A judge was able to issue an injunction to shut down the server, virtually closing Napster.

The really interesting part, however, is that the downloading of music on the Internet has not decreased. Other programs, such as Gnutella and Freenet, that do not rely on a single server to hook up users are available and have gained in popularity since Napster was shuttered. The newer programs will be more difficult to shut both legally and technically. It will be very difficult to stop private users from making copies of material for their own use.

But consider the implications. A user of the Internet could potentially have access to every file on every computer that is on-line at any given point in time. This means not just music files, but files of all kinds, including video and text. This is giving us the ability to get the information, song, or show we want when we want it. A just-in-time global information source.

Other Effects of Global Markets

Globalization is neither a panacea nor the end of the world. It gives us more choices while eliminating others. Another example of global trade is the international drug trade. While many would consider this a negative effect, it shows the power of markets to overcome government resistance. The same government that champions the cause of free markets around the world finds itself helpless to stop a less desirable part of it. After years and untold billions of dollars spent on the drug war, the only noticeable effect is an increase in the prison population at home.

This is a caution flag to governments, established companies, and consumers alike. Markets develop in ways dictated by users and producers. Governments have but limited effects. This is especially true in global markets.

But this caveat is not limited to markets. People have shown themselves capable of throwing out corrupt or entrenched governments that failed to let go when their support waned. In the last thirty years we have seen the ouster of Ferdinand Marcos in the Philippines, President Suharto in Indonesia, and Milosevic in Yugoslavia. We have seen the Berlin wall smashed and former communist dictators in Eastern Europe tried, imprisoned, and executed. Mahatma Gandhi showed that with proper organization, leadership, and will, even the most powerful of governments could be forced to yield. Martin Luther King, Jr., learning from Gandhi, changed the American landscape in ways that no one would have predicted beforehand.

Gandhi and King both relied on the media—newspapers in one case and television in the other—to convey the violence wrought by those in power upon innocent nonviolent protesters. The conscience of a great number of people had to be stirred. And the intended audience needed to have a shared set of values that included justice and equality for all.

Abraham Maslow, who developed the theory of a hierarchy of needs and was discussed in Chapter 13, found that, for the most part, self-actualizing people shared the same values. Recall that when a person's basic needs are satisfied, including his physiological need for food, shelter, and clothing; his need for love and affiliation; his need for security; and his need for esteem there is a possibility of his becoming self-actualizing. What drives them are beyond needs, so he called these metaneeds or metamotivation. This is the desire to live a fulfilling and creative life. This is what humans under the best of circumstances can become. And interestingly, self-actualizing people share the same values. This was not something he theorized, this was something he observed. This is empirical data. And this suggested to him that ethics could be moved from a philosophical discipline, based on what someone believed we should value, to an empirical science, based on observation of the best humanity has to offer.

A better world requires (1) accurate and quick global communications and (2) for great numbers of people to be self-actualizing. This is only possible with a certain level of affluence. Under President McKinley in the early years of the twentieth century, the Philippine uprising was brutally put down using tactics that today would qualify as war crimes. Our actions against Native Americans in the eighteenth and nineteenth centuries could only be called barbaric. In these and earlier cases both the media documenting and broadcasting the events and the necessary affluence were absent. As a result these "wars" were not just tolerated but admired.

What Kind of Global Culture?

It may appear that we are headed toward a global culture with an oversize American influence. The opening of McDonald's restaurants throughout the world lends credence to that notion. It could be argued that such brands as McDonald's, Coke, Tide, and others, along with the promotional and advertising techniques developed in North America and now used throughout the world, are leading to an Americanization of global culture. But it is not quite so simple. As I mentioned earlier, Chinese restaurants outnumber McDonald's in my neck of the woods by twenty to one. When my daughter visited me to celebrate Father's Day, we had her favorite food—sushi. Who would have thought that Americans would be eating raw fish? And not just eating it but loving it. Where are the gourmet restaurants serving American food? The best restaurants claim their cuisine is French, Italian, Chinese, Spanish, Japanese, or Continental. Our taste in foods has undergone a radical transformation, especially among the middle class and the well-to-do. What is American cuisine now, anyway?

We have seen several unexpected shifts in our culture over the last fifty years. Fifty years ago Americans were known as sprinters. Few would have considered jogging more than half a mile—much less running a marathon. Today the marathons of the major cities are forced to turn away runners due to lack of space to accommodate them all. Triathlons are an even more extreme form of competition and probably everyone knows someone who competes. A significant proportion of the population has worked out with weights or some other form of resistance training.

Religious and spiritual views are undergoing profound changes as well. While the Christian fundamentalist movement has made itself visible in the United States through its participation in politics, many parishes of established Christian churches are losing members. The churches of North America are in a crisis. Some don't have enough members to support the parish. Others don't have sufficient priests or ministers for the parishes. On a recent trip to Montreal, I visited a large basilica and the tour guide told us that just 1.5% of the population attends services regularly. About forty years ago Canadians went through a period of disillusionment with the Catholic church, when a scandal similar to the sexual scandals of 2002 in the United States became public. Yet Christianity is flourishing elsewhere. Probably the most dynamic Christian continent is now Africa, where churches and parishes are mushrooming. But in North America more people are meditating, doing yoga, t'ai-ch'i, ch'i gong, or some other form of spiritual practice, most of which have their origins in the East.

Equally startling has been a rash of books about angels, near-death experiences, and past-life experiences. Thirty years ago, anyone claiming to have been visited by an angel or have had a past-life experience was a rarity that invited ridicule. Today these are just as likely to have a sympathetic audience.

There is a shift occurring in the Western view of the cosmos. Roman civilization adopted the religions of two of its conquered peoples. First the gods of Greece, such as Zeus and Aphrodite, were adopted and became the official religion of the state. Later a small sect of another conquered people, the Jews, took the empire by storm, and Christianity became the official religion of the state under the Emperor Constantine. The Native Americans stand in the same relationship to the United States as ancient Greece and ancient Israel stood to the Roman Republic and the Roman Empire. We are seeing a renewed interest in the religious and spiritual practices of the Lakota indians, the Hopi indians, and other tribes. Certainly their respect for Earth, the sense that they are part of nature and not apart from it, is an attitude embraced by more people in North America. While no one can foretell the future, if history is a guide, the influence of Native American culture on the mainstream culture will increase.

Our science, too, is changing. In the early part of the twentieth century, relativity theory and especially quantum mechanics rocked the foundations of Western science. The data were so strange and so contrary to our experience and our beliefs that it induced an existential crisis for the physicists of the time. Interestingly there are strong parallels between quantum mechanics and Taoist and Buddhist philosophy. These were lucidly described by Fritjof Capra in *The Tao of Physics*. Chaos Theory or nonlinear dynamical systems theory, cybernetics, and other theories are influencing and changing other sciences and management theory. While the rest of the world is buying into American culture, on several levels we are going through shifts that are no less significant.

Balance of Trade and Politics

When California was largely undeveloped in the early part of the twentieth century, the federal government adopted policies directing capital to the western states in an attempt to jump-start their development. If we had tracked the balance of trade for most of the twentieth century, the eastern United States would have had a significant balance of trade deficit with the western states.

Today, the western states—especially California—would be considered the equal of any eastern state in terms of wealth and influence. While there still may be more capital and wealth in the East, much of the technological progress is taking place in the West, Southwest, and Rocky Mountains area. As a result of running huge trade deficits and allowing for the westward flow of funds, the West has essentially caught up with the East. Some would say it has overtaken the eastern states. But are the eastern states worse off as a result or are they better off?

I believe most observers would say that the East is better off. Sure there has been some initial loss of population and certain industries have moved west, including filmmaking, semiconductors, and computer programming. But the financial industries of the East have prospered with more companies and more investors to work with. The range of available goods and services for people on both coasts has increased. The whole country—east, west, north, south, and middle—is better off.

Today the same thing is occurring globally. The developed world, especially the United States, is running a balance of trade deficit with the rest of the world. In the case of the United States, the deficit is huge—much larger than anyone thought possible just a few years ago. It consistently has exceeded one hundred billion dollars a year for the last several years. But are we better off or worse off as a result?

Of course if the result is a world where more people are productively employed and on their way to economic independence where there are more customers who can afford our products and more products and services to choose from, we could easily argue this is a very good thing. It is exactly analogous to the economic development of the western United States. But there are several caveats. In the development of the western states, it was the same government that oversaw both the eastern and western states. Anyone living in the East could move west without impunity, even without a passport. It was all "our" country. No one had a sense that the money or the benefits were going elsewhere, except when the East had a major recession. Then there was pressure to readjust the federal mechanism that allocated federal funds to the regions.

But most of us still have a tendency to view nations—perceived as benefiting from our trade deficit—as "them" opposed to "us." This tendency is exaggerated whenever hard times occur. In the last major period of globalization nationalism overtook the dream of a unified world with commerce uniting everyone. The outbreak of World War I pushed people back into their national shells and into a mode of mass killing and destruction. To avoid a recurrence we need to view other people as "us" and not as "them"—or even worse as "it." But we must also allow for people's need for affiliation. We cannot destroy, stomp on, or ridicule people's need to be associated with a religion, nation, ethnic group, or culture.

The world right now can be seen in a broad sense as having three different sectors or super-states with different degrees of development. There is the developed super-state of North America, Japan, Great Britain, the European Union, Australia, and New Zealand. The second sector includes countries who are vying hard to join the developed world. This includes Taiwan, Korea, other Asian nations, parts of South and Central America, and parts of China. The third sector includes countries who are still quite poor. This would include most of Africa, some nations in Asia and the Americas, and parts of China. But there are people in each region who have the wealth and education to be considered part of the developed world.

From the point of view of Maslow's Hierarchy of Needs, each region is centered on a different need. The people of the developed super-state have had most of their needs met. The need for financial security, love, and affiliation are probably two needs that many people are looking to fulfill. But many people are in a position to become self-actualizing. In the developing world there is still the need for material comfort but the need for esteem or status seems more strongly felt. In the poor regions it is still the basic material sufficiency and physical security needs that are paramount.

Each area displays different behavior toward new events and technologies. For instance Asian nations are adopting cell phones faster than North America. In China and Korea it's a craze and people have to have the newest phone. China and Korea do not have the number of landline phones that the developed world has, so a cell phone means more than just a convenient way of communicating. It can represent status and reflect a kind of parity with people in the developed world, the desire to catch up. In North America, on the other hand, phones have been ubiquitous for more than fifty years. The cell phone is a nice addition, but there is little status associated with a new phone.

The developmental needs of each region are quite different. What one sector needs might be totally counterproductive to another. This mimics organizations. A young entrepreneurial organization will experience growing pains. At certain thresholds it needs to make changes to its structure if it is to keep growing. In general, younger corporations need to develop more structure and begin growing metasystems. But the prescription for older companies with a high degree of bureaucracy is totally different. There you need to get rid of excessive structure and force the company to look outward instead of inward. Ichak Adizes examines these issues for corporations in his book *Corporate Lifecycles*.

While greater integration of economies might be desirable among members of the developed super-state, it is not at all clear that the other regions need the same. True, most of those in the developing regions would like to get greater market access for their goods, especially their agricultural and manufactured goods, in the developed super-state. But to force our solutions upon others can lead to a backlash. In my consulting practice I have learned that organizational development requires a sense of timing. Some things happen on their own time and one must wait for signals that a company is ready for the next step before proceeding. This is probably even more true for larger organizations, such as nations. I question a rush to push through additional free trade treaties. I say this from the point of view of someone who believes in free trade, favors greater cultural integration, and believes the trends of globalization are inevitable. But why not do it right even if it takes a few more years—or for that matter, a few more decades?

Economic Integration Leading to Common Destinies

Because of the size of our economy, our military strength, and our leadership in media and technology, the United States has more influence and impact on the world stage than any other single country. And that presents a predicament. During the last U.S. presidential election many citizens of the world felt they should have had a vote even though they were neither U.S. residents nor citizens. After all, who is elected president affects many people outside of our borders. Why shouldn't they, the argument goes, have a vote in their own future?

This is a good question that brings up other questions. If other nations were to vote for the president of the United States, should they also serve in the U.S. military when there is a military conflict? Could they be subject to treason if they fought against the United States? Economic and cultural globalization will inevitably bring up questions of political integration.

Some of the most influential organizations of the world have not been governments, but certain foundations and nonprofit organizations. Amnesty International and Greenpeace are two organizations that come to mind. They rely on credibility and sympathy from people to be effective. But in large measure their credibility and strength also emanate from their independence from any government.

Economic integration brings up some delicate and complex problems. The United States is running a huge trade deficit. The last two decades of the twentieth century were economic boom times. In order for us to run a large trade deficit and maintain a strong dollar, we must be selling something else such as services or investments to the rest of the world. A strong dollar plus a rising stock market enabled the trade deficit to grow with no pain. We became stockbrokers to the world. Our trade deficit stimulated other economies of the world. But there is a downside to this. Should our deficit decline it would force a massive adjustment in certain parts of the global economy. The world is closely linked to the American economy and American valuations of real estate and stocks. Should we suffer a severe downturn that leads to a significant contraction of the trade deficit, the rest of the world will suffer as well.

In the first two years of the twenty-first century, North America went into a recession that severely affected manufacturing and financial services industries. But the trade deficit did not shrink. Indeed, manufacturing continues to move abroad, with U.S. plants closing and that production moving to other countries, most notably China. In addition, rapidly declining interest rates have allowed homeowners to refinance their homes and pull capital out of their home equity. Lower mortgage rates allow buyers to qualify for a larger mortgage that allows them to spend more on a new home. This has helped push house prices higher, making existing homeowners wealthier, at least on paper, and has allowed them to take out some of this equity by refinancing their existing mortgages at lower interest rates. The net result has been that the consumer has felt wealthier and relatively well off with more cash available to him even though unemployment has climbed to 6%. But the rest of the world has seen their economies slow down as well. And many nations are hoping to increase exports to pull them out of a slowdown. The question is, export to whom? Can the U.S. trade deficit continue to grow indefinitely? This is certainly problematic.

Standard economic theory would state that if we lowered the trade deficit, the dollar would become firmer. But with a highly integrated world economy, matters can become much more complex. A smaller trade deficit might lead to a smaller inflow of funds from abroad that are available for investment in real estate and equities. Should this result in lower prices for real estate and equities and stimulate further sales and therefore declines in prices, the net effect could be very negative very quickly. In a highly integrated world economy, a trade deficit for certain economies might be a very positive thing. Attempts to lower the trade deficit might lead to a worse economic condition, not a better one.

But we have a demographic cycle in play that could do just that. Births like most things in nature are not uniformly or randomly distributed. There is a large bulge in the population known as the baby boom. After World War II the United States and Europe experienced a dramatic increase in the formation of families and births, starting in 1946.

That continued until 1964 and then for roughly ten years there was a dramatic decrease in the number of births. In *The Great Boom Ahead,* Harry S. Dent Jr. argued that baby boomers entering their peak earning (and investing) years around 1980 were in large part responsible for the U.S. economic boom that started in the early 1980s as well as the stock market boom. However, when the baby boomers start to retire we will see the opposite economic effects. That is to say they will spend less and will divest their stock portfolios.

If there is even a mild correlation between this demographic trend and economic trends, then we could see some very uncomfortable times starting in the latter years of this decade, not just in the United States but in the global economy. The first boomers turn sixty-two, the traditional early retirement age, in 2008. They can start withdrawing from IRAs at age fifty-nine in 2005. They reach sixty-five in 2011, and from there on in large numbers of Americans reach retirement age.

According to Maslow's observations, self-actualization is found mostly in people in their late fifties and older. As the baby boomers retire it is possible that many of them will experience self-actualization. And since self-actualizers have had most of their needs met they tend not to spend lots of money on material needs. Their egos are not tied up in material possessions—an older car will do just fine, thank you. Besides the strain on social security—a large percentage of the population will be retired—our economy could be much less robust as well. If they drive their cars longer, spend less, draw funds from Social Security, and sell their portfolios, we could see a very different economic period.

CHAPTER 19

NEW ECONOMIC PARADIGMS

Is economics a science or a moral study? John Maynard Keynes, the great economist, referred to economics as a moral discipline since theories could not be directly tested and thus "proved" or disproved. Just consider one of the basic laws, the law of supply and demand. Anyone with formal training in economic theory learns of supply and demand curves. As demand for a product increases, its price increases so demand curves slope upward. As supply of the same product increases, price decreases; therefore supply curves slope downward. Where the two curves meet, supply equals demand. At this price equilibrium is reached. This is the market price.

This seems elegant and logical. But to be science it must be testable and falsifiable. How do we test this theory of supply and demand curves? Demand curves can't be found. Neither can supply curves. They are purely hypothetical constructs with no way of being measured. Further, if we find an example that seems to defy the smooth relationship implied by demand and supply curves, it is explained away. Both demand and supply curves can shift. A change in price can be caused by a shift in supply or a shift in demand and there is no way of telling which. No outcome is sufficient to lead to negation of the theory. It is not falsifiable. This is fatal for any theory if it is to be considered science.

Supply and demand curves seem to provide some insights into market behavior, and therefore one could argue not to throw out the baby with the bathwater. But the insights are not subject to testing. Are they really useful or are we just conveniently deceiving ourselves? If we are to be intellectually honest and rigorous we must discard supply and demand curves as part of the science of economics. They may be part of its history but not part of its science.

The old theory says that when supply and demand remain the same, the price remains the same. But when the oil supplying nations decided to coordinate their actions through the Organization of the Petroleum Exporting Countries (OPEC), the result was an instant increase in the price of oil. Same demand, same supply—higher price. This hints that pricing may be much more than just the impartial working of some objective force. A different kind of example is computer software. When Microsoft offered its first operating system, DOS, it offered it well below the price of other operating systems. There was huge demand for it, yet its price stayed about the same. Higher demand did not lead to higher price.

In the midst of huge amounts of data—numbers of all kinds available for all kinds of markets—the most basic of economic laws must be subject to verification or falsification. While we may not be able to conduct controlled experiments in economics, several other sciences are subject to the same constraints. Geology is one that comes to mind. The geologist makes long-term predictions and then looks for indirect evidence to verify or refute those conclusions.

MetaEconomics

There are areas of any science, including economics, not subject to empirical verification. This can be called the "meta" area of the field, in this case metaeconomics. Metaeconomics would ask questions such as "What is the purpose of an economy?" "Who should benefit most?" "Is equality of incomes a virtue or a worthwhile goal for economic policy?" These are all metaeconomic questions that cannot be tested empirically. They are moral questions based on our values. Since values need not be unique, many sets of values can be in competition at any one time.

Market Economies

In the historical sense market economies are a new invention. For hundreds of thousands of years, perhaps millions of years, man and his predecessors lived in tribes off the land as hunter-gatherers. Agriculture created the need for private property. Hunter-gatherer societies can be quite sophisticated artistically, technologically, and literally. But other than a few personal belongings, such as a knife, tools, and clothing, there is no great need for personal property. Tribe members shared whatever was gathered or hunted. The land, if it belonged to anyone, belonged to the tribe. But with agriculture, things change. A family can farm a parcel of land producing enough to feed themselves and have a surplus left over. If the surplus is theirs and not the tribe's, it is up to the family to determine how to dispose of it. Agriculture made private property and market economies possible.

How much should a family in an agrarian society produce? Who should own the produce they produce? Even the very word "produce" here (in the first use of the prior sentence), meant to represent grown agricultural commodities, is identical to the verb form of production.

In a market economy it is assumed that each person and each family is entitled to whatever they produce as long as something is paid (i.e., taxes) to support the workings of government. Most people would say that is fair. This works well when there is a need in society to produce more. The implication in farming is that since one family works a plot they are responsible for and entitled to whatever is grown on that parcel. If they are rewarded for producing more, they will. That at least has been the experience in many societies. When a society needs maximum production from the land, and the family that owns the land needs maximum production, the needs of society and the family are exactly aligned.

This already has key elements of a market economy. A market economy requires private property and a mechanism whereby the producers can freely exchange their production for other goods and services. What a market does is allow individual companies or people to gain in proportion to how well they perform certain functions. The last twenty years of the twentieth century seemed to be a triumph for market economies on the world stage.

But there is a caveat here. The economies of the developed world are not pure market economies. In farming, the needs of the farmers and society no longer coincide. Many farmers in developed countries obtain significant subsidies from their governments, in some cases outweighing the taxes they pay. These societies need less production from their farms while the farmers still need greater income. The traditional way of making greater income was to produce more, but that is now counter to the needs of society. There was an attempt to return farming to market economics through the removal of farm subsidies from the federal government in the 1990s. But each year saw billions of dollars of emergency funds set aside for farmers. In May 2002, President Bush—whose administration heavily favored free trade—signed into law a $180 billion farm bill increasing farm subsidies by 80%. President Bush and President Clinton, respectively a Republican and a Democrat, both ended up approving massive farm subsidies when they were president. Clearly, farming in the developed countries, particularly the large export crops such as corn, wheat, rice, and soybeans, does not operate under the constraints of a market economy. One of the most serious criticisms of President Bush's bill is that it underwrites exports of these crops, allowing them to be sold on world markets at about half of what it costs to produce them. This undermines those countries that don't pay subsidies and that are trying to develop their own agricultural sector. Is it really in our best interest as a society to dump massive amounts of subsidized agricultural goods on the world market?

Mixed Economies

The term "market economy" is misleading. The economies of the developed nations that have triumphed in terms of wealth creation and power are mixed economies with a large proportion of the services performed by nonmarket entities such as clubs, nonprofit organizations, fraternal organizations, and government agencies. A significant portion of economic activity in the United States, one of the "freest" economies in the world, is performed by these organizations that are not profit seeking. We also have many organizations that are nominally profit seeking, but fail to make a profit. While that is often looked upon as an unintentional effect of the market with these firms being looked upon as marginal, after years of observing them I have concluded that many play an important role in the economy. Many of these are smaller firms providing employment to family members and others. They are often a stepping stone for people entering employment or looking for less stressful employment.

A significant portion of useful activity isn't even considered economic and is not measured. If you clean your own house it is not considered an economic activity. If you have someone else clean the house, it becomes an economic activity. People interacting in the street, giving each other directions, passing on a joke or greeting, have no economic value. Measured economic activity, for the most part, does not measure happiness or satisfaction with life, but aren't these among the main goals of life and of economic activity?

A fuller picture of economic activity needs to look at all the daily functions we perform. Human activity consists of volunteering, social interactions, and human relations, none of which is considered economic under standard terms. Then there is the task of earning a living. But of the total amount of human activity, just a fraction is economic in the sense of making money. Significant production and significant consumption are carried on outside of market activity. A developed society has many institutions that provide a benefit to people, but with little or no measured economic activity. It is better to view all of these as a system. The whole of economic activity must consider all the nonprofit and so-called noneconomic activity if a systemic view is to be adopted. As a system the various parts work together. Looked at individually the parts may seem to be at odds or have no relation to one another, but considered as a system, the nonprofit endeavors and organizations strengthen the profit sector and allow it to operate better.

The nonprofit organizations allow market organizations to do what they do best in those areas where they do it best. Public schools for example help provide an educated work force. Museums and public parks provide recreation and mental stimulation that not only improves the quality of life but helps stimulate the creativity of its users. Because of these institutions the profit-seeking sector does not have to provide basic education or recreation to its work force. Corporations, wealthy individuals, and average-income individuals who work in the for-profit sector donate funds to nonprofit institutions and causes. Consumer laws, standards organizations, and a functioning Securities and Exchange Commission all allow for-profit companies to operate by increasing the size of their markets, the trust of consumers, and the faith of investors, which allow more capital to be raised. In fact we might look at one of the functions of nonmarket companies as optimizing the functioning of the market sector. In turn the market sectors optimize the functioning of the nonmarket sector. Each strengthens and enhances the other.

I would compare these to the interaction between plants and animals. Plants take in carbon dioxide and give off oxygen while animals take in oxygen and give off carbon dioxide. The two appear independent when viewed apart. When viewed as a system, however, interdependence and mutual beneficence emerge. The actual interactive processes are much more complex and involve processes that we barely understand, but together the various forms of life act as a system and regulate the biosphere to a degree in a sophisticated manner that we can only marvel at. Likewise the various organizations in a developed economy also work in a highly sophisticated manner to regulate and enhance the overall system.

Going to either extreme or overemphasizing one sector at the expense of another leads to an unstable situation. We have examples of two extremes in the experience of the former Soviet Union. As a socialist state, the intent of government planning was to assure prosperity, equal distribution of wealth, and a worker's paradise. Every aspect of the economy was to be controlled by the state through bureaucrats who had access to all kinds of data and were the elite of that nation. That clearly failed. The Soviet Union was seen as a viable economic threat to Western democracies for most of the twentieth century. With the dramatic fall of the Berlin Wall, the political dissolution of the Soviet Union, and the renouncement of communism by the countries that emerged we were able to get a real view of Russia and the other countries that used to make up the Soviet Union. The reality was a military superpower with an economy that in many areas could not provide basic services such as running water and roads. It was a poor nation, not a worker's paradise as Soviet propaganda had proclaimed.

On the other hand, with the failure of the Soviet states a totally unregulated economic environment developed without rules, traditions, or counterbalancing organizations. Many free market economists were optimistic that a strong economy would quickly emerge. But here too the reality was very different. A laissez-faire economy turned into a wild west with a handful of individuals, many with connections to the old bureaucracy, stealing or cornering most of the industrial assets of Russia. These people were known as the Oligarchs. The majority of Russians remained in poverty, with many unemployed.

A complete economics must look at all of human society and its workings as the whole economy. The money portion is but a subsystem, and market mechanisms are but a subsystem of that, although a very significant and important part.

Viewing an economy as a self-regulating entity is not totally new. In the classic work *The Wealth of Nations* published in 1776, Adam Smith draws a picture of an economy with each person furthering his own self-interest, yet through some unseen mechanism balance is achieved preventing any one person from dominating. But I am asserting here that the self-regulation takes place not just through market mechanisms but through all the organizations and mechanisms that make up a society. The whole system is much larger than just the markets. Indeed even human society is but a subsystem of the much larger system of all life on Earth.

As mentioned in Chapter 14, in *The Ages of Gaia* James Lovelock builds an ecological computer model of Daisyworld, in which two species of daisies of different colors are able to effectively regulate the temperature of the planet. As more species of daisies are added the model handles the perturbations in solar luminosity with greater stability and robustness.

Robustness here means the ability to survive and prosper under great extremes. It means the ability to bounce back quicker and be less affected by external perturbations. Of course any system has its limits. At great extremes, any self-regulating system perishes. But if we extend the analogy and consider the economy as a self-regulating system, the model argues for the importance of diversity in markets and the economy as a whole. An economy with different companies, with differences of opinion, different strategies, and different managements can better respond to shifts in the environment, economic or otherwise, than a monoculture. When conditions shift those companies that can take advantage of it prosper. They acquire more capital, hire more people, and prevent the shift from becoming onerous. Meanwhile other companies may be doing poorly. But if the environment now shifts in a different way then some of the companies that formerly were suffering now come to life. But if there is just one large company or management system in the country it may not be able to respond to the shift, leading to unemployment and misery.

This model predicts that economies with just one voice or style of management, such as communism and other rigid or intolerant economic systems, would not tolerate extreme external shifts well. Large shifts would lead to collapse or force a crisis leading to radical changes. This proposition is subject to testing.

Perturbations Stability and Diversity

In one of his latter models, Lovelock found that species diversity was greatest when there was a small increase or decrease in warmth, comparable to a shift in the Earth from an ice age to a moderate period like what we are experiencing now.[40] Ice ages have alternated with more moderate times with regularity over the last one million years.[41] They are so common that they cannot be considered an aberration but rather a phase or state of the planet. But when stability persisted for long periods of time in this model, the diversity of species began to decline. Another small perturbation would reestablish greater diversity.

We see something similar and parallel in the diversity of companies in an industry. Long-established industries under stable conditions tend to see a decline in the numbers of companies. But new technology, new markets, or other factors that upset the old order often lead to many new companies entering that industry.

Capital and Capital Creation

What is it that makes for a strong developed economy? Is it capital? Capital is the end result of economic activity. It allows for further economic activity. It is somewhat akin to stored energy. Some capital is necessary for development but it is not the most critical ingredient, nor is it the determining factor. After a certain level additional capital may not make much of a difference. Rather, the ideals, the beliefs, and the knowledge of people are the differences that make the difference. At the beginning of World War II, Germany and Japan were two strong, economically advanced nations. Immediately after the war, their industries lay in ruins and their cities were rubble. Financial capital was nonexistent. A few decades later these two nations emerged as the world's two

[40] *The Ages of Gaia,* by James Lovelock, page 215.

[41] Ibid., 131.

strongest economic powers besides the United States. True the United States provided assistance and some capital, but other nations were helped as well with less dramatic results. Their culture, their beliefs, and their ideals allowed these two nations to reemerge stronger than before. This might be called their intellectual or cultural capital. No amount of capital infusion will allow a poor nation to become developed without a massive shift in the soft capital of knowledge, beliefs, and ideals.

In his book *Growing a Business*, Paul Hawken states that he has seen more companies fail because of too much capital rather than because of too little capital. He tells the story of a friend who started a business. It cost his friend $100,000 to put out a catalog while it cost Hawken just $5,000 to publish his catalog of equivalent size and distribution. When he looked at his friend's costs he found money spent on services Hawken did not even know existed. Anyone can produce a useful catalog by throwing money at it. But a business must develop its processes in a way that cannot be easily duplicated by others at the same price. And then it must keep improving those processes. This allows the company to earn a profit and serve the goals of society. This is how it develops an advantage and this allows it to take over a niche in the ecology we call our economy.

An economy is a reflection of and part of a society. The two cannot be separated. To try and create a modern market economy without being respectful and cognizant of the culture is to invite failure. Many of the critical ingredients that make a modern economy successful are not economic in the conventional sense of the word. A successful modern economy requires organizations, skills, and conventions that are not readily evident, as well as the more obvious ones. It is easy to see a bank, it is more difficult to point out the knowledge of banking that goes against the wind and urges caution when all else have given it up. It is easy to see a factory floor; it is difficult to see the subtle knowledge that keeps the work flowing. A large part of this subtle knowledge is maintained by lesser-paid individuals.

To develop a modern economy it is not enough to develop for-profit businesses. A whole ecology of organizations needs to be developed before the market sectors can function properly. A whole set of attitudes, beliefs, and ideals are also necessary.

Succession

When a field that was formerly forest is abandoned, the forest does not return immediately. Instead grasses first emerge. Once they are firmly established bushes and shrubs appear and in time start to dominate the landscape. Only after several different types of plants with greater complexity have adapted to the field do the trees start coming back. A similar phenomenon exists for organizations and economies. A start-up company needs to go through various distinct stages of development in order to be a mature self-perpetuating organization. Economies and societies too must pass through distinct stages of development. To leave one stage out is not just unhealthy but counterproductive. To expect an agrarian economy to suddenly become a manufacturing one without disruption is unreasonable. It might be given capital and host multinational organizations but it will not behave like a mature economy.

For developing economies there is a rough road map based on the experience of other economies that have gone through a similar progression. Each nation must modify that road map and adapt it to its own culture. The nation must also decide if it wants the same kind of economy as the modern developed nations. As the world economy further integrates, we are already creating abundance in manufactured goods and food. Why duplicate functions that are already performed not just adequately but in abundance? An economy today need not be limited to the models of yesteryear as there are now many more options. Instead of being a manufacturing center, an economy could choose instead to be an eco-tourism or cultural area. But it still must develop its people through training and education. The soft development must occur.

The developed economies are themselves in transition. For an industrial society transforming to a post-industrial society, there is no road map. We have to look to man's common spiritual traditions, psychological theory, and the experience of rich or highly developed individuals of the past. I find it interesting that many individuals who amass great wealth end up giving away large portions of it. This was true even before the income tax added significant financial incentives for charitable contributions. It is not unusual for the heirs of very wealthy self-made men and women to spend their time in "higher" pursuits such as charity, the arts, or cultured leisure. Some very wealthy individuals have spent the latter part of their lives not in business but in philanthropy. Andrew Carnegie became the richest man in the world when he sold his steel company. He then spent the balance of his life involved in philanthropy. One of the beneficiaries of his philanthropy was the public library system. Many self-made people have credited public libraries with having aided them at some point in their lives. Did Carnegie contribute more to the development of American capitalism through his work in creating the company that became US Steel or in his work as a philanthropist?

This would seem to add credibility to a hierarchy of needs such as the one proposed by Abraham Maslow. People in the developed world in large measure have their physiological needs and physical security taken care of. But financial security is far from universal. It is estimated that only 5% of Americans can retire securely. Secure retirement is a function of having sufficient capital or owning an adequate share of the wealth of the nation. This would imply that a more equitable distribution of wealth will become an issue of greater importance as the baby boomers start to approach retirement.

In the old economic model the fight for better income and wealth equality would be seen as a struggle between those who have more versus those who have less. Those with less would feel the need for more and would be leading the fight, while those with more would be resisting and trying to maintain what they have. But in this model it would be the wealthy and the children of the wealthy who would be leading the fight for greater income equality. The poor or those in the middle might very well be resisting the need for greater financial equality.

Of course both could be happening at once since we have people at all levels of the Maslow Hierarchy of Needs in our society. Those primarily driven by financial needs would be seeking better distribution if they were not rich while those who saw themselves as rich would be resisting. Among those motivated not by financial need but by some "higher need" it would be the wealthy calling for greater equality. But as more people find themselves financially secure, we would expect more people calling for greater income equality.

This may appear far-fetched since little of this is evident today. But changes of state can occur rapidly. They are like jumps to a different quantum state; a transition with no in-between state. We have all experienced this to some extent in a change in mood or opinion. At one point we may have felt very strongly one way. Years later we may feel just as strongly, but with the opposite opinion. We might be very cheery one day and depressed another.

Economies and nations have moods and states. A bull market creates wealth. Almost everyone feels wealthier and better. The nation feels buoyant. Certain national attitudes prevail. Business as a profession becomes attractive, investment clubs spring up, and national brands gain preference over generics. There are other interesting and nonobvious effects. Miniskirts, for instance, tend to do better during times of prosperity.

A bear market, on the other hand, brings very different attitudes. Business becomes the villain, stock investments are seen as very risky, and generics and the savings they provide over national brands become of interest again. The national mood is first more like a hangover, then a mild depression, and then an acceptance of drudgery. Bear markets have also been accompanied by longer skirts.

In a sense we are all regulated by our environment and by the greater system, whether that be our culture or even something larger than our culture. Remember that most communication takes place nonverbally and much of what we take in is unconscious. We may be unaware of an impeding change but may sense it unconsciously. It is through our unconscious and in our unconscious that major shifts occur.

Money Supply, Inflation, and Economic Regulation

An attempt to improve on an economy's built-in self-regulation is made by government via monetary policy. The Federal Reserve in the United States and the central banks elsewhere have tools to control the money supply and interest rates. Through these they hope to moderate economic activity according to national goals and interests. There are certain inherent assumptions in monetary policy that are worth examining. Currently there is belief that all inflation is bad for the economy.

This is understandable given the negative experience of many nations with runaway inflation. German society was seriously damaged by runaway inflation after World War I, leading to the rise of Hitler. Although not as severe, the United States also had a negative experience with inflation in the 1960s, followed by stagflation in the 1970s. This coincided with a decline in American influence and prosperity.

Runaway inflation causes a host of problems. It is inherently unstable, making it difficult to plan. The long-term capital markets are destroyed. In extreme cases the bond market can disappear. I had some experience with Brazilian inflation. While the Brazilian government took some very creative steps in the 1960s and '70s to deal with inflation and companies were able to grow, there was no financing available beyond two years. Long-term planning and investment were seriously hampered.

But every instance in this kind of runaway inflation I have studied was accompanied by an uncontrollable increase in money supply by the monetary authorities. It seems clear that when this kind of inflation occurs it produces dislocations in the economy and disrupts long-term planning. This is, I believe, a clear-cut case where the authorities should intervene to bring down the growth of money and bring inflation down to a much lower rate. But if we therefore assumed that inflation of any kind is undesirable we would be making a logical jump that is not justified.

We would also be confusing symptoms and causes. There may be many reasons for inflation that are not negative but represent adjustments in the economic system to events. We could not automatically assume that these would have a negative impact. But let's get some specific examples. Suppose we had a stable economic environment with an average rate of inflation of 1%. Dipping into our MetaKnowledge tool kit tells us that anything measured varies over time. A certain amount of variation due strictly to chance exists in any system.

Suppose I flip a balanced coin 100 times—how many heads should I expect to count? Most people would respond 50 heads. But in reality you would expect anything but 50. Roughly 8% of the time, you might get 50 heads. But you might see 45 heads or 51 or 65 or 35. If you repeated the exercise many times, you would see a full range and distribution for the number of heads. And the point is that even if you only received 35 heads, you could not assume there was anything wrong with the coin. On the very next trial you might get 65 heads or even 50 heads. If you automatically assumed the coin was unbalanced, you would be wasting a lot of time and doing a great deal of harm.

In the case of monetary policy, the rate of inflation might climb to 3% in one month and that might not indicate that anything had changed. It might very well be a mistake for the monetary authorities to take any action. I say might because in order to determine if it is due to chance or not you would need data for several months in which there was no intervention by the monetary authorities.

Some results would indicate that taking action was warranted. If you flipped a coin 100 times and ended up with 100 heads, that is a strong signal that something is amiss. Of course this is not an exact world and it is possible that there is absolutely nothing wrong, but in this case control theory says we should take action. Ironically if in one trial you had 100 heads and in the next you had 0 heads that would be an even stronger signal that something was wrong even though the average is 50.

Dr. Shewhart, the founder of Statistical Quality Control, whose work we discussed in earlier chapters, developed the rules for determining when to take action and when to leave the system alone more than seventy years ago. But how did he determine these rules? He determined them by experimentation. He was looking for a set of rules that would indicate when to intervene so that economic loss would be minimized. Sure there was a great deal of theory involved, but the actual limits were determined empirically. And they have stood the test of time again and again.

Now you might say that interfering in the money supply when the rules say you should not causes no great damage. But that would be incorrect. By intervening when you should not you add additional variation and uncertainty. The system becomes more variable and chaotic. There is no guarantee that the actions of the fed counterbalance the actions of the economy. The variations probably combine. As a result the system would have bigger swings and be less stable. A self-regulating system with random variation does better without intervention. Interventions make things worse.

Yet what happens whenever there is a slight up-tick in the rate of inflation, the money supply, or some other variable? It is often accompanied by a flurry of trading activity. News articles waste words analyzing the change. In actuality nothing in the system has changed and all the analysis is useless.

Self-Regulating Systems

Let's go back to the biological analogy for a moment. We are told the normal temperature for a person is 98.6 degrees Fahrenheit. Does a different temperature indicate sickness? Of course not! In actuality body temperature varies widely depending on the level of activity. Intense physical activity raises the temperature several degrees while starvation or sleep lowers it. Further, the mean of 98.6 is maintained in just a core part of the body. The extremities, such as hands and feet, vary more. It would be unhealthy to try and bring the temperature of someone engaged in a race down to 98.6. This is not random variation but variation of a cybernetic nature and a healthy response to increased physical activity.

Why should we assume that inflation in a boom period needs to be the same as in a contraction or steady state? If we adapt a biological model for the economy then increases in the rate of inflation during boom times—as long as monetary policy was stable—might actually be the healthy response of a self-regulating nature.

And the same question needs to be asked of other variables. How was it determined that 4% unemployment was the lowest level our economy could reach without overheating? We have seen other economies such as Ireland and Japan maintaining unemployment levels well below 4% for extended periods of time without significant adverse consequences.

To some extent we already recognize that some types of inflation have a beneficial effect. When the price of real estate and stocks are rising it is viewed as a good thing. Inflation in the price of capital assets is considered positive. When they rise for a considerable period of time the fed chairman is called a genius. But historically the prices of capital assets rise and fall. We have had great bull markets before and great bear markets as well. We have had periods of economic growth and periods of recessions.

We can introduce another tool from our MetaKnowledge tool kit, dimensionality. A developed economy has a productive sector that includes manufacturing and services. The financial sector clearly has some relation to both of these but they can have a mild correlation. We can experience inflation in manufactured products without necessarily having increasing labor rates or increasing prices for capital such as stocks and bonds. But we can also see stock prices raging ahead, an inflation of financial assets, while the manufacturing sector is not experiencing any kind of inflation, in fact for many products prices might actually be declining. This is what we experienced during the last few years of the 1990s until the first quarter of 2000. The Federal Reserve wanted to slow down the irrational exuberance of the financial markets. And it used its one main tool—interest rates. It brought interest rates up. Higher interest rates initially just fed the financial inflation. If investors could get 8% returns just by lending money on mortgages, they expected much higher returns on stocks and riskier investments. But for the productive sectors this higher interest rate was detrimental and for some companies it eventually proved fatal. A high rate of interest for productive companies when there is an abundance of capital is absurd. The fed's action was like trying to bring the fever down of someone with a headache. This was using one tool to cool the whole economy when only one sector, one dimension, was experiencing increasing prices. We don't know if the markets would have cracked on their own. All past bubbles, whether they were of tulip bulbs, gold, or stocks, have burst on their own and it is reasonable to extrapolate that the stock market bubble of the 1990s would have burst on its own. But the damage to the manufacturing economy—already suffering from overcapacity and lower wage rates in Asia and Latin America—was further aggravated by the fed's actions. The fed now has to frantically backpedal by lowering interest rates as quickly as possible, trying to avoid a price deflation like the one that has stagnated Japan after its central bank took similar action in the late 1980s. At this writing, President Bush is proposing a massive tax cut to stimulate the economy before the elections of 2004. All this is standard political and economic fare. But once again we are returning to massive federal government fiscal deficits. What was needed—if the bubble needed to be burst from without—was something that struck at the heart of speculation, such as increasing the margin requirements for people purchasing stocks on margin.

Is a Long Boom Beneficial?

Is a long sustained period of economic prosperity better than a period where prosperity is interspersed by small recessions? Of course a sustained prosperity makes everyone feel better. Everyone becomes a stock picker. But the mantra that this time it is different and the bear will never return becomes more widely accepted. More people engage in speculation. An old adage on Wall Street advises to not confuse genius with a bull market. When the bear does hit, many more people are hurt. Having intermediate recessions keeps people more cautious and balanced.

There is a similar debate among ecologists about the role and timing of forest fires. For years it was the policy of the Forest Service to put out small fires in our national parks. But those small fires helped clear out the underbrush and debris that had fallen to the forest floor. The fires cleaned out the forest floors while allowing the trees to survive. In extinguishing the small intermittent fires, we set the stage for some of the really big fires that we experienced over the last few decades. The large fires are not bigger versions of smaller fires. They are much more intense and kill the existing trees. But even in this "tragedy" nature comes back as the heat also opens up the pinecones that seed the forest for the next generation of life. But that new forest will not be seen by many of those who are alive today.

A Russian economist in the early part of the twentieth century, Nikolai Kondratieff, discovered three prior cases of systemic collapse of the capitalistic system. He postulated that these occurred with some regularity on average about once every seventy-one years. Such a finding might have made him a hero of the communists who were in power and were predicting the end of capitalism. But Kondratieff was last seen being taken away to a forced labor camp. His work led him to the conclusion that, far from signaling the end of capitalism, these panics, depressions, and breakdowns in the system were inevitably followed by renewal.

It is interesting that when we talk of increasing or decreasing markets we talk of bulls and bears, some of the oldest symbols of the human race. We use symbols that go back to the earliest time of man, and possibly precede our species. These symbols are deeply ingrained in our unconscious. It is ironic that to describe some of the gyrations of what are relatively new economic tools, stock markets—which have been in existence for only hundreds of years—we use the ancient symbols of the bull and the bear.

Is it possible that this cycle of ups and downs, which we have experienced for a few hundred years in the new and sophisticated markets for capital, are part of a much larger and older cycle of life? Ultimately we are a part of the planet and participate in the biosphere and evolution of the planet. The bull and the bear indicate a relationship with the earth dating back to our earliest days.

With the new tools provided by psychology, Chaos Theory, statistics, and self-regulating systems, we have an opportunity to understand our economy not as a lifeless and segregated activity of man but as part of the human ecology. As such we are tied in to global systems and global evolution. Relationships that in the past may have seemed totally irrational may now have some theoretical basis. The resulting model that develops will most likely synthesize from many disciplines. What emerges may be what is needed for our species to take on a new and enlightened role in the self-regulation of life on Earth. This is part of the MetaKnowledge Advantage.

CHAPTER 20

PUTTING IT ALL TOGETHER

In the previous chapters I introduced key concepts to synthesize a new framework for understanding our world in the twenty-first century. Included were statistics, theory of knowledge, a schematic of the economic value of knowledge, a theory of knowledge, a hierarchy of personal beliefs, psychological types, multiple intelligences, human development and self-actualization via peak experiences, self-regulating systems, dynamic system theory (Chaos Theory), dimensionality, and logical levels. These ideas touched on the work of such luminaries as W. Edwards Deming, Walter Shewhart, Gregory Bateson, Robert Dilts, Carl Jung, Howard Gardner, Abraham Maslow, James Lovelock, Fritjof Capra, Bertrand Russell, and others.

The MetaKnowledge Advantage in Management

A working understanding of these principles improves management. In Chapter 4 I demonstrated the dramatic effects The New Management has had in the United States and Japan. Today almost every successful company has embraced some aspect of The New Management. One aspect generally identified with The New Management and widely accepted is process improvement, which can be applied with success even with limited understanding of MetaKnowledge. The shift away from blaming people and firefighting to categorizing problems and then understanding and improving the company's systems is enough to have a dramatic impact on the operations and results of any company. But with greater understanding of MetaKnowledge, process improvement leads to dramatic and even revolutionary changes. As successful as Six Sigma has been at GE, it has not dramatically altered the perception of quality from GE customers. To do that requires a knowledge of variation and pursuing not just process improvement but moving toward a state of statistical control.

I recently bought a new cell phone and decided to try a Motorola after having used Nokia for years. Motorola was an early convert to quality in the 1980s, and used and made famous Six Sigma. Six Sigma aims for extremely high levels of quality in every part and every process. The high goal and its emphasis on statistical terminology seem to have suited Motorola's culture, with its heavy engineering emphasis, and undoubtedly saved the company from extinction in the face of fierce Japanese competition. Motorola's renewal allowed it to become the early leader in cell phone manufacturing. But their lead has steadily eroded.

When I received my new Motorola I was surprised with its complexity. To turn the phone on using one hand I had to turn it upside down. The on button did not always respond. In order to access the internal phone book, the feature I use most often, I had to wade through several menus—on my Nokia it was the first thing to pop up. Only an engineer could love the menu on this phone. These and several other glitches, all minor but irritating, made this phone less useful and desirable than any Nokia I had. Apparently I am not alone because Motorola has consistently lost market share to the extent that they now have about 20% of the market compared to Nokia's 39%.

This appears to be a failure to distinguish between internal and external quality. In some regards the quality of the phone is excellent. It has a lot of good features and my guess is that it will give years of reliable service. But quality of design is missing. Six Sigma essentially focuses on internal processes and internal quality. But external quality is in a subtle way different. It refers to how the customer uses your economic product and what is important to her. A different set of tools is required to understand and improve external quality.

Equally important, not every internal process or external feature is equal. Certain processes are critical for quality and those are the ones that require the greatest efforts. The processes that have minimal effect on quality require minimal effort. The reality is that any organization has a limited amount of time available for improvement efforts. It must pick, choose, and balance carefully where that time is spent. Some processes may end up performing much worse than Six Sigma, but if they have no impact on quality you are better off spending corporate resources elsewhere.

The MetaKnowledge Advantage in Team Building

But The New Management is not limited to process improvement. Building a team that works together opens up great organizational leverage as that term is used in Chapter 11. A fully functioning team can perform incredible accomplishments. But creating a team requires an understanding of people, so once again MetaKnowledge becomes critical. Some understanding of psychological types, appreciation for the theory of multiple intelligences, the hierarchy of needs, and self-actualization are pretty important for putting a team together. Even if a manager has an understanding of these but a poor understanding of variation he still might attempt to grade everyone on a curve and this will have a detrimental effect that prevents the team from reaching its full potential.

A team that functions well together becomes more than the sum of its parts. Managers, coaches, and owners who believe that substituting a high-performing individual for one of the existing team members automatically assures better performance for the team are sorely mistaken. The best teams have a core of players that stay together over time. Notice that in most professional athletic teams, attempts to pay for stronger new players does not lead to consistent championships. The New York Yankees are one example where some good players working together over time formed a dynasty. Trying to replace long-time players with higher performing individuals has not led to more championships.

The same kind of systems thinking applies to departments. Lowering the costs in one department can lead to higher costs for the whole company. The idea is not to maximize the performance of each department, but to optimize the performance of the whole. Measures of costs or profitability of departments can be misleading because they do not show how a cost improvement in one department affects the overall performance. Without systems thinking and an appreciation for the nonlinear relationship between the parts of a system and the whole, process improvement schemes including Six Sigma can lead to higher costs and less profitability for the whole company.

KNOWLEDGE OF VARIATION AND SYSTEMS THINKING. In any kind of performance rating, it is not just the performance of the individual that determines his outcome. Any performance has two factors; some of the results are due to the system and some are due to the individual. We have two unknowns: S, the contribution from the system, and I, the contribution from the individual. But we have only one equation $S + I = R$, the results. How much is due to the individual and how much is due to the system? Much of the result from the system varies considerably. So we can rephrase the question and ask how much of the result is due to the individual and how much is due to chance? The manager who takes individual performance in one period at its face value is assuming there is no system effect and no chance.

SYSTEMS THINKING AND TEAMWORK. Systems thinking, statistical thinking, and teamwork are compatible. One example of teamwork is a crew of eight rowers, four on each side. If one person decides he will pull harder than the others that will only throw the boat off. His greater effort will not contribute to the success or optimal performance of his crew. Here the goal is not maximum efforts, but instead optimal efforts. On any given day one oarsman will be stronger than the others. A system that seeks to have each person give his maximum, perhaps through competition, will inevitably lose to a system where the crewmen harmonize their efforts so that the boat moves smoothly, quickly, and in a straight line.

A Larger System

But systems theory and optimization apply to the whole economy as well. The belief that every company needs to seek maximum profitability for an economy to function well has no empirical support. Systems theory would state that some organizations should not maximize profit and some should not even seek profitability. Which organizations? How about major auditors and accountants? For years their professional code of conduct prevented them from competing on the basis of price. This may have resulted in minimal price competition but it was designed to maintain a professionalism whereby the auditors could maintain independence and serve their societal function to provide accurate financial figures to the public. Every financial statement is to some degree an interpretation. And as we have seen in recent years with the collapse and bankruptcy of major companies, such as Enron and WorldCom (to name just two), the interpretations can be pure fantasy.

But behaviors leading to maximum revenue for one office of a firm or one person can lead to great loss for the auditing firm and even greater loss to society. Encouraging a firm to maximize its revenues can lead to great loss for society. If we encourage self-serving behavior it is predictable that we will get it. Misleading and false financial statements among publicly traded companies are nothing new. It has happened in the past and will happen in the future. Instantly two companies from the past come to mind, National Student Marketing, a high flyer of the 1960s whose CEO landed in jail because of liberal accounting, and Leasco, another high flyer and innovator in creative accounting that lost all its value. There have been hundreds of companies whose financial statements verged on hallucination. And it should be the auditor's role to minimize fantasy and emphasize reality despite objections from clients.

If the auditors of financial statements of major companies are to serve their public function their private profit maximization function may have to be reined in. Auditors need to have the ability, financial strength, and incentives to be an auditor first and a businessperson second. While this might not maximize the profitability or value of accounting and auditing firms it will optimize the results to society.

At the same time we cannot assume that profit is the only incentive for performance. The view that man is only economic in nature, motivated only by money or money maximization, has not stood up to scrutiny. To believe that only profit-seeking firms operate efficiently is also to close our eyes to reality. In New York state, for instance, former lieutenant governor Stan Lundine instituted a total quality management initiative among several key agencies. Years ago getting a driver's license renewed in New York involved long waits on several lines only to be greeted by employees who were curt and angry. A recent visit to the Department of Motor Vehicles, one of the agencies involved in the total quality initiative, was one of the most pleasant interactions I have had with any organization of any kind. Not only was I in and out quickly but the service was courteous, helpful, and accompanied with a smile. Organizations of any kind can benefit from The New Management and from MetaKnowledge.

Please don't misconstrue these comments. I believe the for-profit sector to be one of the most powerful forces developed by the human race. A strong, vibrant for-profit sector is critical for any healthy economy. I am looking to make the profit-making sector stronger and better; I am not advocating it be diminished. But in order to make it work better we must realize its limitations and also the fact that it is part of a larger system that includes nonprofit, clubs, and government agencies. Further, some companies may have to sacrifice their profit maximizing potential and settle on a reasonable profit potential for the good of society to make the rest of the profit-seeking sector stronger and more reliable.

The mistake of the socialists and other advocates of using government to meet every human need was not just to ignore the vital role played by the market economy but also the vital role played by the nonprofit organizations, including charitable organizations, family associations, churches, clubs, and informal organizations of all kinds. The socialists tried to usurp their role as well. From a systems perspective, all of these sectors play an important and complementary role. If they did not they would not survive for very long. Pure voluntarism, the desire to work just to make it better for others without personal compensation, is as much responsible for the success of the developed world as is the self-serving drive to help oneself. No one sector, and that includes government, can do it all.

But even if all these systems—the government agencies, for-profit companies, and the nonprofit—could be imported into a poorer nation (and of course they cannot), it would not lead to the success and wealth characteristic of a developed nation. For even more fundamental than the systems are the people themselves, their own development, their discipline, and their metaknowledge. In this regard the system needs to reinforce constructive values while allowing values to change and grow as the society evolves. There is a co-evolution that takes place between the metaknowledge of a people, its economic and cultural system, and their success and prosperity. Each must reinforce the other. In this regard the educational system plays a special role. And ironically the educational system is made up of organizations from all the sectors: for-profit, nonprofit, government, and pure voluntarism.

The MetaKnowledge Advantage in Research and Interpreting Data

Key aspects of MetaKnowledge were developed during research into quality improvement at the Bell Laboratories by Dr. Shewhart during the 1920s. These ideas had a renaissance in Japan starting in 1950, and in the United States and Europe starting in 1980. They are essential for great management. But the MetaKnowledge Advantage is not limited to management. It is critical in science and government.

One example is surveys of the literature. In many scientific studies the results differ from study to study. Some studies might confirm outcome X; for example, that people prefer cooperation. Others might show outcome Y, let's say this is that people prefer competition, while still others seem to confirm Z, that people have no natural preference.

The usual approach to a survey of the literature is to look at all the studies and then sum up the results; so many showed X, so many showed Y, so many showed Z. Since more studies showed one result, say Y, the authors of the survey conclude and argue that Y is correct. Of course the design of each study and how it was executed will affect the results but there are additional fundamental issues involved.

Suppose there are several statistical populations as defined in Chapter 7. But here the pygmies are naturally cooperative, the Watusi are competitive to a fault, and the typicals have no natural preference. Since those who did the initial studies were unaware of these populations and their associated characteristics, the people who participated in each study were chosen without any regard to which population they belonged to. As a result some studies had a very large percentage of pygmies, some had a very large percentage of Watusi, and others had many typicals. The results from each study were totally dependent on the selection process, which was basically haphazard since it did not take account of the important categories. The survey of the literature is, in turn, totally meaningless.

If there are indeed different statistical populations in the general population it would be more useful to determine first, how many different kinds of statistical populations exist and second, what characteristics identify members of each group. Recent studies have shown the danger in some widely used medical procedures such as hormone replacement and certain kinds of knee surgery. Yet it is possible that these procedures are useful for some very much smaller subset of the general population.

We are spending billions of dollars on medical research that is flawed. At the same time doctors are relying on this research and prescribing medicine to their patients as if there were just one category of patients. It seems to me that in some cases doctors have abrogated their responsibility to know each of their patients uniquely. In medicine we are dealing with a very large population of people who are very likely quite different. We know there are different blood types, psychological types, metabolisms, and so forth. It is highly unlikely that one diet would be optimal for all people. Most likely different statistical groups of people thrive with very different diets, very different exercise regimes, different vitamins, and different treatments for similar symptoms. Taken to the ultimate degree, each person requires different foods and treatments at different times but there are very likely broad categories that most of us would fit in to that could be useful to guide our health.

Is Your Doctor a Doer, Learner, Creator, or Revolutionary?

It is surprising how little research is done on medical procedures. Most surgical procedures have not been put through any kind of statistically rigorous clinical trial. It should not be a surprise when clinical trials show that generally accepted procedures are ineffective in the long-term treatment of the conditions they are supposed to alleviate. One recent trial showed that radical mastectomy, for years the procedure of choice to treat breast cancer, is no more effective than less radical and less invasive procedures. This may come as a surprise but most doctors and dentists are not scientists. They are technicians trained to do procedures developed by others. They are not trained to follow up on and record their results. They certainly have limited statistical knowledge. Yes, there are doctors with the right training and mind-set who could be considered scientists, but this group is a minority and most of these are working on research.

What about quality in hospitals? Is there continual improvement of processes and procedures to lower the incidence of administration of the wrong medicine or performance of the wrong procedure? For most hospitals the answer is no.

The MetaKnowledge Advantage in Economics

I recently read a news piece stating that the debt load of the American family had fallen from 14% of income to 12%. On the surface this seems to be a positive sign. It of course doesn't show the amount of credit card debt that has been replaced by mortgage debt, which would explain the drop. But it also doesn't show the debt load of different segments of the population. The lowest income bracket, the working poor, may not own a house and may not be able to substitute mortgage debt at lower interest rates and better terms for credit card debt. This number does not show the inequality of debt. Some families have too much and it is keeping them poor. Others benefit from that debt.

Another example is the Consumer Price Index. How much prices have increased or decreased is determined by considering a basket of goods that a "typical" consumer might purchase. But once again if there are income categories in the statistical sense, that measure of inflation may not be indicative of different groups. One would expect that the purchasing patterns for senior citizens would be very different than the purchasing patterns of young couples with children. It is therefore possible that the inflation experienced by these two groups could differ significantly. Determining subgroups or statistical populations based on age and/or income might give us a very different picture of inflation for different groups.

The natural inclination in economics is to explain everything as if income distribution were a single statistical population with some being at the "top of the curve" and others at the "bottom of the curve." But this is highly unlikely. The universe is lumpy. Leverage and compounding as covered in earlier chapters will tend to create categories or statistical populations, as we call them, or classes, as they have been called by social commentators. Some kinds of leverage impact everyone in a society. That is what creates a developed and rich economy. In general, the more forms of leverage used in an economy the richer the society.

But some types of leverage only benefit some individuals or organizations. Many people are leverage neutral, meaning that their relative economic success is not affected by leverage. Some individuals are hurt by leverage. Leverage can hurt the wealthy and the poor. Bernie Ebbers, former chairman and CEO of WorldCom, was worth more than $400,000,000 in the late 1990s. He had borrowed to buy as much WorldCom stock as he could. When the stock started to tank he held on and is now faced with hundreds of millions of dollars of debt backed by stock that is worthless. Other corporate executives are facing similar dilemmas. The working poor, who have taken on too much debt because of a lost job or a medical emergency, could spend years toiling as economic serfs to pay off their debt.

Leverage used successfully creates wealth quickly. It puts the person into a different financial state. Various financial thresholds exist. When an individual owns or controls income sources that exceed his expenses, he passes a significant financial threshold. Great success of the person's company, career, or investments can put him into a still different category. Leverage and compounding lead to a few people obtaining a great amount of wealth. They have been put into a different wealth category or class. It should be no surprise then that wealth distribution is not a smooth curve. When an economy is booming, great wealth is created for a few.

In listening to some unsophisticated advocates for free markets, it sometimes seems as if they believe that robust economies develop automatically on their own. The implication is that all we have to do is step aside and markets will take care of themselves. But this just isn't so. The developed economy enjoyed by members of wealthy nations has been learned by each society. A process of trial and error, coupled with some theory and experimentation, has put in structures and organizations that were meant to prevent calamities and breakdowns of the past. A financial collapse in the nineteenth century led to the formation of credit bureaus to disseminate financial information on businesses. The Panic of 1905 led to the formation of the Federal Reserve Board. The Crash of 1929 and the uncovering of shady securities practices led to the formation of the Securities and Exchange Commission (SEC). Disclosure of business practices in the food industry during Teddy Roosevelt's administration was the impetus for consumer protection regulations.

All of these are important elements in the success of the U.S. economy. But none of these was the result of spontaneous combustion. Some of the innovations, like credit reporting organizations, were produced by the private sector; some, like the SEC, were government mandated; and in some, like consumer protection, nonprofits play a major role. In many cases, members of affected industries fought tooth and nail to prevent legislation that has now become an accepted and welcomed part of our "free" economy. Our future economic prosperity rests on the continued pruning of failed ideas and structures. Innovation and experimentation not just within organizations but on the structure of our economy is essential for further economic development.

Three Principles of The New Management as Ecological Principles

In Chapter 4 I brought out three principles of The New Management. These were external quality, internal quality, and internal improvement. These can be expanded into general principles in business. External quality becomes protect your niche; internal quality is operate efficiently and well; and constant improvement is keep improving. A business that violates one or more of these becomes vulnerable and will likely experience problems. McDonald's restaurants built their business by offering quick, satisfying meals at low prices. They used to offer a meal for less than one dollar. But as they grew their strategy became to increase profits by increasing prices. Prices were raised each year. Financial analysts praised their ability to raise prices and thereby increase profits and recommended the stock.

What they were doing, however, was leaving their established ecological niche and trying to occupy a different one. While this can work, it carries significant risks. They were starting to compete against many more restaurants and different formats. Profits and growth have recently stalled. They recently reported their first loss ever. While many reasons for this might be given, the abandonment of the basic niche where their business systems were developed left them exposed. Now they are fighting frequent price wars, trying to recapture at least part of their old niche. Sears, Roebuck and Co. tried the same price strategy in the late 1960s and early 1970s, only to have customers abandon them. That left the door wide open for the discounters. Wal-Mart, on the other hand, has steadily focused on its low-price, guaranteed-return-policy niche and has become the largest corporation in the world based on sales. It now employs more than 1,300,000 people, more people than General Motors or AT&T, the two giants of the industrial economy.

A company can abandon its niche, it can get sick from the inside, or it can fail to keep improving, allowing it to be displaced by a new competitor, or some combination of the three. Niches can also change either gradually or suddenly, and companies that fail to adapt are vulnerable. Digital Equipment, a leader in proprietary minicomputer systems, couldn't make the transition to open systems brought about by the personal computer. They were swallowed by Compaq, who in turn merged with Hewlett-Packard. RCA and ITT both had poor internal quality because of faulty management beliefs. Their demise came about from within.

Changes in State

But the very same principles apply in ecology. Species are constantly growing and dying. Under relatively stable conditions, there is a stable rate of birth and death of species as niches change slowly. When the environment jumps to a different state—such as when an ice age occurs or ends—there is flux in the number of species and greater diversity. When there is an extreme event the ecology experiences mass extinction of species. After a mass extinction many new species are quickly (from a geological perspective) created. This infers periods of great stability interspersed with periods of flux when great numbers of species come on the scene, from a geological perspective, all at once. There is evidence that evolution occurs in just this manner.

Economies also jump to different states. One measure of an economy is the average price-earnings (PE) ratio of some major group of companies. For instance we could take the price-earnings ratio of the Dow Jones Industrial Average or Standard and Poor's 500 Index. When the PE ratio is in single digits the economy is in one state. PE in the teens is another, and PE in the twenties is the third. A bull market takes an economy from one state to a higher PE state. A bear market takes an economy to a lower PE state. Stable markets maintain the state. Doing business in a single-digit, stable PE state is very different from doing business in a stable 20X PE state—and both are different from a bull and bear market. In each state different sectors of the economy prosper and different strategies are optimal.

As I am writing this the U.S. economy is in recession and President Bush is proposing a significant tax cut to stimulate the economy. His justification is understandable—if we are still in a recession in two years his prospects for reelection dim considerably. If a recession is just a matter of weak demand and too high a tax level then a fiscal stimulus might make some sense. But with a $435 billion dollar balance of trade deficit, fiscal stimulus might just lead to greater demand for foreign goods and an even larger trade deficit. At the same time it would create huge fiscal deficits and pour billions of dollars into foreign hands. Yet by the end of this decade enormous demands will be made on government as baby boomers begin to retire. Running huge fiscal deficits will leave the federal government in a weakened position. It is ironic that an administration that ran on a platform of less government interference for business feels compelled to help our "free" economy do better each time there is a problem.

And suppose that a recession is not just caused by less demand, but is in fact a different state. It could be a reaction to an excess of some kind, perhaps intoxication. During the boom of the 1990s all sorts of silly ideas took hold, such as profits were unnecessary; profits were what you said they were; good technology was everything; good management didn't matter; and so on. A recession might be a necessary part of economic self-regulation: a cleansing phase that creates a base for new growth. It might force each company and each industry to make necessary adjustments. Have a little faith in the self-regulating ability of our economy to correct itself and pull through the difficult times, such as hangovers as well as periods of intoxication.

Changes of State Due to Growth

In addition to different cyclical states, economies and the global ecosystems experience growth. Over time significant changes occur allowing us to distinguish between one ecological period and another. We can also distinguish between different economic periods, the Middle Ages versus the Renaissance versus industrial times, for instance. When an economy jumps to a different price-earnings state we have a cyclical change of state. With growth and evolution, economies and social structures experience a different kind of change of state: one induced by growth and evolution.

I asked in Chapter 1 if we are now experiencing a new change in state. I believe the answer is yes. The human race has gone through several changes of state in the past. Some of the markers of the different growth-based economic and social states are the communication technology: nonverbal communication, verbal communication, written communication, printed communication, electronic communication—and now all of these combined in the Internet. Each is associated with particular social structures: nonverbal with tribes, verbal with tribes and villages; written with towns, city-states, and empires; printed with nation-states and empires; and electronic communication with powerful nation-states and regional alliances.

Growth-Based Changes in State Require New Metaknowledge

When human society is transitioning to a new social and economic state metaknowledge must change. Early on magical thinking gave way to a sense of personal control or at least tribal control. In early empires the people identified with the king. The written word promulgated systematic learning. The development of the high-speed printing press shifted thinking from Earth as the center to the Sun as the center. Religious justifications gave way to some kind of empirical validation. Science in the era of the printed word has also undergone some drastic reformulations. Statistics, non-Euclidian geometry, the separation of mathematics from science, germ theory, evolution, genetics, the periodic tables, atomic theory, quantum mechanics, and relativity theory are some of the major revolutions in thought.

We now need a new metaknowledge as a basis for business, economics, social systems, and politics. In a period of instantaneous communications with scientific and technical knowledge spreading around the globe, weapons of mass destruction are no longer the province of the military of a few powerful nations. The nation-state has a limited future. Foreign policy today is largely based on foreign policy of an earlier age. With mercantilism, nations tried to achieve a positive balance of trade, by force if necessary. The European powers carved empires for themselves. Britain knew she could not conquer the continent and instead played a balance of power game to keep any of her rivals from becoming too strong. With the circumnavigation of the globe by either

Ferdinand Magellan or Juan Sebastian Del Cano, depending on your point of view, in either 1521 or 1522, we began moving from an open foreign political system to a closed one. And the rules and strategy for effective foreign policy must change. What has become painfully evident is that in a closed system any action taken abroad eventually reverberates at home. The distinction between foreign and domestic, between at home or away is disappearing. Nations such as Poland, the Czech Republic, and Latvia, once controlled by the Soviet Union, now look to the United States as their role model and look to Russia with distrust. Iran, where American foreign policy circumvented free elections to support someone more inclined to be an American ally, is now closed to the United States, which is looked upon with suspicion.

Our foreign policy must change from one where a nation's best interests were paramount to one where human and global interests are paramount. In my opinion that means the United States must actively support and aid representative government even if the elected officials are not our friends in the short-term. For each elected government will pass and ultimately it will be the relationship that the people of the United States have with the people of that country that determines our long-term relationship.

In the past a bellicose or brutal dictator could be allowed to stew in his own country. Regional politics and war remained regional. That clearly is no longer the case. And there must be some force to police inhumane and inexcusable behavior. For the time being that role falls to the United States more than any other nation. It is something most Americans, myself included, are uncomfortable with but that is the new reality. And if we are to promulgate stability, we will have to engage in long-term nation building. While that is something we have not historically done and may not be particularly competent at right now, it is a change of no greater magnitude than prior changes. In the 1940s the United States went from being a peace-hugging nation that wished to avoid war at any cost to the most powerful war machine on Earth in just two years. We have gone from sprinters to marathoners; from pork eaters to beef eaters to sushi lovers; from a segregated society to an integrating society; from a white nation to a diverse nation; from strongly defined sexual roles and occupations to greater diversity; from a domestic economy to an international economy. Taking on a new role will feel difficult at first. We must pass through the stages of conscious incompetence and conscious competence before we can experience unconscious competence. But we need not do this alone. The comments of the last few paragraphs are applicable to all the countries of the developed super-state. And in a closed system all our interests are aligned.

A Changing Perception of Animals

What was most striking to me as I investigated and thought through the material in this book was the change in status of animals throughout the world. The scientific research that continues on chimpanzees, gorillas, dolphins, orca whales, and other creatures continues to surprise us. Chimpanzees, for instance, have been taught arithmetic and to understand zero. A continued expansion of animal rights to me seems inevitable. I am not an animal rights activist. I am merely looking at the data—the trend in animal rights popularity and the increasing body of evidence of animal intelligence—and drawing inferences. As I am writing this (February 2003), the Colorado legislature is beginning to discuss a bill that would give pets status as companions, the implications being that harming a pet would be considered legally equivalent to harming a person.

All these elements inevitably draw us to the question of ethics. How should we behave as individuals toward one another, toward people of different classes and nations, toward other species, and toward the environment? How should nations and regions behave toward each other? These are all related and based upon our presuppositions: our beliefs of reality, who we are, and how the world functions. As our material well-being reaches a critical stage, communications continue to improve, and more of us identify with humanity—perhaps even with all of life and not just one single nation—our presuppositions, our metaknowledge must change.

Ethics and MetaKnowledge

The great economist John Maynard Keynes, in an essay called "Economic Possibilities for Our Grandchildren," written in the midst of the Great Depression, predicted that in a hundred years the economic problem for the industrialized nations would be solved. He compared the standard of living in 1930 with the past and projected, based on capital accumulation and technological innovation, that in one hundred years wealth would increase eightfold. The pace by which the economic problem would be solved depended on four factors: society's ability to control population; its ability to avoid major wars and civil dissensions; its willingness to rely on science where appropriate; and the rate of capital accumulation.

With an eightfold increase in average wealth, the basic issues of food, clothing, and shelter—the main concern of humans for hundreds of thousands of years—would be in large measure taken care of. Of course this would not solve other problems associated with being human. Keynes broke down our needs into two categories: absolute needs, which we feel regardless of what others feel; and relative needs, which are those that we feel only if their satisfaction lifts us above other human beings. Roughly speaking the absolute needs correspond to Maslow's physiological needs.

To Keynes the possibility of solving our economic problem was startling given that for eons it had been the "most pressing problem of the human race," indeed of the whole biological kingdom. Solving the economic problem therefore presented some very real problems. The adjustment could be painful. Spouses of the well-to-do, for instance, deprived of their traditional tasks and occupations, were unable to "find anything more amusing"[42] to do with their time. Looking at the wealthy of his day, who might be called the advanced guard of this trend, the outlook was depressing, for most of them had "failed disastrously."[43]

But he was optimistic that with more experience, different and better ways to live life without the pressing need for survival would be found. And this was extremely important, for now we would be facing the permanent problem of the human race: How to use the freedom from economic cares to live "wisely and agreeably and well."[44] In his words, "it will be those peoples, who can keep alive, and cultivate into a fuller perfection, the art of life itself and do not sell themselves for the means of life, who will be able to enjoy the abundance when it comes."[45] He seems to be hinting at what it is to be self-actualizing, and

[42] *Essays in Persuasion,* "Economic Possibilities for Our Grandchildren," by John Maynard Keynes, page 367.

[43] Ibid., 368.

[44] Ibid., 367.

[45] Ibid., 368.

this should be no surprise. Keynes was a wealthy self-made investor who pursued economics not as an occupation but out of his passion and joy for the subject. From his words we must conclude that he was self-actualizing.

Keynes believed that when the economic problem was solved we would be free to return to principles of "traditional virtue—that avarice is a vice, that the exaction of usury is a misdemeanour, and the love of money is detestable."[46] And, "We shall once more value ends above means and prefer the good to the useful."[47] It must have pained him, then, when he concluded, "The time for all this is not yet. For at least another hundred years we must pretend to ourselves and to every one that fair is foul and foul is fair; for foul is useful and fair is not. Avarice and usury and precaution must be our gods for a little longer still. For only they can lead us out of the tunnel of economic necessity into daylight."[48]

I won't quibble with Keynes whether in the past avarice and greed were necessary ingredients of capital accumulation. I disagree, but the past, for our purposes, is moot. The position based on MetaKnowledge is distinctly different. I believe that the best results are obtained by aligning our interests with those of customers and with those of society. Economics is not a zero-sum gain, where one gains at the expense of others. Customers and vendors are not adversaries to be defeated, but partners to work with to expand the pie. By working together, with knowledge of variation, systems thinking, and the other parts of Meta-Knowledge business becomes a win-win proposition. By giving more we get more. By working with vendors and sharing information we both gain.

Yes, with MetaKnowledge there is competition and it is fierce. But there is also cooperation. Indeed the two are not opposites—they must and do coexist. Even competitors must cooperate. The aim is not to beat up someone else but to become the best you can be, and in so doing serve the needs of society. At times there are direct fights for a given market or war. But in most cases companies increase their market share by providing customers more or something new that customers then discover they really want. By serving society you gain not just

[46] Ibid., 371.

[47] Ibid., 372.

[48] Ibid., 372.

financially but with the satisfaction that comes from being useful and from the intrinsic value of the work itself.

With MetaKnowledge there is no dichotomy between good business and ethics. We, as a society, must stop using the smoke screen of maximizing capital or profit for actions that are unethical on their face. Lying about results to the public, creating shoddy products or poor service, avoiding real ecological and social concerns in approving projects cannot be justified in the name of good business or making money. The astute businessperson recognizes that we are all connected, we are all part of a system, and any action that creates loss for society in some sense harms him as well and is not a justifiable business option.

If the economy is an ecology, there will be innumerable ways of earning a living. There are many niches that may require very different behaviors. Some unlikely ways of earning a living can produce great wealth. I am reminded of stories I heard when I was growing up of rag merchants who were millionaires. It seemed unlikely that these early recyclers who took away our unwanted rags and had little status could earn so much, but apparently some did. For an ecology to work there needs to be freedom to pursue activities that we might not understand or agree with. I will not lay claim to the assumption that all companies in all niches must follow the same ethics. But certainly for leading firms and public firms, a high level of ethics must be required. And there is a certain minimal ethical and legal system that all must adhere to. Not only is this good ethics it is good business. And the same ethics applies in government and the other sectors of our economy as well.

The Economic Problem Today

We are pretty close to the developmental point predicted by Keynes. Our society as a whole produces enough to feed, clothe, and shelter everyone. Even among the middle class the economic problem has been largely solved. As an example, a car built today could with reasonable care last ten to fifteen years. But most people will buy a car well before the previous car expires. It is not the need for transportation that is being fulfilled by a new car when the old one still works well. It is the need for esteem or status or affiliation. It is to satisfy you or your family's desires. Increasingly it is not material needs that are motivating our behavior. Higher needs in the Maslow hierarchy are calling to be fulfilled.

The beauty of MetaKnowledge is that its principles apply in all sectors. While not every organization has customers in the traditional sense, every organization has beliefs, people, and systems. One principle is continual and never-ending improvement. Improvement has become a science. We could keep improving efficiency to create more goods with fewer people, but at some point relatively soon we must ask, "Why?"

The farming population is already less than 2%. Would there be any meaningful gain if that were brought down further? I think that would be a very difficult case to make. On the other hand, improvement in the quality of farm goods—that is to say healthier, with more minerals and nutrients, with less impact on the environment—does make sense. At some point quantity becomes immaterial and then quality becomes paramount. We are already seeing significant trends along these lines. Organic products, even though they may cost more, are grabbing a significant share of the market. Although water is free right out of the tap, Americans and Europeans are spending significant amounts on bottled water.

Other Problems

Even if we do solve the economic problem there is no shortage of other problems to deal with. Income inequality and opportunity for poorer segments of our society are two. But in the latter part of this decade, we will be facing an enormous demographic shift. The largest population bulge in our history, the baby boomers, begin to retire. They begin to reach the traditional early retirement age of 62 in 2008. In 2011 they start turning 65. At that point we will have severe internal challenges. A strain on resources will occur as proportionately more people become eligible for social security. If they also begin to withdraw funds from stocks, lower valuations for stocks and a reversal, at least in part, of the wealth effect that helped power the booms of the 1980s and '90s will occur.

Global Concerns

With greater material wealth, large numbers of older people, the possibility of having many more self-actualizing people, and international communications giving us vivid pictures of famine, war, and suffering in other parts of the world, it will be virtually impossible for the people of the developed world to turn their backs on the rest of the world. The wealth, prosperity, and political freedom of the developed world are in stark contrast to conditions in other parts. But technology can be used by anyone, not just those with high morals. It should be evident to everyone that the period of American isolation from the rest of the world is but a naïve wish at this point. We will face severe external challenges as well.

With global communications and globalization, the problems of other parts of the world become our problems. We cannot choose and pick some of the consequences of these major trends. We get the whole package, the desirable and the undesirable. If we choose to advocate free trade and the free flow of funds and open communications we must remember that that becomes a two-way street. Economically, politically, and increasingly socially we are becoming one world. We have already seen the deterioration of national sovereignty as all nations are being forced to behave in a manner consistent with the mores of other nations. We will be called upon to help, in some form, other parts of the world on a regular basis. And there is little question that force will be used. We must continue to improve our ability to use it wisely.

We have already been called on to prevent massacre and genocide in Eastern Europe. And it will be to our great disgrace if we cannot—with our wealth, power, education, people, and management acumen—persuade opposing sides to come to the table and bargain in good faith instead of continuing to kill each other in the Middle East.

Truly Global Concerns

But our challenges are not limited to the human sphere. Systems thinking applies not just to the global economic system but to the whole planetary biosphere. Life on Earth has shown itself to be self-regulating to an incredible degree. Key variables such as temperature and oxygen levels have held at remarkably stable levels for extended periods of time. It is possible that almost anything we do to the land, ocean, and atmosphere will be corrected by these self-regulatory forces. But those corrections may be done in geological time, that is to say hundreds of thousands or millions of years, not human time of years and decades. In the meantime the short-term consequences to the environment may not be to our liking.

The attitudes toward other life forms and the planet in general are changing. Dolphins, whales, and other large creatures are protected by international treaties. Ecological impact studies are required for major construction projects. If we believe that many higher animals are sentient, as many people do, then they must be treated differently and their standing in human law will continue to evolve, giving them more rights.

When man was an inconspicuous part of life, another animal eking out an existence, we had the luxury of believing that humans were above nature, that our role was to conquer and bend her to our will. Commerce was distinct from nature and had nothing to do with ecology. As the human population expanded and their organizations became more complex, our actions toward other humans and other ecologies were sometimes brutal and uncaring. But human success and growth now means that our actions have consequences—not just on others but on the natural ecology—and that may come back to harm us or our grandchildren. We need to view humans and human commerce as extensions of nature, a part of the larger ecology.

The economic success of the developed world means that we are looking at a time when the major economic problems that were the main reason for working during the lives of our grandparents are largely solved. The main reason for commerce used to be survival, that is to say to earn a living. But increasingly, other needs—particularly the need to do worthwhile work—are entering the picture. Our best trained young people want more than money, they want to do something meaningful.

We are on the threshold of a new era where economic needs are not as pressing, where our actions have irreversible consequences for us and our grandchildren. The role of business is not diminishing, it is changing and expanding. A shift in thinking is occurring from the purely atomistic, mechanical view of independent actions to a balanced appreciation for the whole, with interdependence among parts and biological models for economics, politics, and personal action. More than ever wisdom is called for in our most important human endeavors. And the best proxy we have for wisdom is MetaKnowledge.

THE RELATIONSHIP BETWEEN QUALITY AND PROFITABILITY

I want to graphically illustrate the relationship between quality and profitability. In simple terms, profit is the difference between revenues and the costs associated with those revenues. Conceptually profits are a measure of the increase in value of an enterprise over a period of time. Profit is backward looking. Accountants measure the profit of the last year or of the last quarter.

There are two kinds of statistical studies: enumerative and analytical. An enumerative study measures some quantity (profit, sales, heat, population, etc.) in the past, or real time, which is the very recent past. An analytical study attempts to predict what will happen in the future, either under similar circumstances or if circumstances change appreciably. An analytical study predicts and therefore requires a model. All financial statements are enumerative: they measure, they do not predict. The belief that financial statements predict future results is a logical and conceptual error and the source of considerable confusion in financial decision making.

Predicting financial results in the short-term requires a different model than one used to make long-term predictions. Here I want to focus on relatively short-term predictions. Every company has fixed costs. For our purposes, fixed costs are those costs that will be incurred next month if we open our doors prepared to do the current volume of business. A better term might be fixed operating costs but for brevity's sake I will stick with fixed costs. Fixed costs include items such as rent, insurance, and salaries for all our work force (not just production people, but all sales, marketing, finance, administration, and support people as well). If we have a store it includes all the sales people we need to adequately run the store as well as all support. Even if we have zero sales, these costs will be incurred as long as we are in business ready to sell and produce at current levels.

Excluded from fixed costs in this model are variable production costs. In a manufacturing operation this includes materials, supplies, some energy costs, all overtime, and any other variable costs. In a retail operation variable costs include any product costs. If a store sells nothing, then merchandise doesn't move, inventory doesn't decline, no new products are ordered, and there is no cost of goods sold, but the store still incurs costs to keep its doors open.

Fixed and variable costs as defined here are different than a cost accountant's definition. For cost accountants, variable costs include the labor associated with production. But since most production people are working for the company and will report in to work whether you have a lot of work or little, it is important to include these salaries as part of fixed costs for the purposes of this model.

Let me take some numbers from a real example. Brooktrout Enterprises (fictitious name, real company) had a fixed cost of $450,000 a month. Their variable costs were out of control (they were not in statistical control, numerical control, or even visual control) and varied considerably from month to month and from job to job but on average were about 50% of sales. If costs are 50% then gross margin or gross profit is (100% (sales) – 50% (variable costs) =) 50%, so each dollar of sales generates a gross profit of 50¢. This 50¢ of gross profit begins to cover fixed costs. In order for gross profits to cover the fixed costs of $450,000, the company needed to sell $900,000 in a given month ($900,000 of sales x 50% = $450,000 = fixed costs). This is graphically illustrated in Chart I on page 253.

Because of the recessions and missteps by the company, sales were averaging $830,000 a month, below the $900,000 breakeven. They were hemorrhaging money. They had lost money the prior year as well on higher sales. The last two years represented the first slowdown in business after a decade of strong growth. A company close to or below breakeven experiences an emotional roller coaster. In good months they pull out a little profit and feel some calm. The next month, however,

Chart I
Break-even Analysis: Cost vs. Profit

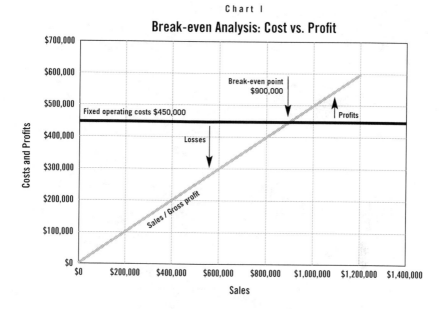

they can lose quite a bit of money leaving the managers and associates feeling distraught.

We took a number of steps to bring them back to profitability. Leases, lending arrangements, supplies, and material costs were renegotiated. We also started to improve internal quality and bring their processes under control. Since their systems became more efficient we didn't need to also replace people who left. This had the effect of bringing fixed costs down to $420,000. If the gross margins had remained at 50% their break-even sales level would have been $840,000, still above average monthly sales. This is illustrated in Chart II.

We were also actively working to improve internal quality thereby lessening internal waste and improving external quality. One example of how improving internal quality lessens waste comes from another client, a printer. Customers demanded that color on the printed product closely match some standard—either earlier printed products, artwork, or an industry standard color-matching book. The pressmen were adjusting the inks to try and match the standard. When I queried pressmen concerning the quality of incoming ink, I received very different responses. Some liked the ink, others thought it was terrible. We did some research and determined what specifications were important and then started measuring incoming ink. We found that it was out of con-

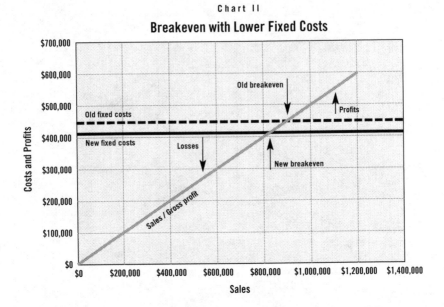

Chart II

Breakeven with Lower Fixed Costs

trol in all important specifications such as viscosity, density, pH, and hue. Immense variation from batch to batch forced pressmen to constantly adjust the ink on the presses. This resulted in extra copies that didn't match and had to be thrown out—creating waste that ate up paper, ink, press time, plant capacity, and capital.

We started working with the ink supplier to bring these key specifications into control. The original supplier wasn't able to respond adequately so a new supplier was found who could provide a consistent product. This led to a significant reduction in waste during production, and this was just one of hundreds of initiatives that were taken to improve internal quality and lower variable costs.

At Brooktrout variable costs dropped from 50% to 40%. Now gross margins were 60% instead of 50%, and as a result the monthly breakeven sales level had dropped to about $700,000. The company could make a profit on lower sales and therefore could get through the recession. This is illustrated in Chart III.

Capacity

There is something more to consider and that is capacity. Under Brooktrout's old systems (or lack thereof) capacity was about $950,000 a

Chart III

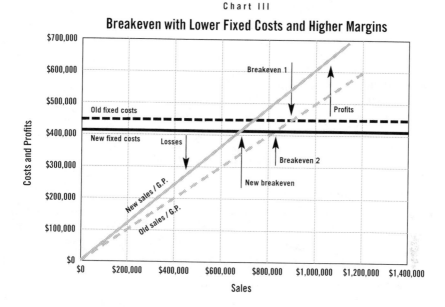

month. When sales exceeded that level, significant overtime was necessary. In addition, its systems, already stretched, were pushed beyond their limits resulting in greater inefficiencies. They could get some additional work out above $950,000, but waste increased exponentially. In the past they had managed to lose money in months when they shipped more than $1,000,000.

When capacity of $950,000 a month is compared to a breakeven of $900,000, it shows there was little room to make money. Like all businesses their sales vary from month to month. In months below breakeven they would lose money, but even at capacity they stood to make only $25,000. With a capacity to break-even ratio of 1.06 (950,000/900,000) there is no way they could earn healthy returns even with strong sales.

While Brooktrout's costs decreased and margins increased with improvements in internal quality, capacity had not been decimated. On the contrary, capacity had actually increased. Before, a lot of capacity was taken up making waste and rejects. As internal quality was improved capacity was freed up to make usable products. Capacity was now closer to $1,250,000. A capacity to break-even ratio approaching 2.0 indicates a strong and healthy operation that can withstand economic variability. Ideally the company should be able to make money or break even during very slow months. The best way of achieving this is through the three main principles of The New Management: internal quality, external quality, and continual improvement. This is illustrated in Chart IV.

External Quality

Clearly, improving internal quality improves external quality, leading to fewer returns and disgruntled customers and therefore greater customer satisfaction. But when we started surveying customers, we found that contrary to the company's perception, price was not the leading motive for customers doing business with the company. In fact, price was rarely mentioned. There were a few very boisterous customers who frequently complained to the owner, trying to get a better price. Often they were successful. But when an accurate representative sample was taken—aimed at giving a better picture of the whole customer base—we discovered that price was not an issue for many loyal customers. Instead it turned out that delivery times and the inability to give sufficient warning when a delay was imminent were the most troublesome issues to customers. And all this time the company had operated under the assumption that price was the leading issue.

Chart IV
Breakeven with Lower Fixed Costs, Higher Margins, and Capacity

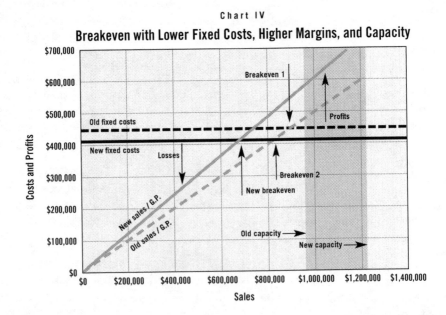

Armed with this data and this insight, we could begin to focus on delivery and design the company to be more flexible, offering quicker, more reliable delivery and notifying the customers in advance when a delivery date was threatened.

Break-Even Analysis for Knowledge Companies

Chart IV shows constraints of capacity. In most operations, when capacity is reached or exceeded a new plant or store needs to be opened. And now the company is dealing with a new round of fixed costs and new risks. What if demand is so strong that a new store or a new plant is justified, but when it does open several months or several years later, the excess demand can fill up just 25% of the new plant's capacity while the break-even point for the new plant is 50%? Profitability becomes compromised and a deterioration in sales might lead to losses.

From an operations point of view, if demand is strong enough to support a plant or store operating at close to full capacity you should be competitive even if you have fewer plants or stores than a much larger competitor. The size advantage of the larger player is due to his ability to spread research and development costs over more units, meaning his fixed costs per unit are lower and therefore his costs are somewhat lower. Size may also confer an advantage in advertising and marketing, since a larger player may have more dollars to spend in this area. But size also has disadvantages. A little complacency can easily slow down a larger competitor and make it more difficult for them to respond to radical shifts in the marketplace.

But what happens if the business has no capacity constraints? That is effectively the case for software companies. In addition, the variable costs are negligible. Microsoft can stamp out another disk of the Windows operating system quickly and cheaply. It may contract out all or a portion of the actual disk creation. Their cost per disk is probably pennies. If the computer manufacturers do the installation, the cost to Microsoft of additional replication is zero. If distribution of software takes place over the Internet, the marginal cost is also zero. For a knowledge company with products to sell, all its costs are fixed costs as we have defined them here. And it is possible for a knowledge company to have revenues that are 3, 5, or 50 times its break-even costs. Since variable margins approach 100% of sales, profit margins can be enormous. As evidence of that, consider that for 2001, Wal-Mart had sales of $220 billion and profits of $6.7 billion while Microsoft had sales of $25 billion and profits of $7.3 billion.[1]

The same holds true to some extent for other knowledge products such as records and books. A superstar author who sells millions of copies or a superstar group that sells millions of albums can be more profitable than many lesser stars who sell just hundreds of thousands each, even though their combined sales volume is greater. A new voice will produce much smaller revenues. These economics help foster the star system as studios and publishers have a financial incentive to invest marketing dollars in those titles and artists who are likely to sell millions over others who may just do well.

---

[1] *Fortune* magazine, "Fortune 500 listing for 2002," April 15, 2002.

A SAMPLE
CONTROL CHART

Suppose a crack quality control team goes into a hospital to investigate the level of quality. They secretly track six workers for four months and note the number of errors each makes each month. Their results are in the table below.

These results seem pretty clear-cut. Barbara is the best worker, although even she had plenty of errors, while Lenny was the worst performer. Some managers would be ready to let him go. Cathy might have gotten a warning in the first month, but given her sterling performance in the fourth month she might have been recognized as the most improved worker. What possible good could a control chart do here?

The average number of defects for every worker over the four months is *215 / 24 = 8.96*, which we can round off to 9. Each worker

NAME	MONTH 1	MONTH 2	MONTH 3	MONTH 4	TOTAL	RANK
Ken	8	10	12	9	39	5
Barbara	6	4	11	7	28	1
Lenny	11	11	11	8	41	6
Noboru	8	11	8	11	38	4
Cathy	15	5	12	4	36	3
Steve	5	9	9	10	33	2
Total	53	50	63	49	215	

was checked 50 times during the month, so the average incidence of errors, *p*, is *9 / 50 = .18.* The Upper Control Limit (UCL) is computed as follows:

UCL = 9 + 3 (the square root of *(9 (1–.18))*)
UCL = 9 + 3 (the square root of *7.38*)
UCL = 9 + 3 *(2.7) = 17.15 = 18*

The Lower Control Limit (LCL) is computed as follows:
LCL = 9 – 3 (the square root of *(9 (1–.18))*)
LCL = 9 – 3 *(2.7)*
LCL = 9 – 8.1 = 1

Graphing the results each month, starting with Ken and working down on the table above to Steve produces the following graph:

At no point is anyone above the Upper Control Limit or below the Lower Control Limit. This indicates strongly that all the differences are caused by the system or by chance. These results are taken from page 55 of my earlier book, *Dr. Deming: The American Who Taught the Japanese About Quality*. The numbers were actually generated by each one of the individuals dipping a paddle with 50 holes into a bowl containing 20% black beads and 80% white beads and then counting the number of black beads in the paddle. In a live situation the results generate

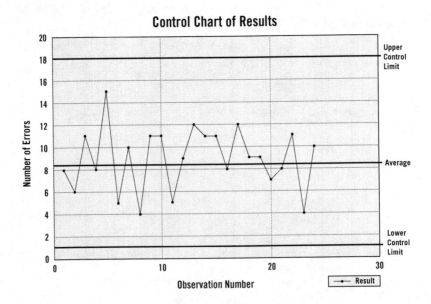

Control Chart of Results

greater variation from day to day and from person to person as even the supply of beads changes.

This should at the very least give pause to managers who are quickly on top of "poor" performers and praise and reward "good" performers. The manager needs to ask, how much of the results are due to chance? This is equivalent to asking how much of the results are due to the system. Only by doing systematic improvements that lessen the incidence of errors for everyone will the number of mistakes decline on a regular and permanent basis. An additional benefit is that improvements to the system also lessen the variation from person to person and from day to day.

Additional sources of information about variation and control charts can be obtained from the following: *Understanding Variation: The Key to Managing Chaos,* by Donald J. Wheeler; *Understanding Statistical Process Control,* by Donald J. Wheeler and David S. Chambers; and *Statistical Quality Control Handbook,* of AT&T.

BIBLIOGRAPHY

Adizes, Ichak. *Corporate Lifecycles.* Prentice Hall, Englewood Cliffs, New Jersey, 1988.

Aguayo, Rafael. *Dr. Deming: The American Who Taught the Japanese About Quality.* Fireside, Simon & Schuster, New York, 1990.

Asimov, Isaac. *I, Robot.* Bantam Books, New York, 1950.

Attenborough, David. *Life on Earth,* a series of videos produced by BBC in association with Warner Brothers and Reiner Moritz Productions. The John D. & Catherine T. MacArthur Foundation Library Video Classics Project. Approximately thirteen hours.

Baker, Gregory L., and Jerry P. Golub. *Chaotic Dynamics: An Introduction.* Press Syndicate of Cambridge, New York, Copyright Cambridge University Press, 1990.

Bandler, Richard, and John Grinder. *The Structure of Magic I.* Science and Behavior Books Inc., Palo Alto, California, 1975.

Bandler, Richard, and John Grinder. *The Structure of Magic II.* Science and Behavior Books Inc., Palo Alto, California, 1976.

Bandler, Richard, and John Grinder. *Frogs into Princes.* Real People Press, Moab, Utah, 1979.

Bandler, Richard, and John Grinder. *Trance-formations.* Real People Press, Moab, Utah, 1981.

Bateson, Gregory. *Mind and Nature: A Necessary Unity.* E. P. Dutton, New York, 1979.

Bauer, Henry H. *Scientific Literacy and the Myth of the Scientific Method.* University of Illinois Press, Urbana and Chicago, 1992.

Black Elk, Wallace, and William S. Lyon. *Black Elk: The Sacred Ways of a Lakota.* Harper and Row, San Francisco, 1990.

Brennan, Michael J. *Theory of Economic Statics.* Prentice Hall, Inc., Englewood Cliffs, New Jersey, 1965.

Campbell, Joseph. *The World of Joseph Campbell: Transformations of Myth Through Time.* Produced by William Free Productions and Mythology Ltd. in association with Holoform Research, Inc., 1989. Approximately thirteen hours of videotapes.

Capra, Fritjof. *The Tao of Physics.* Shambhala, Boston, 1975.

Capra, Fritjof. *The Turning Point.* Simon & Schuster, New York, 1982.

Capra, Fritjof. *Uncommon Wisdom.* Simon & Schuster, New York, 1988.

Capra, Fritjof. *The Web of Life.* Anchor Books, Doubleday, a division of Bantam Doubleday Dell Publishing Group, Inc., New York, 1996.

Capra, Fritjof, and David Steindl-Rast with Thomas Matus. *Belonging to the Universe: Explorations on the Frontiers of Science and Spirituality.* HarperCollins Publishers, Inc., New York, 1991.

Carroll, Lewis. *The Complete Sylvie and Bruno.* Mercury House, Inc., San Francisco, 1991.

Chopra, Deepak. *The Seven Spiritual Laws of Success.* Amber-Allen Publishing, San Rafael, California, 1993.

Chowdhury, Subir. *The Power of Six Sigma.* Dearborn Trade Publishing, Chicago, 2001.

Collins, James C., and Jerry I. Porras. *Built to Last: Successful Habits of Visionary Companies.* HarperCollins Publishers, Inc., New York, 1997.

Collins, Jim. *Good to Great: Why Some Companies Make the Leap . . . and Others Don't.* HarperCollins Publishers, Inc., New York, 2001.

Dalai Lama XIV. *The Four Noble Truths.* Mystic Fire Video, Inc., New York. Four-tape series, approximately six hours.

Davenport, Thomas H., and Laurence Prusak. *Working Knowledge: How Organizations Manage What They Know.* Harvard Business School Press, Boston, Massachusetts, 1998.

Dawkins, Richard. *Unweaving the Rainbow.* Houghton Mifflin Company, New York, 1998.

Deming, W. Edwards. *Sample Design in Business Research.* John Wiley & Sons, New York, 1960.

Deming, W. Edwards. *Quality, Productivity and Competitive Position.* Massachusetts Institute of Technology Center for Advanced Engineering, Cambridge, Massachusetts, 1982.

Deming, W. Edwards. *Out of the Crisis.* Massachusetts Institute of Technology Center for Advanced Engineering, Cambridge, Massachusetts, 1986.

Deming, W. Edwards. *The New Economics.* Massachusetts Institute of Technology Center for Advanced Engineering, Cambridge, Massachusetts, 1993.

Dent, Harry S., Jr. *The Great Boom Ahead.* Hyperion, New York, 1993.

Dent, Harry S., Jr. *The Roaring 2000s.* Touchstone Books, Simon & Schuster, New York, 1998.

Dharma, Krishna. *Ramayana.* Torchlight Publishing, Los Angeles, 1998.

Dilts, Robert. *Changing Belief Systems with NLP.* Meta Publications, Cupertino, California, 1990.

Dyer, Wayne W. *You'll See It When You Believe It.* William Morrow and Company, Inc., New York, 1989.

Dyer, Wayne W. *Real Magic.* HarperCollins Publishers, Inc., New York, 1992.

Freud, Sigmund. *Introductory Lectures on Psycho-Analysis.* W. W. Norton & Company, New York, 1920, 1935, 1964, 1965, 1966.

Freud, Sigmund. *Therapy and Technique*. Collier Books, Macmillan Publishing Company, New York, 1963.

Friedman, Thomas L. *The Lexus and the Olive Tree*. Farrar, Straus and Giroux, New York, 1999.

Gardner, Howard. *Frames of Mind: The Theory of Multiple Intelligences*. Basic Books, a Division of HarperCollins Publishers, Inc., New York, 1993.

Gleick, James. *Chaos: Making a New Science*. Penguin Books, Viking Penguin Inc., New York, 1988.

Grebogi, Celso, and James A. Yorke, editors. *The Impact of Chaos on Science and Society*. United Nations University Press, The United Nations University, Tokyo, 1997.

Grove, Andrew S. *Only the Paranoid Survive: How to Exploit the Crisis Points That Challenge Every Company and Career*. Currency, a division of Bantam Doubleday Dell Publishing Group, New York, 1996.

Hagstrom, Robert G. *The Warren Buffet Way*. John Wiley & Sons, Inc., New York, 1995.

Hawken, Paul. *The Next Economy*. Holt, Rinehart and Winston, New York, 1983.

Hawken, Paul. *Growing a Business*. Collins Publishers, Don Mills, Ontario, Canada, 1987.

Heller, Robert. *Warren Buffet: The Man Who Made Billions with a Unique Investment Strategy*. Dorling Kindersley Limited, London, 2000.

Hill, Napoleon. *The Master-Key to Riches*. Fawcett Crest Book, Ballantine Books, New York, 1965.

Hopkins, Claude C. *My Life in Advertising & Scientific Advertising*. NTC Business Books, Lincolnwood, Illinois, 1995.

Jackson, Phil, and Hugh Delehanty. *Sacred Hoops*. Hyperion, New York, 1995.

James, William. *The Principles of Psychology*. Dover Publications, Inc., New York, 1890, 1918, 1950.

Jung, C. G. *Psychological Types*. Princeton University Press, New Jersey, 1971. *Originally published in German in 1921*.

Jung, C. G. *On the Nature of the Psyche*. Princeton University Press, New Jersey, 1960.

Kehoe, John. *Mind Power into the 21st Century*. Zoetic Inc., Vancouver, British Columbia, Canada, 1997.

Kelly, Kevin. *New Rules for the New Economy: 10 Radical Strategies for a Connected World*. Viking, Penguin Group, Penguin Putnam Inc., New York, 1998.

Keynes, John Maynard. *Essays in Persuasion*. W. W. Norton & Company, Inc., New York, 1963.

Lewis, Clarence Irving. *Mind and the World Order: Outline of a Theory of Knowledge*. Dover Publications, Inc., New York, 1929.

Lindsay, Robert Bruce. *Introduction to Physical Statistics*. Dover Publications, Inc., New York, 1941.

Lorenz, Edward N. *The Essence of Chaos.* University of Washington Press, Seattle, Washington, 1993.

Lovelock, James. *Gaia: A New Look at Life on Earth.* Oxford University Press, New York, 1979, 1987, 1995.

Lovelock, James. *The Ages of Gaia: A Biography of Our Living Earth.* The Commonwealth Fund Book Program of Memorial Sloan-Kettering Cancer Center, W. W. Norton & Company, Inc., New York, 1988, 1995.

Machiavelli, Niccolo. *The Prince and the Discourses.* The Modern Library, Random House, New York, 1950.

Magee, David. *Turn Around: How Carlos Ghosn Rescued Nissan.* HarperCollins Publishers, Inc., New York, 2003.

Malthus, Thomas Robert. *An Essay on Principle of Population.* Penguin Books, Ltd., Harmondsworth, Middlesex, England, 1798, 1831, 1970.

Marston, William Moulton. *Emotions of Normal People.* Reprinted by Persona Press, Inc., Minneapolis, 1979. *Original publication 1928.*

Maslow, Abraham. *Toward a Psychology of Being, second edition.* Van Nostrand Reinhold, New York, 1968.

Maslow, Abraham H. *Maslow on Management.* John Wiley & Sons, Inc., New York, 1998.

Monden, Yasuhiro. *Toyota Production System.* Industrial Engineering and Management Press, Norcross, Georgia, 1983.

Moore, Geoffrey A. *Crossing the Chasm.* HarperBusiness, New York, 1991.

Neef, Dale, editor. *The Knowledge Economy.* Butterworth-Heinemann, Boston, 1998.

Neef, Dale, G. Anthony Siesfeld, and Jacquelyn Cefola, editors. *The Economic Impact of Knowledge.* Butterworth-Heinemann, Boston, 1998.

Neihardt, John G. *Black Elk Speaks.* University of Nebraska Press, Lincoln and London, Nebraska, 1982. *Originally published in 1932.*

Niednagel, Jonathan P. *Your Key to Sports Success.* Laguna Press, Laguna Niguel, California, 1992, 1997.

O'Dell, Carla, and C. Jackson Grayson Jr. *If Only We Knew What We Know.* The Free Press, Simon & Schuster, 1998.

Ohmae, Kenichi. *The End of the Nation State.* The Free Press, Simon & Schuster, New York, 1995.

Ohno, Taiichi. *Toyota Production System: Beyond Large-Scale Production.* Productivity Press, Cambridge, Massachusetts and Norwalk, Connecticut, 1978, 1988.

Ohno, Taiichi with Setsuo Mito. *Just-In-Time For Today and Tomorrow.* Productivity Press, Cambridge, Massachusetts and Norwalk, Connecticut, 1986, 1988.

Packard, David. *The HP Way.* HarperBusiness, New York, 1995.

Palmedo, Philip F., and Edward Beltrami. *The Wines of Long Island: Birth of a Region.* Waterline Books, Great Falls, Virginia, 1993.

Palmedo, Philip F, and Eliza Hicks. *Voices in Bronze.* Rutledge Books, Inc., Danbury, Connecticut, 1998.

Peck, M. Scott. *The Road Less Traveled*. Touchstone, Simon & Schuster, New York, 1998.

Pei, Mario. *The Story of Language*. J. B. Lippincott Company, Philadelphia and New York, 1949, 1965.

Penrose, Roger. *The Emperor's New Mind*. Penguin Books USA, Inc., New York, 1991. *Copyright Oxford University Press, 1989*.

Reichheld, Frederick F. *The Loyalty Effect*. Harvard Business School Press, Boston, 1996.

Ries, Al, and Jack Trout. *Positioning: The Battle for Your Mind*. McGraw-Hill Book Company, New York, 1981, 1986.

Ries, Al, and Jack Trout. *Marketing Warfare*. Penguin Books USA Inc., New York, 1986.

Rifkin, Jeremy. *The End of Work*. G. P. Putnam's Sons, New York, 1995.

Robinson, Alan, editor. *Continuous Improvement in Operations*. Productivity Press, Cambridge, Massachusetts, 1991.

Ruiz, Don Miguel. *The Mastery of Love*. Amber-Allen Publishing, San Rafael, California, 1999.

Russo, Edward, and Paul J. H. Schoemaker. *Winning Decisions: Getting It Right the First Time*. Currency Doubleday, New York, 2002.

Schroeder, Keith A. *Life and Death on the Internet*. Supple Publishing, Menasha, Wisconsin, 1998.

Schumacher, E. F. *Small Is Beautiful: Economics as if People Mattered*. Blond & Briggs Ltd., London, 1973; Perennial Library, Harper & Row, New York, 1975.

Shewhart, Walter A. *Economic Control of Quality of Manufactured Product*. D. Van Nostrand Company, Inc., New York, 1931. *Republished by American Society for Quality Control, 1980*.

Shewhart, Walter A. *Statistical Method from the Viewpoint of Quality Control*. Graduate School, USDA, Washington, D.C., 1939.

Sloan, Alfred P., Jr. *My Years with General Motors*. Currency Doubleday, New York, 1963.

Smith, Adam. *The Wealth of Nations*. The Modern Library, New York, 1937.

Stewart, Ian. *Does God Play Dice?: The Mathematics of Chaos*. Basil Blackwell, Cambridge, Massachusetts, 1990.

Stewart, Thomas A. *Intellectual Capital: The New Wealth of Organizations*. Doubleday, a division of Bantam Doubleday Publishing Group, Inc., New York, 1997.

Stewart, Thomas A. *The Wealth of Knowledge: Intellectual Capital and the Twenty-First Century Organization*. Currency, a division of Random House, Inc., New York, 2001.

Sveiby, Karl Erik. *The New Organizational Wealth: Managing & Measuring Knowledge-Based Assets*. Berrett-Koehler Publishers, Inc., San Francisco, California, 1997.

Thomas, D. W., handbook committee chairman and others. *AT&T Statistical Quality Control Handbook*. Western Electric, 1956.

Thurow, Lester C. *Building Wealth*. HarperCollins Publishers, Inc., New York, 1999.

Walton, Sam, with John Huey. *Made in America: My Story*. Bantam Books, New York, 1992.

Wheatley, Margaret J. *Leadership and the New Science: Discovering Order in a Chaotic World, second edition*. Berrett-Koehler Publishers, San Francisco, California, 1999.

Wheeler, Donald J. *Understanding Statistical Process Control*. SPC Press, Inc., Knoxville, Tennessee, 1986.

Wheeler, Donald J. *Understanding Variation*. SPC Press, Inc., Knoxville, Tennessee, 1993.

Womack, James P., and Daniel T. Jones. *Lean Thinking*. Simon & Schuster, New York, 1996.

ACKNOWLEDGMENTS

This book would not have come into being without the assistance of Philip F. Palmedo. While I may be the author, he was the midwife who helped give birth. Phil is an author himself and when I told him I was having difficulty getting words on the page, he gave me just the right bit of advice to encourage me to push forward.

Over the next couple of years I met with Phil and used him as a sounding board to hash out and clarify the ideas in this book. Phil is one of those rare individuals who can easily cross disciplines. He holds a PhD in physics from MIT. He's an avid art collector and an author on such diverse topics as the wines of Long Island and the creative process in art. He's also a successful entrepreneur and angel investor who has advised nations and entrepreneurs on issues of technology and management. Phil was remarkably generous with his time and wisdom. Thank you, Phil.

I need to thank my neighbor, Virginia Bloch, for introducing Phil and I and for her warmth and wit.

Another friend of mine, Craig Hane, was instrumental in stimulating some of the ideas in this book. Craig is also a versatile individual who holds a PhD in mathematics from Indiana University and is a serial entrepreneur. He has formalized his management knowledge into an axiomatic-based system called QPI, for Quality and Productivity Improvement. His seminars and newsletters, along with our private conversations, have been a constant source of stimulation and new ideas.

Other friends were instrumental along the way, including Patrick Fletcher, Anthony Robbins, Donna Martini, David Pinkowitz, and Kimberly Jennings.

What is presented here is based on more than thirty years of management experience, the last thirteen as a consultant to companies large and small. I need to thank all my consulting clients who allowed me to use their companies as a laboratory, by trying and adopting ideas and suggestions. It is extremely gratifying to have an idea or method implemented by a client, to witness it improve his operation, and to receive some appreciation. But every time an idea or method is implemented is an opportunity to improve it. With each iteration it becomes better and takes less time so that future clients benefit from clients of the past and the present. The continuous improvement of methods, theories, and applications, plus the dissemination of this knowledge through consultants and consulting firms, must certainly be one reason why a developed economy continues to develop and change and can be resilient to dramatic changes. This spreads the improvement process throughout the economy and puts pressure on companies that are resistant to change.

Among the most enjoyable aspects of consulting are the wonderful clients, many of whom have become friends. I would like to thank them all, especially Steve Headrich, Norman Mayne, Calvin Mayne, Dr. Jacobo Sabbaj, Paul Lepercq, Francois Letaconnoux, Bill Vignola, Frank Kitchens, Doug Does, Chris Freddo, Christina Falsetta, Robert Mione, Richard Gardner, Bob Gerst, Terry Ortynsky, George and Robin Hallohan, John Harkins, Jeff Martini, Mike Bartosz, Hal Wicke, Larry J. Maltin, Daniel J. Glenn, and Ramon Abad.

A book project of this kind requires intense effort for long periods with little in the way of feedback or compensation. Friends and family were vital to me and I would like to thank Margaret Bottine, Estelle Solotoff, Brendan Aguayo, Alexis Aguayo, Justin Goldstein, Kay Posillico, Susan Weatherbee, Julie Simpson, Nic Mauro, John and Joanne Merenda, Denise Martorana, Alyse Parise, David Ochoa, Carole Roberts, Don Levine, Ed Diaz, Nancy Sternbergh, Ann-Marie Scheidt, Marcy Tublisky, Norman Weingart, Ed Scheine, Ellen Volpe, Heather Hanson O'Neill, Hope Delane, Howard Tollin, Lauren L. Mazar, Maria Morales-Prieto, Mary Jane Hartigan, Richard Isaac, Rick Foster, Ronald Roel, Russell von Frank II, Steven Lichtenstein, Sybil Taylor, Tim Lefebvre, Tom Moore, Jeff Keller, Peter Reiss, Randy Davis, Mitchell Zachary, Tomas McMillan, Ed Pruit, Hal Cherney, John Youngman, and Mary Ann Deriso.

My thanks to Robert Wallace of The Free Press, who believed and encouraged the project, and Liz Stein, the most efficient editor I have ever worked with, for bringing this to fruition.

Special thanks to Kathy Mulder, photographer and friend.

INDEX

abilities, 132
Abraham & Strauss, 29
absolute needs, 244
abundance, 34, 91, 178, 219, 244
accountants, 21, 231–32
adaptation, 18, 24, 33, 41, 164, 181, 239
Adizes, Ichak, 206
Adler, Alfred, 120
adoption, 40, 181
Africa, 203, 205
agriculture, 31, 172, 173, 212–13. *See also* farming
AIWA, 27
Allen, Paul, 98
Allied Signal, Inc., 4
American industry: rebirth of, 40
American Online, 200
American Society for the Prevention of Cruelty to Animals, 195
Amnesty International, 207
analytical statistical studies, 54
animal rights, 243
animals, 243, 249. *See also specific type of animal*
AOL Time Warner, 19–20, 101
Apple Computer, 28, 32, 33, 38
Argentina, 198–99
Aristotle, 2, 68, 161, 193
art, 177, 180
Ashe, Arthur, 142
Asia, 190, 205, 225
Asimov, Isaac, 140

assignable causes, 61–62, 65, 66, 78
assumptions, 54, 55–56, 68, 82, 139–41. *See also* propositions
AT&T, 36, 239
atomic theory, 241
auditors, 231–32
Australia, 205
automobile manufacturing, 26
autopoiesis, 157–58, 159
axioms, 68

baby boomers, 209, 240, 247
banking, 150
Bartlett, Craig, 46
Baryshnikov, Makhail, 141–42
Bateson, Gregory, 56–57, 67, 228
bear markets, 85, 221, 224, 226, 239
beat-them-over-the-head approach, 81, 83
being in the zone, 143
beliefs: becoming, 81–82; and capital, 217, 218; changing, 115; and health, 115, 116; hierarchy of, 115–16, 228; and identity, 116–17; and knowledge, 67, 79; and learning, 115; and Meta-knowledge Advantage, 247; and model for transformation, 191; and New Economic paradigms, 217, 218; about organizational purpose, 153–54; about people, 153; and proto-life, 158; and reality, 70–71; in science, 116;

A B O U T   T H E   A U T H O R

RAFAEL AGUAYO is an internationally recognized expert in quality and management. Currently, Mr. Aguayo is a full-time consultant and works with large and small companies to help them transform their business into dynamic, quality conscious, and profitable enterprises. His clients have included Bell Canada, Merck, MCI, Hewlett-Packard, Digital Equipment, Northern Telecom, and Newsday. Mr. Aguayo can be contacted at rafael@rafaelaguayo.com. For additional articles and information on MetaKnowledge visit his website, rafaelaguayo.com.